D0713155

THE CATALOGUE OF THE SHIPS IN HOMER'S *ILIAD*

THE CATALOGUE OF THE SHIPS IN HOMER'S *ILIAD*

BY

R. HOPE SIMPSON

AND

J. F. LAZENBY

OXFORD
AT THE CLARENDON PRESS
1970

Oxford University Press, Ely House, London W. 1

GLASGOW NEW YORK TORONTO MELBOURNE WELLINGTON
CAPE TOWN SALISBURY IBADAN NAIROBI DAR ES SALAAM LUSAKA ADDIS ABABA
BOMBAY CALCUTTA MADRAS KARACHI LAHORE DACCA
KUALA LUMPUR SINGAPORE HONG KONG TOKYO

PRINTED IN GREAT BRITAIN
AT THE UNIVERSITY PRESS, OXFORD
BY VIVIAN RIDLER
PRINTER TO THE UNIVERSITY

Just one word in the *Iliad*—and that word doubtful . . .
Thrown down here like the gold sepulchral mask.

GEORGE SEFERIS, *The King of Asine*
(tr. Rex Warner)

PREFACE

THE idea of writing this book came to us during a glorious spring visit to the Spercheios Valley in 1957, which led in the spring of 1958 to a more thorough exploration of the area.[1] Later, in the summer of 1958, Hope Simpson, with his wife and Miss D. H. F. Gray, travelled extensively through Boeotia, Locris, Thessaly, and Aetolia,[2] and with his wife in Elis, Triphylia, Messenia, and Arcadia in September, while Lazenby visited Turkey, and in particular Boghazköy and Xanthos, in the same year. In 1959 Hope Simpson and his wife again travelled extensively, together or separately,[3] in the Argolid, Corinthia, Boeotia, Phocis, and Locris, and in 1960 and 1961 the two of us toured first the Dodecanese,[4] and then central Greece, Thessaly, and the Peloponnese.[5]

None of these journeys would have been possible without the generosity of the British School of Archaeology at Athens, the Craven Committee, Magdalen College, the Michael Ventris Memorial Foundation, and the Universities of London, Birmingham, and Newcastle upon Tyne (formerly King's College in the University of Durham). Our thanks are due to all these bodies for their financial aid, and to the chairman and members of the various committees concerned for their kindness and interest in our projects.

We should also like to thank all those who have given us help, advice, and encouragement, especially Miss D. H. F. Gray, Mrs. Elizabeth French, Mrs. Helen Waterhouse; Professors G. L. Huxley, M. H. Jameson, W. A. McDonald, C. M. Robertson, E. B. Turner, and T. B. L. Webster; and Messrs. J. Chadwick, J. N. Coldstream, V. R. d'A. Desborough, W. G. Forrest, D. H. French, M. S. F. Hood, R. Meiggs, and H. L. Sackett. We are grateful, too, to Dr. R. Raper for his help in preparing the plates, to Mrs. Elizabeth M. Lazenby for assisting in typing

[1] Cf. 'The Kingdom of Peleus and Achilles', *Antiquity* 33 (1959), pp. 102–5. Hope Simpson was School Student of the British School of Archaeology at Athens in 1955–7, during which time he completed a survey of prehistoric Laconia which had been started by Mrs. Helen Waterhouse. Lazenby was Thomas Whitcombe-Greene Scholar in the University of Oxford for 1956/7 and 1957/8, and Senior Demy at Magdalen College, Oxford, for 1957–9, studying Mycenaean survivals in Homer.

[2] This travel was assisted by a generous grant from the Oxford University Craven Fund.

[3] Mrs. Hope Simpson was accompanied on separate occasions by Miss A. Burford and Miss L. S. Garrard.

[4] Cf. 'Notes from the Dodecanese', *BSA* 57 (1962), pp. 154–75.

[5] Cf. *JHS Arch.* for 1961/2, pp. 30–1.

the manuscript and for preparing the Index, and to all those concerned at the Clarendon Press for their helpfulness and skill in the preparation and publication of this book.

We also owe our thanks to The Bodley Head for permission to quote the lines from Rex Warner's translation of George Seferis's *The King of Asine* (*Poems*, 1960, p. 71), which appear at the beginning; to Macmillan & Co. Ltd. for permission to quote the passage by Blegen from *A Companion to Homer* (edited by A. J. B. Wace and F. H. Stubbings, 1962, p. 386) which appears at the beginning of Part I; and to the Clarendon Press for permission to quote the passage from N. G. L. Hammond's *A History of Greece to 322 B.C.* (1959, p. 67) which appears at the beginning of Part III.

Finally, we should like to dedicate this book to all our many friends in Greece, both archaeologists and ordinary people, who have been alternatively interested or irritated by our inquiries, but who have always used us with the friendliness and hospitality for which their country is justifiably famous.

Kingston, Ontario R. HOPE SIMPSON

Newcastle upon Tyne J. F. LAZENBY

May 1969

CONTENTS

LIST OF PLATES

(AT END)

LIST OF MAPS

For the areas covered in Maps 2–7 please see Contents

LIST OF ABBREVIATIONS

AA	*Archäologischer Anzeiger* (Beiblatt zum Jahrbuch des deutschen archäologischen Instituts).
ADelt.	*Ἀρχαιολογικὸν Δέλτιον τοῦ Ὑπουργείου τῶν Θρησκευμάτων καὶ Παιδείας.*
AE	*Ἀρχαιολογικὴ Ἐφημερίς.*
AEM	*Ἀρχεῖον Εὐβοϊκῶν Μελετῶν.*
AH	*Achaeans and Hittites*, G. L. Huxley (Oxford 1960).
AJA	*The American Journal of Archaeology.*
AJP	*The American Journal of Philology.*
AM	*Mitteilungen des deutschen archäologischen Instituts, Athenische Abteilung.*
Ann.	*Annuario della Reale Scuola archeologica di Atene.*
ATL	*The Athenian Tribute Lists*, B. D. Merritt, H. T. Wade-Gery, and M. F. McGregor (Cambridge, Mass. 1939–53).
AU	*Die Aḫḫijavā-Urkunden*, F. Sommer (*Abhand. bayer. Akad. Wiss.*, phil.-hist. Abt., N.F. 6 (1932), pp. 1–469).
BCH	*Bulletin de Correspondance hellénique.*
BICS	*Bulletin of the Institute of Classical Studies* (University of London).
BSA	*The Annual of the British School of Archaeology at Athens.*
CH	*A Companion to Homer*, ed. A. J. B. Wace and F. H. Stubbings (London 1962).
Chron. MP	*The Chronology of Mycenaean Pottery*, A. Furumark (Stockholm 1941).
CPh.	*The Journal of Classical Philology.*
CR	*The Classical Review.*
CVA	*Corpus Vasorum Antiquorum.*
EMF	*Das Ende der mykenischen Fundstätten auf dem griechischen Festland*, P. Ålin (*Studies in Mediterranean Archaeology*, Vol. 1, Lund 1962).
Ergon	*Τὸ Ἔργον τῆς Ἀρχαιολογικῆς Ἑταιρείας.*
GBA	*Greece in the Bronze Age*, Emily Vermeule (Chicago 1964).
GL	*Die griechischen Landschaften*, A. Philippson (ed. Kirsten: Frankfurt am Main 1950–9).
Gazetteer	*A Gazetteer and Atlas of Mycenaean Sites*, R. Hope Simpson (University of London Institute of Classical Studies, *Bulletin*, Supplement No. 16, 1965).
HCS	*The Homeric Catalogue of the Ships*, T. W. Allen (Oxford 1921).
HHC	*Homer and his Critics*, J. L. Myres and D. H. F. Gray (London 1958).

HHI	*History and the Homeric Iliad*, D. L. Page (Berkeley and Los Angeles 1959).
HM	*Homer and the Monuments*, H. L. Lorimer (London 1950).
ILN	*The Illustrated London News.*
JdI	*Jahrbuch des deutschen archäologischen Instituts.*
JHS	*The Journal of Hellenic Studies.*
JHS Arch.	*Archaeological Reports* published by the Society for the Promotion of Hellenic Studies and the British School of Archaeology at Athens.
KMK	*Die kretisch-mykenische Kultur* (2nd edn.), D. Fimmen (Leipzig and Berlin 1924).
LAAA	*Liverpool Annals of Archaeology and Anthropology.*
LMTS	*The Last Mycenaeans and their Successors*, V. R. d'A. Desborough (Oxford 1964).
MH	*From Mycenae to Homer*, T. B. L. Webster (London 1958).
MP	*The Mycenaean Pottery. Analysis and Classification*, A. Furumark (Stockholm 1941).
MV	*Mykenische Vasen*, A. Furtwängler and G. Loeschke (Berlin 1886).
NK	'*Neon Katalogos*', V. Burr (*Klio*, Beiheft 49 N.F., 1944).
ÖJh.	*Jahreshefte des Österreichischen archäologischen Instituts.*
OpArch.	*Opuscula Archaeologica* (Skrifter utgivna av Svenska Institutet i Rom: Acta Instituti Romani Regni Sueciae).
OpAth.	*Opuscula Atheniensia* (Skrifter utgivna av Svenska Institutet i Athen: Acta Instituti Atheniensis Regni Sueciae).
PAE	Πρακτικὰ τῆς Ἀρχαιολογικῆς Ἑταιρείας.
PG	*Protogeometric Pottery*, V. R. d'A. Desborough (Oxford 1952).
PI	*The Poet of the Iliad*, H. T. Wade-Gery (Cambridge 1952).
PPS	*Proceedings of the Prehistoric Society.*
PT	*Prehistoric Thessaly*, A. J. B. Wace and M. S. Thompson (Cambridge 1912).
RA	*Revue archéologique.*
RE	*Real-Encyclopädie der classischen Altertumswissenschaft*, Pauly–Wissowa–Kroll.
Rev. Ét. Gr.	*Revue des études grecques.*
RhM	*Rheinisches Museum für Philologie.*
SH	*The Songs of Homer*, G. S. Kirk (Cambridge 1962).

PART I · INTRODUCTION

When we find that Troy VIIa, which immediately followed Troy VI, with continuity of culture and a re-use of the great fortification walls, was actually destroyed in a great fire, which apparently brought violent death to more than one human victim, it does not seem too bold to draw the logical conclusion.

CARL W. BLEGEN

WHEN Schliemann began to excavate at what he took to be the site of Troy,[1] he was inspired by the belief that the poems of Homer told of events which had actually happened, and probably few would now dispute that there is a kernel of historical truth, however small, in the story of the Trojan War: one of the successive settlements on the site—Troy VIIa—*was* sacked at about the time Herodotus, at least, said Homer's Troy had been sacked,[2] and although it cannot be proved that Greeks were responsible, they were certainly in contact with the settlement at the time. Since Schliemann's day, moreover, archaeology has given us an increasing knowledge of the Greek world at that time, and although archaeologists and Homeric scholars alike may sometimes have gone too far in seeing everywhere resemblances between this real world and the heroic world, there clearly is some connection between them.

Because our knowledge of the Greek world in the Late Bronze Age comes almost entirely from archaeological evidence, the most striking similarities between it and the heroic world are in material things. Thus, with rare exceptions,[3] the weapons and tools of the heroes are made of bronze, and although bronze continued to be used by the Greeks during the Iron Age, iron became increasingly common after the collapse of Mycenaean civilization in the twelfth century B.C. Iron, it is true, is often mentioned in the poems, but in many cases these references are not strictly anachronistic—for example, when it is mentioned in a simile or metaphor:[4] here the whole point is to conjure up a striking image for the audience, not to describe the world in which the heroes lived. Similarly, references to iron in a magical or marvellous context[5] may not be anachronistic in poems ostensibly about the Bronze Age, since iron was known and prized as a precious metal long before it came into common use.[6]

But when we try to compare the material setting up of the poems with the real Mycenaean world, in detail, we come up against considerable difficulties: Homer's references to weapons and armour, for example, are usually not detailed enough for us to be sure exactly what is envisaged, and in any case, such things often did not change appreciably during the centuries which separated the Mycenaean world from the time at which the poems probably reached substantially their present form.[7] It is probably fair to say that there is hardly a single object in the *Iliad* and *Odyssey* for which a parallel cannot now be found from the Mycenaean period,[8] and such recent discoveries as the Dendra panoply[9] and the Keos temple[10] should be a warning against arguments *e silentio* where the Mycenaeans are concerned. But it is probably equally fair to say that, generally speaking, the material setting of the poems could reflect the Early Iron Age.

Hence it is necessary to concentrate on the objects described or implied in Homer which, on our present evidence, must reflect either the Late Bronze Age or the Early Iron Age. Mycenaean objects in Homer are fairly numerous: the 'boar's-tusk' helmet in Book 10 of the *Iliad*,[11] Nestor's cup,[12] Penelope's couch,[13] Helen's silver work-basket on wheels,[14] the huge 'body-shield' which seems to underlie several passages,[15] the numerous references to metallic greaves and armour,[16] silver-studded swords.[17] Nor should we forget Odysseus' palace, although as Kirk has recently emphasized,[18] this type of house-plan could have survived into the Early Iron Age, for example at Athens.

Kirk[19] lists, as possible post-Mycenaean phenomena in the poems: cremation, the use of a pair of throwing-spears, the absence of scribes and writing, the references to Phoenicians, Odysseus' brooch, Athene's golden lamp, separate, roofed temples, the Gorgon-head, and the one or two possible descriptions of hoplite tactics. Of these, he admits that Odysseus' brooch and Athene's golden lamp are uncertain criteria,[20] and the discovery of the Mycenaean temple on Keos with its cult statues, some of them life-sized, has shown that references to temples in Homer *may* not be anachronistic. It may be that the four references to the Gorgoneion betray the popularity of this motif in the Orientalizing period,[21] but as Webster points out,[22] the epithet βλοσυρῶπις for Gorgo in the description of the Gorgoneion on Agamemnon's shield (*Il.* 11. 36), is certainly archaic and may have originated in the Bronze Age, and we cannot be sure that the Gorgon myth was not already current in Mycenaean times —the monster Huwawa with whom Gilgamesh fought was evidently thought of as looking like Gorgo.[23]

The alleged 'hoplite passages' are also of doubtful significance. As Kirk says,[24] 'references to masses of troops—to "walls", "lines", or "ranks" (πύργοι, στίχες, φάλαγγες)—do not necessarily imply hoplite order, since the drawing up of troops in lines or columns must have been a commonplace of warfare at many different periods'. Even the three passages he cites as going beyond 'the usual vague language for general fighting' (*Il.* 13. 130–5 and 145–52, 16. 211–17) perhaps do not imply anything more than a close-packed mass of warriors: they clearly contain an element of poetic exaggeration—even in a hoplite phalanx the helmets of the soldiers would not literally touch!—and both contexts are unusual. In the first the Greeks are marshalling to make a last desperate stand after Hector has stormed the wall, in the second the Myrmidons are about to issue forth under Patroklos' command, for the first time in the *Iliad*.

The references to Phoenicians possibly reflect the establishment of Phoenician trade-routes to the west in the ninth century B.C.,[25] but they do not amount to very much; apart from one mention in the *Iliad* (23. 744), they appear only in reminiscences and false tales in the *Odyssey*, and it is noticeable that Sidon is the only Phoenician *city* which appears in the poems. As Miss Lorimer pointed out,[26] Sidon was destroyed at the end of the Bronze Age, and although the site was reoccupied, Tyre was far more important in the Early Iron Age. Yet Tyre is not mentioned in Homer. This would seem to suggest that part at least of the Homeric tradition about the Phoenicians goes back to the Bronze Age.

We are thus left with cremation, the use of a pair of throwing-spears, and the absence from the poems of scribes and writing. Of these, the second is crucial; if it is true, as is generally claimed,[27] that the standard equipment of a warrior in Mycenaean times included only a single thrusting-spear, then Homeric warfare is certainly very different. But is it true? Do we really know how the Mycenaeans used their spears in battle? The only representations of Mycenaean warriors actually in action occur on gems mostly of early Mycenaean date, depicting duels between single warriors, and although they all show warriors armed with a single spear and using it for thrusting, it is difficult to see how artists *could* have depicted fighting at long range on such tiny objects. In any case, they really tell us nothing about the practice of the thirteenth and twelfth centuries B.C. From this period we have a number of representations of soldiers,[28] but no battle scenes like those depicted on Late Geometric vases. Admittedly, there is no certain representation of a warrior carrying two spears,[29] but although we may agree with Snodgrass[30] that the carrying of two spears 'may well be taken as a sign that one of them at least is to be thrown', is the converse true? Must we assume that the carrying of a single spear indicates that it is to be used for thrusting?

Nor is the Homeric picture as clear as is sometimes suggested. There are only eleven passages in the *Iliad*[31] and three in the *Odyssey*[32] in which a hero is expressly stated to be carrying two spears, and some of the heroes in question certainly did not always carry two spears. Thus Hector, the hero most often said to have two spears,[33] has only a single one, eleven cubits long, when he goes to visit Paris (*Il.* 6. 318–20), and to his cost, has only one in his last fight with Achilles (*Il.* 22. 289–93). Instructive, perhaps, is the passage describing Paris going out to battle in the third book of the *Iliad* (lines 16–19): with his leopard skin, his bow, sword, and two spears, the gallant prince is clearly only lightly armed, but for his duel with Menelaus he puts on greaves and corselet borrowed from his brother Lykaon, and takes sword, shield, and a single ἄλκιμον ἔγχος (*Il.* 3. 328–38)—which he then proceeds to throw! The two-spear equipment, in short, seems to be almost as rare in Homer as it apparently was in the Bronze Age.

An analysis of the actual way in which the heroes use their spears suggests that they were normally thought of as armed with a single spear which they could use indifferently for throwing or for thrusting. The choice before a hero is well brought out by a passage (*Il.* 13. 557–9) in which Antilochos is described as wondering whether to throw his spear or to keep it for thrusting, and that this was a feasible weapon is shown by Tacitus' account of the German *framea*:[34] 'hastas vel ipsorum vocabulo frameas gerunt, angusto et brevi ferro, sed ita acri et ad usum habili ut *eodem telo, prout ratio poscit, vel comminus vel eminus pugnent.*' Now, admittedly, the Late Geometric battle-scenes provide a good parallel for Homeric warfare in one respect, but they do not do so in another: the throwing-spear is certainly there, as are warriors armed with two spears, but there are no duels at close quarters with spears used for thrusting.[35] Yet in Homer the thrust is almost as common as the throw,[36] and can we be certain that this is either because we have in Homer an older tradition in which the thrusting-spear predominated, overlaid by a later tradition in which the throwing-spear took its place,[37] or because Homeric warfare reflects a time when the spear was normally thrown, but could be used for thrusting in an emergency?[38] Certainly it is rash to conclude that the thrusting-spear was the normal weapon of Mycenaean warriors to the exclusion of the throwing-spear, in view of the lack of evidence,[39] and, for all we know, the tactics employed by the heroes on the field of battle may have been in use before the collapse of Mycenaean civilization.[40]

The same is true of the way the heroes normally use their chariots in battle. It is sometimes suggested[41] that the large numbers of chariots listed in the Linear B tablets from Knossos and Pylos show that the Mycenaeans used their chariots for massed charges, as did the Egyptians and Hittites, and Nestor's statement (*Il.* 4. 303–9) that it was by the massed chariot charge that 'the men of old sacked cities and fortresses' is held to be a garbled memory of the way the Mycenaeans used their chariots, while the normal heroic use for transportation purposes is thought to reflect the Iron Age usage, or to betray a complete misunderstanding of the way in which chariots were used in war.

But the truth of the matter is that we really do not know how the Mycenaeans used their chariots in war, for the crude carvings on the shaft-grave stelai are the only representations of the chariot in battle, and these tell us nothing.[42] It may be admitted that the Mycenaeans adopted the war chariot from the Near East,[43] but it is dubious whether they could have used it for massed charges in a country like Greece, and they might have used it in very much the way that Homer describes. For it is quite untrue to say that the chariot was never used like this in war: Caesar's description of the way the Britons used their chariots[44] is very reminiscent of Homeric usage. Nor can we be certain that the way the heroes use their chariots reflects the usage of the Early Iron Age, for the representations of chariots in battle on Late Geometric pottery may in fact be an attempt to depict heroic warfare.[45]

It is more difficult still to determine how far the heroic world resembles the Mycenaean in non-material things, mainly because, as we have said, our knowledge of Mycenaean Greece depends largely on artefacts. At first sight, however, there is an obvious dissimilarity in burial customs—one of the few non-material matters upon which archaeology can provide reliable evidence. The Mycenaeans undoubtedly normally buried their dead, although it appears that towards the end of the Mycenaean period cremation was beginning to be sporadically adopted.[46] In the poems, on the other hand, the dead are normally cremated, though there are some passages which seem to refer to burial, such as the beautiful lines (*Il.* 3. 243–4) which explain why Helen cannot see her brothers among the Greeks:

τοὺς δ' ἤδη κάτεχεν φυσίζοος αἶα
ἐν Λακεδαίμονι αὖθι, φίλῃ ἐν πατρίδι γαίῃ.

Such passages would probably still have been meaningful to people who practised cremation, partly because they still thought of the dead as going to dwell underground, partly because a tumulus was often raised over the remains of the pyre, or over the jar in which the collected bones were placed.[47] But they probably do, nevertheless, refer to inhumation.

It is, however, a natural conclusion that the usual heroic custom of burning the dead reflects the period after the collapse of Mycenaean civilization, when cremation became the normal rite in many parts of the Greek world.[48] But, as Kirk points out,[49] most of the references to cremation in Homer concern the practice of soldiers serving in a foreign land: can we be sure that, in such circumstances, the Mycenaeans buried their dead? Would they not have been afraid that the tombs would be insulted and rifled when they withdrew, just as Agamemnon feared that the Trojans would insult the tomb of his brother (*Il.* 4. 174–7)? Furthermore, it may not merely be a coincidence that one people with whom the Mycenaeans were in contact and who certainly practised cremation were precisely the people of Troy VI–VIIa.[50] Thus we cannot really be sure that the practising of cremation by the heroes does reflect post-Mycenaean custom.

Our knowledge of the religious beliefs and customs of the Mycenaeans in general is, in the nature of things, too slight and uncertain[51] for us to tell whether heroic belief and custom reflects the religion of the Mycenaeans or rather that of the Early Iron Age Greeks. The predominance of Zeus in Homer seems, at first sight, to conflict with the apparent predominance of a female deity or deities in Mycenaean times, but most of the Homeric male gods do in fact also appear in the Linear B tablets, though not always under their common Homeric names.[52] It may be significant, for example, that Poseidon appears to have been an important deity at Pylos,[53] and that it is to Poseidon that Nestor and his people are sacrificing when Telemachos comes to visit them (*Od.* 3. 4–11). But many cults clearly survived into historical times, as Nilsson made clear,[54] and when, for example, in one of his fabricated reminiscences, Odysseus mentions the cave of Eileithyia at Amnisos (*Od.* 19. 188), even though a Linear B tablet from Knossos seems to record the offering of honey to Eileithyia at Amnisos,[55] we still cannot be sure whether this is a genuine Mycenaean reminiscence, or rather a reflection of the practice in later times, for the cult of Eileithyia certainly survived into historical times.

The decipherment of Linear B has, on the other hand, shown that the Mycenaean kingdoms, or at least those centred on Pylos and Knossos,[56] were highly organized, even bureaucratic, and although much is still unclear, it is already obvious that life was much more complicated and sophisticated than it is in the heroic world, and that the latter reflects hardly anything of the political, social, or economic details of Mycenaean life.[57] It has been suggested that, in fact, the heroic world rather reflects the apparently simpler and less sophisticated world of Protogeometric and Geometric Greece,[58] and on this view the Mycenaean reminiscences in the poems are seen as few and isolated, 'distorted beyond sense or recognition'.[59]

The chief difficulty in assessing this view is our comparative lack of knowledge of the Protogeometric and Geometric periods, but one wonders whether it is not, in any case, based on a fundamental fallacy. The world depicted in the poems is, after all, essentially a *poetic* world, not a real world at all, though the *material setting* is largely realistic: can we really believe that real Greeks ever did behave as the heroes behave? that, for example, there was ever a time when one Greek king would have sent for another, on the battlefield, to attend to his brother's wound, or a real Greek princess have gone down to the shore to do the family washing? Even the prominence of the heroes on the battlefield, although there probably was a time, before the appearance of the hoplite phalanx, when the few who could afford horses and armour did dominate the fighting, surely does not merely reflect this: the heroes occupy the limelight because it would be *poetically* unthinkable for a hero to fight, let alone be killed by, some nameless 'private', though this must have happened often enough in real life.

Throughout the poems the interest is focused on the heroes as personalities and on their personal relationships, not on the way they command their forces or organize their kingdoms, or on the positions they occupy in some elaborate and complicated hierarchy. Indeed, although some rule more powerful kingdoms or are better fighters than others and so have more authority, basically, with the single exception of Thersites, they are all regarded as *equals*, and thus there is no room for the technical terms which seem to have been applied to the various gradations of rank within the Mycenaean kingdoms. There *is* a vast difference between the life the heroes lead and the lives of their ostensible Mycenaean counterparts, but this is not because the heroes reflect a simpler, less sophisticated aristocracy, but because they are essentially not real men at all. It has, for example, been argued[60] that 'the lords of Mycenae . . . organized the work on their properties through an elaborate hierarchy of men and operations, requiring inventories and memoranda and managerial controls; but Eumaeus could carry the inventory of Odysseus' livestock in his head'. But surely the point of the passage in question (*Od.* 14. 96–108) has really nothing to do with the way he rules his estates; it is simply a vivid way of presenting the homely character of the old swineherd and his feelings for his absent master, and the point could have been made in the same way whether the audience was accustomed to Linear B accounting or not. Similarly, the fondness of the heroes for the giving and receiving of gifts surely does not reflect a society in which gift-giving was an integral part of the economy:[61] the giving and receiving of gifts is rather an integral part of the heroic ideal. The fact that the poems betray little if any knowledge of the quasi-feudal bureaucracy of the tablets may not be so much due to the disappearance of the system as to the fact that it was something quite alien to the poetic tradition, and therefore failed to impinge upon it, however fundamental it may have been to real life.

But in fact one wonders whether the very complexity and comprehensiveness of the organization revealed by the Linear B tablets may not be giving a false impression of what life was really like in Mycenaean Greece. It is fairly certain, for instance, that the actual writing of the tablets was in the hands of professional scribes,[62] and it by no means follows from the fact that they made use of such documents that even the rulers of the Mycenaean world could read or write.[63] Thus the scene in the *Iliad* (7. 170 f.) in which the heroes 'make their mark' before drawing lots to see who is to fight Hector is just as likely to have been true of the champions of Mycenaean Greece as it apparently was of the Early Iron Age. Still less is it likely that the ordinary people of Mycenaean Greece were literate, and many a Mycenaean swineherd must in fact have carried the inventory of his master's flocks and herds in his head. We do not even have any evidence, as yet, that the more 'provincial' communities, such as Odysseus' kingdom, knew anything about writing at all. So the fact that there is no reference to writing in the poems, except in the story of Bellerophon where some such device was essential (*Il.* 6. 168–9), is not by any means necessarily another sharp cleavage between the Homeric world and the Mycenaean,[64] and the obscurity of the reference to writing in the Bellerophon story may just as easily betray the lack of understanding of the average Mycenaean as the ignorance of later generations.[65]

The question remains whether the undoubted Mycenaean reminiscences in Homer were preserved through the medium of Mycenaean poetry, or through a more general folk memory. Kirk has recently argued[66] that there is little if any cogent evidence for the existence of Mycenaean epic poetry, and suggests instead that the poetic tradition grew up during the 'Dark Ages' when some memory of Mycenaean Greece still lingered on. He emphasizes the crucial importance of the Catalogue of the Ships in the argument,[67] and this we will discuss in Part III of this book. But one wonders whether, the Catalogue apart, the existence of Mycenaean poetry is not in any case the simplest explanation of the Mycenaean reminiscences elsewhere in the poems. It is easy enough to suppose, for example, that the Greeks of the Early Iron Age could have remembered that their ancestors used weapons made of bronze, even that they wore bronze corslets (χαλκοχίτωνες) and conspicuous greaves (ἐϋκνήμιδες). But is it really likely that they would have remembered a time when men fought naked from the waist up, protected only by the great body-shield, when probably for several generations even before the fall of Mycenae body-armour and the smaller round shield had become standard equipment? Is it likely that they would have remembered the boar's-tusk helmets with such accuracy that they could even put in the detail that the curve of the plates faced a different way in each row (*Il.* 10. 264)? It seems more likely that oral poetry was already being composed in Mycenaean Greece, and that the memories were preserved because each generation of bards learned the techniques of composition from its predecessor, and was incapable of inventing a whole new set of formulas, even if it wanted to. Indeed we would argue that, for the Homeric scholar, one of the most important results of the archaeological discoveries of the past century has been precisely to indicate when the oral tradition began.

But if there was Mycenaean poetry, we should bear in mind the possibility that such poetry was being composed before the time of the historical Trojan War. It has, in fact, often been pointed out[68] that many of the more certain Mycenaean reminiscences in the poems seem to go back to comparatively early Mycenaean times—for example, the body-shield and the boar's tusk helmet itself. In Aias, son of Telamon, we may perhaps discern a hero of such earlier poetry,[69] and one wonders whether even Achilles may not belong to an older, more primitive type of story in which magic and the miraculous played a larger part than they do in Homer. It is even possible that the siege of a city was the subject of heroic poetry before the Trojan War, for it certainly seems to have been a motif in Mycenaean art from the time of the silver vase from Shaft Grave IV to that of the frescoes from the megaron at Mycenae.[70] And if there was poetry about heroes and their exploits before the thirteenth century B.C., it becomes easier still to understand why the life the heroes lead is so unlike the life their Mycenaean originals led. For the heroes and their behaviour will, as it were, represent a distillation of what generations of bards *imagined* the lives of heroes to be like, and some of the modern Russian epics about the Revolution show vividly how epic poets will describe even contemporary persons, places, and events in traditional language.[71]

In short, the main reason for the dissimilarity between the heroic world and the world of the tablets may lie in the nature of the epic tradition itself. One characteristic of this tradition seems to have been to attempt to create an impression of reality by giving the heroes real weapons and armour, having them live in real houses, use real furniture, and so on—it is noticeable that there are very few magic *things* in the poems. But the lives the heroes live and the way they use the real equipment they possess could not, in the nature of things, be ordinary. Hence the contrast between the apparent reality of the *material* setting of the poems and the unreality of the lives the heroes live in this setting: the *material* setting is, at least in part, Mycenaean, and we have tried to show that hardly any of it need necessarily be later. But the political, social, and economic life of the heroes is neither Mycenaean nor Early Iron Age: it may represent an amalgam of elements from all the centuries during which the epic tradition flourished, and it may also represent an ideal towards which the aristocratic societies looked before the reopening of trade-routes in the eighth century ushered in the dawn of a new era. But essentially, in its non-material aspects, the heroic world is an imaginary world, only loosely tied to reality.

Given the nature of the evidence, it is impossible to be certain how far the *Iliad* and *Odyssey* preserve a memory of Mycenaean Greece, how far they reflect the centuries immediately prior to their reaching their present form. We have tried to show that there is certainly some reason to think that the tradition which lies behind them goes right back to the Mycenaean era, and that many of the arguments which have been advanced for believing the Mycenaean element to be confined to a few isolated details are not as strong as is sometimes thought. If these conclusions are accepted, there is nothing intrinsically improbable in the view that the Catalogue of the Ships in the second book of the *Iliad* in some sense preserves a memory of Mycenaean Greece, and in the succeeding pages we shall try to show how far and in what sense it may be said to do so.

NOTES TO PART I

1. Blegen is surely right in arguing (*Troy* iv. 10–11) that, if there ever was a historical Troy, it must be identified with the site at Hissarlik.
2. Herodotus (2. 145. 4) dates τὰ Τρωικά about 800 years before his own time, i.e. about 1250 B.C.—for other 'traditional' dates see Forsdyke, *Greece Before Homer*, pp. 28 f. For the date of the destruction of Troy VIIa cf. especially Blegen et al., *Troy* iv. 10 f., though doubts have been expressed about Blegen's conclusions, e.g. by Nylander (quoting Furumark) *Antiquity* 37 (1963), p. 7.
3. Examples of iron weapons or implements referred to or implied are: *Il.* 4. 123, 18. 34, 23. 30, and 23. 826 f. (Areithoos' iron mace, *Il.* 7. 141, might have been a lump of meteoric iron attached to a wooden haft). In the *Odyssey* there are the famous axes of Odysseus himself and the reduplicated line αὐτὸς γὰρ ἐφέλκεται ἄνδρα σίδηρος (16. 294 = 19. 13), which implies that the weapons hanging on the walls of the megaron in Odysseus' palace were of iron.

   Iron is also referred to as a sign of wealth, especially in the repeated line χαλκός τε χρυσός τε πολύκμητός τε σίδηρος (*Il.* 6. 48 = 10. 379 = 11. 133 = *Od.* 14. 324 = 21. 10), where the epithet πολύκμητος probably betrays a knowledge of iron-working. (Cf. also *Il.* 7. 473, 23. 850–2; *Od.* 1. 184.)
4. e.g. the comparison of Odysseus and his comrades twisting the stake in the Cyclops' eye to a smith tempering an axe or hatchet in water—τὸ γὰρ αὖτε σιδήρου γε κράτος ἐστίν (*Od.* 9. 391–3).
5. e.g. the iron axle of Hera's chariot (*Il.* 5. 723).
6. An iron ring, for example, was found in the Vaphio tholos (*AE* 1889, p. 147). Lorimer, *HM*, pp. 111 f., lists and discusses other early examples of iron found in Greece.
7. We agree with those who argue that the 8th century is the most likely date for this to have happened, e.g. Kirk, *SH*, pp. 282–7. We do not propose to venture upon the question of authorship, which does not matter for our purposes; we shall use the term 'Homer', without prejudice, to refer to the received texts of the *Iliad* and *Odyssey*.

   An example of a piece of equipment which did not change between the 13th and 8th centuries B.C. is the circular shield with central hand-grip (Lorimer, *HM*, p. 181).
8. Odysseus' brooch (*Od.* 19. 226–31) and Agamemnon's 'Gorgoneion' shield (*Il.* 11. 32–7) are possibly the only exceptions—but see above, p. 2, and nn. 20–2 below.
9. Verdelis, *AE* 1957, p. 15; *BCH* 85 (1961), p. 671; *AJA* 67 (1963), p. 281; Vermeule, *GBA*, pp. 135–6; etc.

10. Vermeule, *GBA*, pp. 285–6; 217–18; etc.

11. *Il.* 10. 261–5; Lorimer, *HM*, pp. 212–19; etc.

12. The famous cup from Shaft Grave IV still remains the best parallel, though not an exact one; cf. Lorimer, *HM*, pp. 328–35; Kirk, *SH*, p. 395 (n. 4 to p. 111).

13. Webster, *MH*, p. 27.

14. Kirk, *SH*, p. 111.

15. *Il.* 7. 219, 11. 485, 17. 128 (Aias' σάκος ἠΰτε πύργος): cf. 14. 404–5, where the fact that Aias' sword- and shield-belts are implied as crossing indicates that he is carrying a body-shield (Lorimer, *HM*, p. 182); and 13. 709–11, where we are told that Aias' comrades used to relieve him of his shield; *Il.* 6. 117 (Hector's shield); *Il.* 15. 645–6 (Periphetes' shield); *Il.* 5. 793–8 (where Diomedes only has to lift his telamon to get at his wound—i.e. he is naked from the waist up, protected only by his body-shield, as, for example, are the warriors on the lion-hunt dagger. The same thing is implied by *Il.* 2. 388–9).
    It must be emphasized that these heroes are not consistently described as equipped with the body-shield: even Aias' shield when described in detail (*Il.* 7. 219–23) is probably of a different type (Lorimer, *HM*, pp. 182–3), and when Diomedes was actually wounded he was wearing a corslet (*Il.* 5. 98–100). But *taken in isolation* all these passages seem originally to have described or implied a body-shield.

16. As implied by the epithets ἐϋκνήμιδες and χαλκοχίτωνες for the Achaeans, and by numerous more explicit passages. There is increasing evidence for the use of metallic armour by the Greeks in the Late Bronze Age, but so far no evidence that they used it between the time of the Sub-Mycenaean helmet from Tiryns (*BCH* 82 (1958), p. 707; Kirk, *SH*, Plate 4*a*) and that of the panoply from Argos (*BCH* 81 (1957), pp. 322 f., esp. 340 f.; Kirk, *SH*, Plate 6*b*).

17. Lorimer, *HM*, pp. 273–4.

18. *SH*, pp. 111–12.

19. *SH*, pp. 183–8. Elsewhere (op. cit., pp. 123–5) Kirk argues that there are two other discrepancies between the poems and the Mycenaean world—the lack of reference to the complex Mycenaean bureaucracy, and the alleged failure to understand the use of the chariot: see above, pp. 6–8, and 4–5.

20. *SH*, p. 185. For the brooch cf. also Webster, *MH*, p. 111, where it is argued that the *decoration* possibly reflects Mycenaean inlay techniques. For the lamp of Athene cf. Webster, op. cit., p. 107.

21. Kirk, *SH*, p. 186.

22. *MH*, pp. 94, 128, 213.

23. Webster, *MH*, p. 82.

24. *SH*, p. 187.

25. Kirk, *SH*, p. 185.

26. *HM*, p. 67.

27. Cf., for example, Lorimer, *HM*, p. 256; Gray, *HHC*, p. 182; Kirk, *SH*, p. 183; Snodgrass, *Early Greek Armour and Weapons*, pp. 115–16.

28. Most notably the so-called 'Warrior Vase' of LH IIIC (cf. Lorimer, *HM*, Plate III 1*a*, 1*b*; Webster, *MH*, Plate 7).

29. As Snodgrass suggests, op. cit., p. 115, the twin spears allegedly carried by the 'Captains of the Blacks' on the Knossos fresco may be a single spear depicted in outline: there is a rather similar case of a possible representation of twin spears on a sherd in the National Museum at Athens (No. 1141). The men undoubtedly carrying two spears on a fresco from Tiryns are, as Miss Lorimer says, *HM*, p. 256 n. 5, almost certainly hunters.

30. Op. cit., p. 115.

31. 5. 495 = 6. 104 = 11. 212; 3. 18–19, 10. 76, 11. 43, 12. 298, 12. 464–5, 13. 241, 16. 139, 21. 145.

32. 1. 256, 12. 228, 22. 101.

33. Four out of the eleven passages in the *Iliad* refer to him: 5. 495 = 6. 104 = 11. 212; 12. 464–5.

34. *Germania* 6. 1–2. When Tacitus goes on to say 'eques quidem scuto frameaque contentus est, pedites et missilia spargunt', he leaves no doubt that the *framea* was a real dual-purpose weapon, not merely a throwing-spear sometimes used for thrusting or vice versa, and strongly implies that each *eques* had only a single *framea*.

35. Lorimer, *HM*, p. 257.

36. In the *Iliad*, on a rough count, there are 81 cases of a hero throwing a spear, as against 69 cases of one thrusting, while there are some 15 references to volleys of spears thrown, as against some 10 cases of more than one person thrusting.

37. As, for example, Lorimer, *HM*, p. 259, and Kirk, *SH*, pp. 183–4, suggest.

38. As, for example, Lorimer, *HM*, p. 257 (cf. p. 463), suggests.

39. Snodgrass, *Ancient Greek Armour and Weapons*, p. 245 n. 3, lists some possible examples of Minoan and Mycenaean throwing-spears. To these should probably be added some of the spear-heads from the LM II 'Warrior Graves' at Knossos (*BSA* 47 (1952), p. 256—spear-heads AJ (4) and I (11); and *BSA* 51 (1956), p. 96—spear-heads nos. 9–13).

40. Cf. Wace and Stubbings, *CH*, p. 518.

41. e.g. by Kirk, *SH*, pp. 124–5; cf. Finley, *The World of Odysseus* (Pelican Books 1962), p. 52.

42. They may even be representations of chariots used for racing: see Mylonas, *AJA* 55 (1951), pp. 134 f.

43. Lorimer, *HM*, p. 307. In this connection it is interesting to note that the brother of a king of Aḫḫijavā may have gone to the Hittites for chariot instruction (cf. the Tavagalavaš Letter: Huxley, *AH*, p. 2).

44. *De Bello Gallico* 4. 33; cf. Anderson, *AJA* 69 (1965), pp. 349–52.

45. Snodgrass, *Ancient Greek Weapons and Armour*, p. 160. As Webster pointed out (*BSA* 50 (1955), pp. 41–3; cf. *MH*, pp. 169 f.), the Dipylon shield may be due to a similar desire on the part of Geometric artists to depict heroic warfare (cf. Snodgrass, op. cit., pp. 58–60).

46. To the example of a Mycenaean cremation at Prosymna (*HM*, p. 104), must now be added two near Pylos (*Ergon* for 1957, pp. 89 f.), five or six near Perati (*HHC*, p. 270; *JHS Arch.* for 1958, p. 3; for 1961/2, p. 6), and others from Rhodes, Naxos, and Crete (Vermeule, *GBA*, pp. 301–5).

47. e.g. at Colophon (*AJA* 27 (1923), p. 67), Samos (Boehlau, *Aus ionischen und italischen Nekropolen*, pp. 12–13, 32–4; *JHS* 53 (1933), pp. 170–1), and Halos in Achaea Phthiotis (*BSA* 17 (1910/11), pp. 1 f.).

48. Cf. Lorimer, *HM*, pp. 103–10; Webster, *MH*, pp. 109–10, 140, 164–6, 290.

49. *SH*, p. 183.

50. Lorimer, *HM*, p. 107; Mylonas, *AJA* 52 (1948), pp. 56 f.

51. The fundamental work is probably still Nilsson's *The Minoan–Mycenaean Religion* (2nd edn., Lund 1950), but much has been added as a result of the decipherment of Linear B, and of such discoveries as the Keos temple (cf., for a general discussion, Vermeule, *GBA*, pp. 280–97).

52. Cf. Vermeule, *GBA*, pp. 291–7.

53. Vermeule, *GBA*, p. 295; Webster, *Antiquity* 29 (1955), pp. 10–14, esp. 11–12.

54. Op. cit., *passim*.

55. *DMG*, p. 127.

56. To which, presumably, must be added Mycenae and Thebes on the evidence of the scattered tablets from these places.

57. Cf. especially Finley, *Historia* 6 (1957), pp. 133–69; *The World of Odysseus* (Pelican Books, 1962), pp. 165–8; Kirk, *SH*, pp. 36–9.

58. e.g. by Finley, *The World of Odysseus*, pp. 55–6; Kirk, *SH*, pp. 36–9, 139–56.

59. Finley, op. cit., p. 52.

60. Finley, op. cit., p. 166.

61. As suggested by Finley, op. cit., chapter 3 (pp. 58–84).

62. *DMG*, p. 110.

63. Similarly, many a medieval baron was unable to read or write.

64. As Finley again argues (op. cit., pp. 165–8); cf. Kirk, *SH*, pp. 184–5.

65. It is noticeable that there is similarly only one reference to writing in Beowulf (H. M. Chadwick, *The Heroic Age*, p. 212), and none at all in Bronze Age Near Eastern epics (Webster, *MH*, p. 73).

66. *SH*, especially Chapters 5 and 6 (pp. 105–25 and 126–38).

67. Op. cit., pp. 109–10.

68. Cf., for example, Wace and Stubbings, *CH*, p. 329.

69. Lorimer, *HM*, p. 182; Page, *HHI*, p. 235; Webster, *MH*, p. 58; Kirk, *SH*, p. 181.

70. Webster, *MH*, pp. 58 f.

71. Cf., for example, Bowra, *Heroic Poetry*, pp. 116–17, 186, 221, 335, 340, 469 f., 513 f.

PART II

THE CATALOGUE

Ἔσπετε νῦν μοι, Μοῦσαι Ὀλύμπια δώματ' ἔχουσαι—
ὑμεῖς γὰρ θεαί ἐστε, πάρεστέ τε, ἴστε τε πάντα,
ἡμεῖς δὲ κλέος οἶον ἀκούομεν οὐδέ τι ἴδμεν—
οἵ τινες ἡγεμόνες Δαναῶν καὶ κοίρανοι ἦσαν.

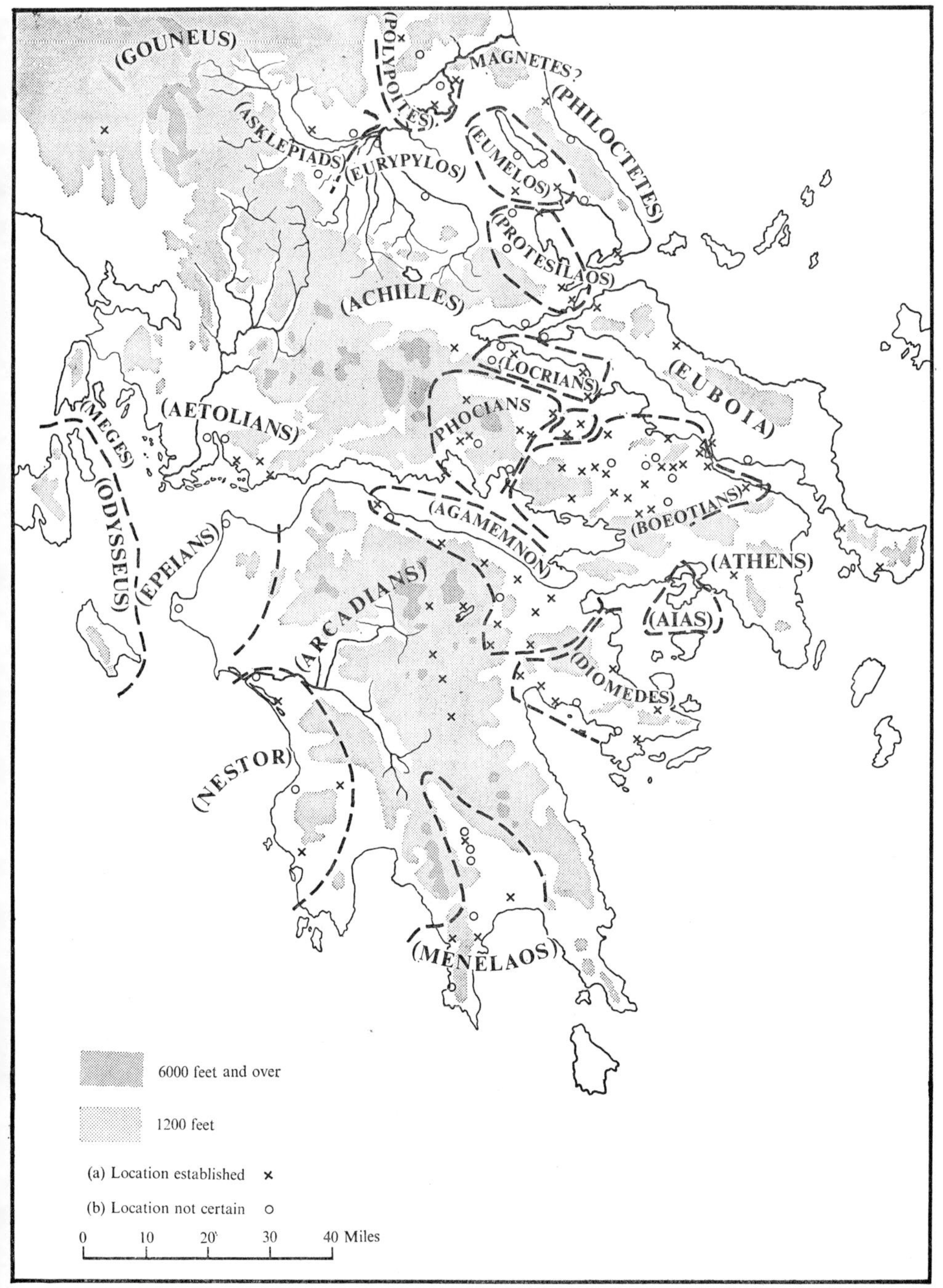

Map 1: Mainland Greece according to the Homeric Epics

THE 'Catalogue of the Ships' forms part of the second book of the *Iliad* (lines 494–759), and is a list of the leaders of the Greek army, the places from which their men came, and the numbers of ships they commanded. For the moment we propose to leave aside all questions concerning the origins of the Catalogue, and simply to discuss each place mentioned in it in turn, paying particular attention to the location of the place and the evidence for its occupation at various times. At the end of the section on each group of places we shall discuss the frontiers implied and the period which appears to be reflected, but the general question of the picture of Greece which emerges will be postponed to Part III.

For the sake of convenience we shall head each group of places either with the area where they are located, or with the name of the people who inhabited it, or with the names of their leader or leaders. Where appropriate we shall endeavour to give a map reference for places discussed, and these will be to the War Office G.S.G.S. 1 : 100,000 Series, prepared during the Second World War. Sets of these maps are most readily available at the Library of the Societies for the Promotion of Hellenic and Roman Studies (31–4, Gordon Square, London W.C. 1), and at the British School of Archaeology in Athens. In order to help with the identification of the sites we shall also try to give their local names (toponyms).

Map references will be given to individual sheets in the form, for example, for Dramesi (Hyrie): 'I.9 Khalkis 309E/904N'. Other references for a particular site, given at the beginning of the discussion upon it, are not intended to be complete, particularly in the case of the more important sites. Places mentioned in the Catalogue will normally be referred to in a transliterated form, and we make no claim to being consistent in the form of the transliteration, but the discussion on each will be headed by the nominative form of its name as it appears in the Oxford Text of the *Iliad*, followed by the number of the line in which it occurs.

THE BOEOTIANS

Ὑρίη (2. 496) MAP 2

REFS. *Gazetteer*, No. 432; *ADelt.* 1 (1915), parart., p. 55; *PAE* 1911, p. 142; *JHS* 54 (1944), p. 24; *Hesperia*, Suppl. viii (1949), pp. 39–42; *AE* 1956, parart., pp. 26–7, figs. 9–11; Ålin, *EMF*, p. 120.

Strabo (9. 404) says that there was a place called Hyria, in his day in the territory of Tanagra, though formerly in that of Thebes, and that it lay near Aulis. It has been securely identified with the large mound site (about 300 metres by 100) on the northern edge of the village of Dramesi (I.9 Khalkis 309E/904N). Pottery found at or near the site covers all periods from Neolithic to LH IIIB, including LH I from tombs, and LH IIIA–B sherds on the surface. But no Protogeometric or Geometric has yet appeared.

The site is also famous for the stone carvings of ships which are usually thought to be Mycenaean, and which Blegen[1] suggested may once have been a special monument, set up in a tomb, possibly in connection with an overseas expedition, such as that against Troy.

Strabo (loc. cit.) also records the variant theory that the Hyrie of the Catalogue referred to Hysiai, but he evidently did not accept this, and there is no reason to doubt his opinion.

Αὐλίς (2. 496) MAP 2

REFS. (1) *General*: Frazer, *Pausanias* v. pp. 72–3.

(2) *Sanctuary of Artemis*: *Ergon* for 1958, p. 60; for 1959, pp. 24–31; for 1960, pp. 49–53; for 1961, pp. 48–51; cf. *JHS* and *BCH* reports for these years.

(3) *Mycenaean settlement*: *Gazetteer*, No. 433; *Ergon* for 1959, pp. 30–1; *AE* 1956, pp. 21–7; *JHS Arch.* for 1959–60, p. 13; Ålin, *EMF*, p. 120.

The excavations at the sanctuary of Artemis have confirmed the traditions about the location of the town of Aulis (as distinct from the bay), and of the shrine. As Frazer surmised, it lay on the peninsula which divides the bay of Aulis (Megalo Vathy) from the smaller bay of Mikro Vathy to the north (I.9 Khalkis 053E/944N). The later acropolis was probably Megalo Vouno to the north-west,[2] but trial excavations have revealed LH III pottery associated with walls of large stones, on the western slopes of the hill called Nisi or Yeladhovouni to the east of the sanctuary. The Homeric epithet πετρήεσσα is certainly suitable to Yeladhovouni and the hills around the Bay of Aulis. There is also evidence for continuity of occupation into the Early Iron Age at the site.

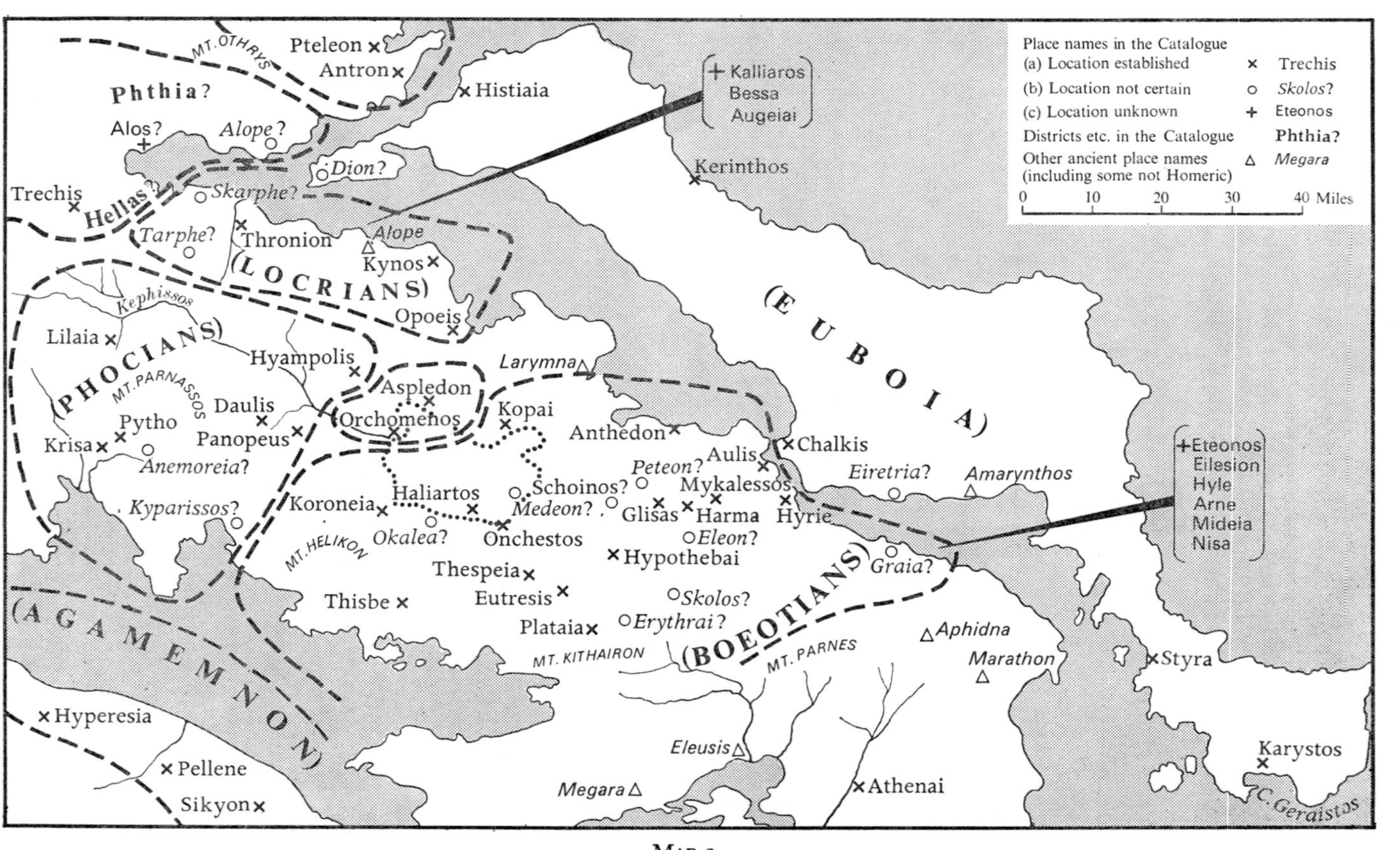

Place names in the Catalogue
(a) Location established
Trechis
(b) Location not certain
Skolos?
(c) Location unknown
Eteonos
Districts etc. in the Catalogue
Phthia?
Other ancient place names (including some not Homeric)
Megara
0
10
20
30
40 Miles
Phthia?
MT. OTHRYS
Pteleon
Antron
Histiaia
Kalliaros
Bessa
Augeiai
Alos?
Alope?
Dion?
Kerinthos
Trechis
Hellas?
Skarphe?
Tarphe?
Thronion
Alope
Kynos
(LOCRIANS)
Kephissos
Opoeis
(EUBOIA)
Lilaia
(PHOCIANS)
Hyampolis
MT. PARNASSOS
Larymna
Aspledon
Daulis
Kopai
Pytho
Orchomenos
Krisa
Panopeus
Anthedon
Chalkis
Anemoreia?
Peteon?
Aulis
Eiretria?
Amarynthos
Eteonos
Eilesion
Hyle
Arne
Mideia
Nisa
Haliartos
Schoinos?
Mykalessos
Kyparissos?
Koroneia
Medeon?
Glisas
Harma
Hyrie
Okalea?
Onchestos
Eleon?
MT. HELIKON
Hypothebai
Graia?
Thespeia
(BOEOTIANS)
Thisbe
Eutresis
Skolos?
(AGAMEMNON)
Plataia
Erythrai?
Aphidna
MT. KITHAIRON
MT. PARNES
Marathon
Styra
Hyperesia
Eleusis
Karystos
Pellene
Megara
Athenai
Sikyon
C. Geraistos

MAP 2

Σχοῖνος (2. 497) MAP 2

This place has not yet been securely located, though it was certainly still in existence in classical times.[3] Strabo (9. 408) says that it was fifty stades from Thebes on the road to Anthedon, so it should be sought somewhere in the region of the north-eastern edge of Lake Likeri, to the south-west of the village of Mouriki.[4]

Burr[5] gives an erroneous reference to Strabo 9. 410, and the location suggested on his Skizze 1 conflicts with the one given on his Karte 3.

Σκῶλος (2. 497) MAP 2

Skolos is usually placed near Darimari, the village about 9 kms. to the east-north-east of Kriekouki (modern Erythrai).[6] The site which appears to agree most closely with the directions given by Strabo (9. 408) and Pausanias (9. 4. 4) is that of the ruined Metochi of Ayios Meletios, less than a kilometre west of Darimari, on the road to Kriekouki (I.9 Khalkis ♁ at 107E/757N).

To the description of the site given by Frazer[7] may now be added the recent discussions by Pritchett.[8] The 'rocky table-height at the foot of a spur of Mt. Kithairon' (in Frazer's words), with a spring near by, is ideal for Mycenaean occupation, as we noted in our visit in 1961, and although we found only tile fragments and fine-quality black-glazed sherds, we now learn that Professor Vanderpool has found here 'the stem of a Mycenaean kylix'.[9]

Pritchett, however, now argues that Ayios Meletios is the site of Erythrai (see below), and he offers a new site for Skolos, *north* of the river Asopos. But Pausanias says πρὶν δὲ ἢ διαβῆναι τὸν Ἀσωπόν (for those going from Plataea to Thebes), and this, if anything, seems to indicate the *south* bank of the Asopos, agreeing better with Strabo's description ὑπὸ τῷ Κιθαιρῶνι. The speed of movement of marching armies (Herodotus 9. 15, and Xenophon, *Hellenica*, 4. 4. 48–9) is an unreliable guide. Clearly Skolos was sufficiently far from Plataea to be at times subject to Theban rapacity (Herodotus, loc. cit. and 6. 108); yet it might also be reckoned as lying in Plataean territory (Strabo 9. 409 and *Ox. Pap.* v. 170–1, col. xii, lines 12–14, where Skolos, Erythrai, and Skarphe, i.e. Eteonos, are said to have been formerly one state with Plataea). It is clear from Herodotus (6. 108) and from Strabo (loc. cit.) that there was some warrant for regarding the Asopos as the *normal* boundary between Theban and Plataean territory.

Ἐτεωνός (2. 497) MAP 2

Strabo (9. 408, cf. 409) placed this town in the Parasopia, though he says that its name had changed to Σκάρφη. Beyond this there is no evidence for its position, and there is certainly no warrant for locating it near Dervenosialesi, as Burr does:[10] such a position would hardly agree with the ancient grouping of Skolos, Eteonos, Erythrai, and Plataea.[11] The Homeric epithet πολύκνημος suggests a position somewhat similar to that of Skolos.

Θέσπεια (2. 498) MAP 2

REFS. *Gazetteer*, No. 418; *RE*, Suppl. vi. 609 (Mycenaean sherds found by Heurtley); *Hesperia* 20 (1951), pp. 289 f.; *BCH* 76 (1952), p. 219; *BCH* 79 (1955), p. 257; Frazer, *Pausanias* v. 140–2.

The historic city of Thespiai lay on the right bank of the Kanavari stream (the ancient Thespios), south of the road from Thebes to Domvraina, and south of and below the modern village of Thespiai. An important Neolithic settlement has been discovered in the region now known as 'kastro' or 'magoula' (I.8 Levadhia 895E/828N), the higher, eastern end of which appears to have formed the centre of the ancient city. It was presumably here that Heurtley picked up his Mycenaean sherds, but we could find none in 1961, and it is difficult to define the extent of the Mycenaean settlement. So far there is no evidence for Protogeometric or Geometric occupation of the site.

Γραῖα (2. 498) MAP 2

REFS. *Gazetteer*, No. 430.

Pausanias (9. 20. 2) records a typical claim by the people of Tanagra to the name of Graia, but Strabo (9. 404) mentions an actual place called Graia near Oropos, and this is supported by Stephanus of Byzantium (s.v. *'Ορωπός*) and by Eustathius (ad *Il.* 2. 498). Stephanus adds that 'according to others' it was a seaside place in the district of Oropos, opposite Eretria.[12]

In view of this testimony, it seems more than a coincidence that a Mycenaean site should have been discovered near Oropos which exactly fits this description. It lies in the vineyard of one Nikolaos Nikolaou, at a point where a narrow-gauge railway leads to an old coal-mine, to left (seaward) of the road from Skala Oropou to Markopoulo (I.10 Nea Psara 462E/821N). It was discovered by V. Petrakos, now a member of the Greek Archaeological Service, and although it has not yet been published, its discoverer very kindly informed Hope Simpson that he had picked up many sherds of Minyan ware and Mycenaean pottery on the surface.[13]

Μυκαλησσός (2. 498) MAP 2

REFS. *BSA* 14 (1907/8), pp. 226–318; *RE*, Suppl. vii (1940), pp. 495–510.

The ancient remains near the modern village of Rhitsona are probably those of Mykalessos. The site occupies a low knoll about 400 metres south-west of the modern hamlet, and 300 metres west of the road from Thebes to Khalkis (I.9 Khalkis △ 195 at 218E/933N). The knoll, which is about 120 metres long, north to south, by 80 metres, bears traces of circuit- and other ancient walls.[14] Since the excavations of the British School[15] were mainly concerned with the ancient cemetery, the precise position and extent of the city were not determined, but the knoll presumably marks its approximate centre.[16]

Despite the statements of Burr,[17] no certainly Mycenaean sherds had been recorded from this site until recently, and we were still unable to find any in 1964. However, we did come across one or two chips of obsidian, and

Mycenaean sherds have now been found on the surface.[18] The site is certainly suitable for Mycenaean occupation, and its position is a strategic one, commanding the Anephorites pass to the west.

The cemetery, which appears to have first come into use in the mid-8th century B.C. and to have flourished in the latter half of the 6th century, provides some evidence to support the story (cf. Thucydides 7. 29. 2–4) that Mykalessos had declined by the end of the 5th century. It is not mentioned by the Oxyrhynchus Historian as providing a Boeotarch in 395 B.C.,[19] and Pausanias (1. 23. 3 and 9. 19. 4) found it in ruins. Yet in the Catalogue it is *εὐρύχορος*, and it is mentioned in the *Hymn to Apollo* (line 224) as lying on the way from the Euripos to Thebes. It also figures in the Cadmus legend (cf. Pausanias, 9. 19. 4).

Ἅρμα (2. 499) MAP 2

REFS. *Gazetteer*, No. 428; Frazer, *Pausanias* v. 62–3; Philippson, *GL* i. 742, No. 210.

Strabo (9. 404) says that Harma was in his time a deserted village near Mykalessos, and Pausanias—who saw it in ruins, like Mykalessos (9. 19. 4)—enumerates it in sequence between Glisas (see below) and Mykalessos. Strabo, Pausanias, and Plutarch (*Moralia* 307a) all relate the name to the legend of Amphiaraos, who was swallowed up by the earth, together with his chariot (*ἅρμα*), on his flight from Thebes.

The place is probably to be identified with a barren and scrub-covered hill, now known as 'Kastri', which commands the main route from Thebes to Khalkis at the point where the road begins to ascend towards the Anephorites pass (I.9 Khalkis △ 298 Kastro Likovouno at 190E/913N). The hill, which now lies on the *left* of the main road—it used to lie on its right[20]—rises some 200 metres above the level of the plain, and its extensive summit (about 300 metres north to south) is criss-crossed with ancient wall-foundations of rough polygonal blocks, including what appear to be the foundations of a small square tower on the south. At one point there are the remains of a circuit-wall made of large blocks with a rubble core, but much of the walling seen by Frazer seems now to have disappeared.

Most of the sherds on the top and on the slopes are classical, and there is a plethora of purple-glazed tiles, but in 1959 Hope Simpson found some obsidian and a few LH IIIA–B sherds of normal type. So far there is no evidence that the place was occupied in Protogeometric or Geometric times.

Εἰλέσιον (2. 499) MAP 2

The location of this place is quite uncertain, and Strabo (9. 406) only confuses the issue by connecting *Ἕλος*, *Ἐλεών*, and *Εἰλέσιον* by a specious piece of etymology. Burr[21] places it at the site of some remains of polygonal walling a little to the west of Chlembotsari, on the old road from Thebes to Tanagra, but it has also been sought at the village of Bratsi, and even placed on the coast.[22]

Ἐρυθραί (2. 499) MAP 2

REFS. *Gazetteer*, No. 424; Philippson, *GL* i. 742, No. 198; Fimmen, *KMK*, p. 6; *RE*, Suppl. vi. 609; Frazer, *Pausanias* v. 2–6; Pritchett, *AJA* 61 (1957), pp. 9–28 and map; Ålin, *EMF*, pp. 119f.

This place has unfortunately still not been exactly located, although classical Erythrai, together with Hysiai, must have been in the vicinity of modern Kriekouki (now called Erythrai). Pausanias (9. 2. 1.) enumerates Hysiai after Plataea and before Erythrai, and hence Pritchett[23] equates Hysiai with the ancient site to the south-east of and above the chapel of Pantanassa, about two kilometres east of Kriekouki (I.9 Khalkis ♁ at 050E/736N), and formerly located Erythrai at the chapel of Ayia Triadha, about a kilometre further to the east. He would now, however, locate Erythrai at Ayios Meletios (see above, on Skolos). But Erythrai is generally closely coupled with Hysiai in our sources (cf. Pausanias 9. 2. 1., and Strabo 9. 404 πλησίον Ἐρυθρῶν). Hysiai lay on the road to Athens via Eleutherai (Pausanias 9. 1. 6), and it is perhaps not impossible that it lay to the south of Erythrai, rather than to the west of it. Erythrai is, indeed, more usually located at the Pantanassa site,[24] and presumably the two Mycenaean sherds from 'Erythrai' found by Bölte[25] were from this site. The ridge above the Pantanassa chapel is a lower spur of Mt. Kithairon, and the position is both commanding and defensible.[26] Mycenaean occupation was revealed, if not by Bölte, by the sherds collected by ourselves in 1961, which included a much worn fragment of a (?) Mycenaean animal-figurine and some LH III *Deep Bowl* handles, among others which seemed to be Mycenaean.

Ἐλεών (2. 500) MAP 2

REFS. *Gazetteer*, No. 427; *RE*, Suppl. vi. 609 (Mycenaean sherds found by Bölte); Philippson, *GL* i. 742, No. 209; Frazer, *Pausanias* v. 63–5; Ålin, *EMF*, p. 120.

According to Strabo (9. 405, cf. Pausanias 1. 29. 6), Eleon bordered on Tanagra and lay near a marsh, though it is not clear whether he relied on fact or merely on etymology for this latter piece of information: at all events, there does not seem to be any very compelling reason to look for a marsh here, whether seasonal or perennial, as Frazer did.

The place is probably to be located on the flat top of a steep-sided hill, immediately to the north-west of the modern village of Eleon (formerly called Dritsa), and overlooking the eastern part of the Theban plain (I.9 Khalkis 173E/877N approx.). The flat area on top of the hill measures about 200 metres north-west to south-east by about 120 metres, and in the Archaic period was protected on the east—the only side where it is not naturally defensible—by a beautifully constructed wall of Lesbian masonry.

The prehistoric surface-sherds are of uniformly excellent quality, especially the *Grey* and *Yellow Minyan* ware, and the LH IIIA–C:1. There is an enormous quantity of such sherds on the eroded south-eastern slopes, together with obsidian, while the extensive slopes towards the plain on the north are also strewn with sherds, very few being later than Mycenaean: so far no Protogeometric or Geometric sherds have been found. The extent of the site and the quantity and quality of the Mycenaean pottery indicate that during the Mycenaean period this was a settlement second only to Thebes in the Theban plain.

Ὕλη (2. 500) MAP 2

The name of this place naturally suggests that it lay on or near the shores of Lake Hylike (cf. Strabo 9. 407–8), although it is doubtful whether the proposed location on the barren peninsula of Κληματαριάς[27] can be right. *Iliad* 5. 707 f., however, suggests a position bordering on Lake Copais, and it is possible that it should be sought in the region of the ancient Akraiphnion—at all events, on the eastern side of the lake. But for the present its location must remain quite uncertain.

Πετεών (2. 500) MAP 2

Strabo (9. 410) says that Peteon was a village in Theban territory, near the road to Anthedon. Burr[28] accepts the conjecture that it should be located at the hill of Ayios Elias, above and to the north-east of the village of Mouriki (I.9 Khalkis ♁ at 082E/963N), and describes the walls on the north-west of the chapel as 'sicher Mykenisch'. But Hope Simpson, who visited the place in 1960, is of the opinion that these walls are in fact of the Hellenistic period, when such neat polygonal masonry was common. The narrow and rocky ridge on which the tiny chapel and the walls are perched seems hardly suitable for a settlement of any size, but there are sporadic classical sherds to be found on the slopes between the hill and the outskirts of the village, though Hope Simpson could find nothing earlier.

The identification with Peteon is, then, unsupported, but remains a possibility.

Ὠκαλέη (2. 501) MAP 2

Strabo (9. 410) says that Okalea lay midway between Haliartos and Alalkomenion, thirty stades from each, and this is partly confirmed by the *Hymn to Apollo* (lines 242–3), in which Apollo is said to pass 'Okalea of the many towers (πολύπυργος)' on his roundabout route to Haliartos. The location of Haliartos is, of course, certain, and Alalkomenion probably lay somewhere near Mamoura, as is suggested by the inscriptions carrying decrees of the Boeotian confederacy found in the village.[29] Frazer identified as the ruins of the temple of Itonian Athena some polygonal foundations on the rocky tip of the spur south of the main road, and a little to the north of the village of Soulinari:[30] since his day a new hamlet called Kato Agoriani has sprung up just west of the site (I.8 Levadhia 751E/945N).

The inconsiderable height of the ridge and its proximity to the plain do not materially contradict Strabo's description (9. 413) of Alalkomenion as being 'neither large, nor lying in a defended position, but in the plain', and accords well with Pausanias' statement that it lay at the foot of a low mountain (9. 33. 5). Hope Simpson found some LH and other Bronze Age sherds here in 1959.[31]

If, then, the site at Kato Agoriani is that of Alalkomenion, we should look for Okalea somewhere to the west of the modern Siacho, if we follow Strabo's directions precisely, but no ancient site has yet been found here.

Μεδεών (2. 501) MAP 2

REFS. *Gazetteer*, No. 407; S. Lauffer, 'Medeon', in *AM* 63/4 (1938/9), pp. 177 f.; Burr, *NK*, p. 23; Ålin *EMF*, p. 121.

The location given by Strabo (9. 410)—'near Onchestos and below the mountain Phoinikios (= ? the modern Phagas)'—makes it probable that Medeon is to be identified with the small acropolis, now known as 'Kastraki', to the west of Dhavlosis (I.8 Levadhia Dhavlosis at 915E/933N). It is well placed to survey the drainage canals and dykes of the bay of Dhavlos.

The site was excavated by Lauffer, and MH *Grey Minyan* and *Matt-painted* wares, together with LH IIIB, are common. There are also a few black-glazed classical sherds, but so far no evidence for Protogeometric or Geometric occupation. According to Strabo (loc. cit.), the town later changed its name to 'Phoinikis'.

A Mycenaean cemetery was noted at Mt. Sphingion near by, and LH sherds and house-remains on the hill of Kalimpaki, near Dhavlosis.

Κῶπαι (2. 502) MAP 2

REFS. *Gazetteer*, No. 401; Philippson, *GL* i. 742, No. 163; Frazer, *Pausanias* v. 131–2.

The meaning of the name Kopai ('oars') possibly reflects the time when the normal method of transport to the place was by boat (cf. Pausanias 9. 24. 1), and there can be little doubt that it is to be located at the modern village of Topolia (I.8 Levadhia 911E/048N): Frazer records that, until a few years before 1895, the hill on which the village stands was an island accessible only by boat, and *IG* vii, No. 2792, found at the north end of the promontory of Mytika, north of the bay of Kardhitsa, records this as the boundary between the men of Kopai and those of Akraiphnion. Thucydides (4. 93. 4) refers to Kopai in the form *Κωπαίῃ*.

The polygonal walls and the causeway on the north side of the village, recorded by Frazer, seem to have disappeared, but Hope Simpson found a few Mycenaean sherds on the eastern slopes in 1959, and the site looks exactly suitable for Mycenaean occupation. No evidence has yet appeared that it was inhabited in Protogeometric or Geometric times, but this negative evidence from surface-sherding is, of course, hardly significant.

A possible derivation for the modern name, 'Topolia', is suggested by *CIG*,

No. 2703 (built into the village church of the Panayia), which reads *Δαματρ[ι] Ταυροπολω*.

Εὔτρησις (2. 502) MAP 2

REFS. *Gazetteer*, No. 417; H. Goldman, *Excavations at Eutresis in Boeotia* (Harvard University Press 1931); *JHS Arch.* for 1958, pp. 10–11 (Neolithic and EH); Åkin, *EMF*, pp. 123 f.; Desborough, *LMTS*, p. 120.

The location of Eutresis was proved by an inscription bearing part of the name, found during the excavations carried out by Miss Goldman. The site lies at the northern end of the plain of Leuktra, near the spring of Arkopodhi ('Bear's Foot'), and about midway between Thebes and Livadhostro (I.9 Khalkis 328 at 952E/795N). It may thus lie on a branch of the possibly Mycenaean road of which traces have been found running up from Livadhostro.[32] The extensive Mycenaean circuit-walls of Cyclopean masonry bear out the tradition of the walls built by Zethus and Amphion (Stephanus of Byzantium, s.v. *Εὔτρησις*; cf. Strabo 9. 411), and show that the town was important in LH IIIB, though apparently more populous in the Middle Helladic period. The site was abandoned towards the end of LH III (the latest pottery being LH IIIC:1 from House V), and its history only begins again in the 6th century.[33]

Since the location of this place is as certain as any such location can be, the apparent gap in its occupation between *c.* 1200 B.C. and the 6th century is a strong indication that the Catalogue's reference to it is a reminiscence of the Mycenaean period, since no one, presumably, would maintain that it reflects the 6th century. It might be argued that the Catalogue refers to some other place of the same name, or that when the site was re-occupied, the name 'Eutresis' was simply given to it arbitrarily, as ancient names are now sometimes given to villages in Greece. But such arguments would seem to be those of desperation.[34]

Θίσβη (2. 502) MAP 2

REFS. *Gazetteer*, No. 419; Evans, *JHS* 45 (1925), pp. 1–42 (the 'Treasure'); *BSA* 26 (1923–5), pp. 41 f.; Frazer, *Pausanias* v. 160–4; *AM* 73 (1958), pp. 17 f. (Neokastro walls); Åkin, *EMF*, p. 124.

This place is certainly to be located at the village which used to be called Kakosi, though its name has now been changed to Thisvi. The Mycenaean settlement occupied the acropolis, now known as Palaiokastro, rising behind the village on its north-west side (I.8 Levadhia 723E/805N). Its total length (north-west to south-east) is about 300 metres, and the width of the summit is about 100 metres, tapering to the south-east. At the north-west end are the remains of a corner built of massive blocks, which looks like the inner face of part of a Cyclopean circuit-wall. The top surface and the extensive slopes are strewn with Mycenaean pottery of the finest quality, but there are very few recognizable classical or later sherds—the earliest noted comes from a Late Corinthian *Skyphos*.

In fact it appears likely that the classical site was mainly centred on the plateau-like lower hill to the south of the village, now called Neokastro, which bears impressive remains of fortifications in good isodomic masonry (?4th century B.C.), including a well-preserved tower. At the south foot of this hill, and in the soft rock of other slopes in this vicinity, remains of chamber-tombs can be seen, some of which were Mycenaean.[35]

A fertile plain stretches to the south (about 3 kilometres east to west by 2 kilometres), and Heurtley[36] noted the importance of Thisbe in relation to the Steveniko pass leading from the harbours at Vathy or Khorsiai, via Thisbe over Helikon, to Lake Copais and Orchomenos. There is also a long but gentle route from Thisbe via Thespiai to Thebes. The remains of an ancient dyke seen by Pausanias,[37] dividing the plain of Thisbe into two, may have carried a road from the harbour.

The Homeric epithet *πολυτρήρων* is apposite, the cliffs in the vicinity of the acropolis being honeycombed with the nests of wild pigeons, as Frazer noted, though Strabo (9. 411) says that the epithet was derived from the port which was *πετρῶδες περιστερῶν μέστον*.

Κορώνεια (2. 503) MAP 2

A multiplicity of ancient references suffices to establish the location of Koroneia (I.8 Levadhia 244 at 728E/948N), and as Burr remarks,[38] the acropolis was probably occupied in Mycenaean times: the position is superb, and the site conforms to the pattern of Mycenaean settlement round Lake Copais. But surface exploration has so far failed to produce any evidence of early occupation, and the site has unfortunately not been excavated.

Strabo (9. 411) preserves a tradition that the Boeotians took possession of Koroneia only *after the Trojan War*, at the same time as they occupied Orchomenos, and the same tradition probably lies behind Thucydides' statement that the Boeotians did not enter Boeotia until sixty years after the Trojan War (1. 12. 6). We shall discuss these traditions and their possible bearing on the question of the period reflected by the Catalogue in Part III.[39]

Ἁλίαρτος (2. 503) MAP 2

REFS. *Gazetteer*, No. 409; Frazer, *Pausanias* v. 164–6; *BSA* 27 (1925/6), pp. 81–91 (especially p. 82); *BSA* 28 (1926/7), p. 129; *JHS* 46 (1926), pp. 234 f.; *BSA* 32 (1931/2), pp. 190 and 205–6; *JHS* 64 (1944), p. 89; Ålin, *EMF*, p. 121.

The Mycenaean acropolis lay at the western end of the long ridge upon which ancient Haliartos was situated: here there is a higher knoll, some 250 metres east to west by 150 metres, originally surrounded by a Cyclopean circuit-wall, remains of which can be seen on the south side. A sherd picked out from the fabric of the wall 'was thought by Mr. Forsdyke to date from about 1400 B.C.' (i.e. LH IIIA),[40] and sherds picked up on the surface by Hope Simpson in 1959 included EH, MH *Grey* and *Yellow Minyan*, and LH IIIB. A 'Mycenaean area' at the east end of the sanctuary also produced sherds ranging from LH II to

LH IIIB,[41] and it is thus apparent that the Mycenaean site continued for a considerable distance along the ridge to the east: there were even some LH IIIB sherds in evidence in 1959, at a point some 300 metres east of the higher knoll on the western end. This was therefore a large Mycenaean settlement, and the impression given is that it would have had a population second only to that of Orchomenos in the Copais basin.

There can be no doubt that the Haliartos of the Catalogue is this place, but there is evidence that it was also occupied in the Geometric period. The Homeric epithet *ποιήεις* perhaps refers to the lush water-meadows (Strabo 9. 407), and it must be remembered that the drainage of Lake Copais in ancient times[42] would have benefited the area around Haliartos as does the present scheme, which has its headquarters there.

The *Hymn to Apollo* (lines 239 f., 244–76, and 375–87) indicates the prominence of Haliartos in early traditions, and it became an important member (one of the earliest) of the Boeotian League, with the honour of providing a Boeotarch in turn with Levadhia and Koroneia.[43]

Πλάταια (2. 504) MAP 2

REFS. *Gazetteer*, No. 423; *RE* 20 (1950), s.v. 'Plataiai', pp. 2255–2332, especially p. 2282 and plan on p. 2266; Skias, *PAE* 1899, pp. 42–56, especially pp. 50–1; cf. *AJA* 7 (1891), p. 404; Frazer, *Pausanias* v. 8–13; Frazer and Van Buren, *Graecia Antiqua*, pp. 136 f.

This entry in the Catalogue presumably refers to a town on the site of the historic city of Plataea. The area which was earliest inhabited seems to have been the north-western part of the forward spur of the site, where the ground is higher.[44] Here trial excavations by Skias revealed 'Pre-Mycenaean', Mycenaean, Geometric, and Early Corinthian sherds, the Geometric sherds and bronze fibulae providing some evidence of continuity at the site.

It is interesting that this higher, north-western part of Plataea was enclosed separately, and apparently formed an inner citadel, although it is naturally exposed to attack from the south, along the line of the spur:[45] from it there is a fine view over the plain towards Thebes.

The Mycenaean occupation was, presumably, mainly in the LH III period, to which the little horse-figurine found by Skias,[46] at least, seems to have belonged.

Γλισᾶς (2. 504) MAP 2

REFS. *Gazetteer*, No. 426; Frazer, *Pausanias* v. 60–1; Philippson, *GL*, i. 742, No. 192.

Strabo (9. 412) describes Glisas as being a *κατοικία ἐν τῷ Ὑπάτῳ ὄρει* (the modern Sagmatas), and it should probably be identified with the little acropolis, now called Tourleza, on the rocky hill above the village of Syrtzi, north of the Thebes–Khalkis road (I.9 Khalkis 110E/919N): the hill is in fact a spur of the Sagmatas range.

The small area of the summit was once enclosed by a wall of polygonal masonry, and here the sherds are mainly classical, but lower down, on the south-west slopes above the village, Hope Simpson found in 1959 sherds from LH IIIB *Kylikes*, together with part of the rim of an LH I/II 'Vaphio Cup'. Obsidian is plentiful both here and on the summit. There is so far no evidence that the site was occupied in Protogeometric or Geometric times.

Ὑποθῆβαι (2. 505) MAP 2

REFS. (1) *The Cadmeia*: *Gazetteer*, No. 416; *AE* 1909, pp. 58–122; *AE* 1930, pp. 29 f.; *PAE* 1911, pp. 143 f.; *PAE* 1912, pp. 85 f.; Rodenwaldt, *Tiryns* ii. 188 f.; Furumark, *Chron. MP*, p. 52; *AA* 63/4 (1948/9), pp. 240 f.; *AA* 68 (1953), pp. 16 f.; *Kadmos* iii, pp. 25 f.; *ILN* for 28/11/64 and 5/12/64; *JHS Arch.* for 1963/4, p. 13, for 1964/5, p. 15, and for 1965/6, p. 12; Ålin, *EMF*, pp. 118 f.; Desborough, *LMTS*, p. 121.

(2) *The Kolonaki Cemetery*: *ADelt.* 3 (1917), pp. 123–209; Ålin and Desborough, locc. citt.

The name Ὑποθῆβαι (which suggested to Stephanus of Byzantium an analogy with Ὑποχαλκίς in Aetolia) presumably refers to a settlement *below* the former citadel of Thebes on the Cadmeia (cf. Strabo 9. 412 and Pausanias 2. 6. 4). This accords with the tradition that the Epigonoi had sacked Thebes shortly *before* the Trojan War (cf. *Il.* 4. 406), and the excavation of part of the Cadmeia has in fact shown that the Mycenaean 'first palace' here *was* destroyed before Troy VIIa.[47] If, however, the sack of Troy VIIa took place about the middle of the LH IIIB period, and still more if it took place in LH IIIC,[48] it could hardly be literally true that, for example, Diomedes took part in both exploits. In fact it looks as though the tradition has here compressed history.[49]

The evidence from the cemeteries shows a continuity of occupation at Thebes after the sack of the Cadmeia, so that it would appear to be historically possible for men from here to have taken part in the sack of Troy VIIa.[50] But whether or not this entry in the Catalogue can be used to decide which period it reflects is another question.[51]

Ὀγχηστός (2. 506) MAP 2

REFS. *Gazetteer*, No. 408; Frazer, *Pausanias* v. 139–40; Philippson, *GL*, i. 742, No. 172; *JHS Arch.* for 1961/2, p. 31.

Onchestos has been identified with a rounded hill now called Kasarma (from the ruined Turkish building standing upon it), immediately north of the main road from Thebes as this enters the south-east corner of the Copais basin (I.8 Levadhia 889E/906N). It thus commanded the route from the Theban plain to Lake Copais, and would have made a useful staging-post for travellers (cf. *Hymn to Apollo*, lines 229 f.).

On the south side of the hill, some 20 metres north of the road, there are some ancient blocks which appear to be the foundations of a small square building. Pausanias (9. 26. 5) claimed that the sacred grove—(cf. the Catalogue's reference to the Ποσιδήϊον ἀγλαὸν ἄλσος here)—as well as the shrine and image of Poseidon, existed in his day, but Strabo (9. 412) vehemently asserted that the place was bare of trees—as it certainly is to-day! The tradition of this sacred grove may very well go back to Mycenaean times, when such places often seemed to have been regarded as holy.[52]

In any case, Onchestos was certainly inhabited then: on a visit in 1961 we picked up EH, MH (*Minyan*), and some LH IIIA–B sherds on top of the hill and for a radius of about 50 metres in all directions. We also found some classical and later sherds, but no Protogeometric or Geometric.

Ἄρνη (2. 507) MAP 2

Noack's view that Arne should be identified with the great Mycenaean fortress of Gla[53] has been revived, despite the strong arguments advanced by Gomme,[54] as a result of the recent excavations at the site.[55] These led the excavator, Threpsiades, to maintain[56] that his discoveries had shown that De Ridder was wrong to regard the site merely as a sort of military barracks.[57]

The remains unearthed, however, still do not appear to be inconsistent with De Ridder's view: the so-called 'palace' is made up of numbers of abnormally small apartments, and the 'agora' could easily be interpreted as military quarters, the soldiers perhaps occupying the long 'megaron',[58] with stables in the long buildings on the south and east of the courtyard.[59] In any case, the rectangularity of the ground-plan is really rather unlike what we should have expected in a Mycenaean settlement, and conjures up a picture of something much more like a Roman fort or camp, though this might merely be due to the flatness of the site. The scarcity of sherds, upon which Desborough remarks,[60] also seems inconsistent with Gla's being an ordinary settlement. In fact, the most likely explanation for the surrounding of such a bare, rocky, and waterless site, with Cyclopean walls over two kilometres long, is surely a military one, and as was seen long ago by De Ridder, and later also by Kenny,[61] Gla is best explained as the headquarters for the maintenance of all the forts in the north-western bay of Lake Copais and the look-out posts on Mt. Ptoon.

If, then, Gla was a fortress rather than a town, it is unlikely to be the *πολυστάφυλος Ἄρνη* of the Catalogue—the epithet being singularly inappropriate—and Gomme's hypothesis that it was the stronghold of the Phlegyians (cf. *Il.* 13. 301–2, and Pausanias 9. 9. 2 and 36. 1–3) is attractive, particularly because, according to Pausanias, the Phlegyians were from the Minyan district, and Gla seems likely to have been controlled by Orchomenos.[62]

It is better, therefore, to look elsewhere for Arne, but that even the ancients did not know where to look is indicated by their disagreements about it: Pausanias (9. 40. 5–6) says that Arne was the old name for Chaeronea, but we cannot be sure that this means anything more than that the people of Chaeronea had hit upon this method of securing a mention in the Catalogue. Strabo (9. 413) reports three different theories: that Arne was the old name for Akraiphnion; that Arne, like Mideia, had been swallowed up by the lake; and that Zenodotus wrote *Ἄσκρην* for *Ἄρνην*—Strabo rightly pours scorn upon the last, in view of what Hesiod has to say about his home! In short, the search for Arne appears to be hopeless.

Μίδεια (2. 507) MAP 2

The search for Mideia is equally hopeless. Pausanias (9. 39. 1) says that this was the ancient name for Lebadeia, but as in the case of Arne, one cannot help but be suspicious of this claim, particularly since Strabo (9. 413) records the quite different tradition that Mideia had been swallowed up by Lake Copais. If we may dismiss Pausanias' view as being based on nothing more than the spurious claims of the people of Lebadeia, we should, presumably, look for Mideia in the region of Lake Copais, and it is conceivable that the name may once have been attached to one of the ancient settlements on the north shore of the lake.[63]

Νῖσα (2. 508) MAP 2

According to Apollodorus (ap. Strabo 9. 405), Nisa *οὐδαμοῦ φαίνεται τῆς Βοιωτίας*, and as Strabo saw, the conjecture *Ἴσον* involves a false quantity. There is, unfortunately, a lacuna in the text of Strabo at this point, but however it is to be filled, it does not seem likely to provide any warrant for connecting the Nisa of the Catalogue with Nisaia in the Megarid, for that is several times mentioned elsewhere by Strabo (e.g. 9. 391), and never in conjunction with Nisa. In fact, as Allen saw,[64] the number of ancient variants for *Νῖσαν* reported by Strabo show an actual unwillingness to make the connection with Nisaia, though the Megarians were supposed to have adopted it after Leuctra, out of anti-Boeotian sentiment (cf. Polybius 20. 4. 1 and 6. 5). The tradition of a founder Megareus from Onchestos[65] has a fabricated look about it, and as we might have expected, the Athenians had a counter-tradition (Pausanias 1. 39. 4) that the Megarid originally belonged to Athens, and that Nisaia was named after Nisos, son of Pandion.

There is nothing intrinsically improbable about early connections between Megara and either Boeotia or Attica, but as Page saw,[66] the position of Nisa in the Catalogue is against the idea that it lay in the Megarid. Oldfather[67] thought that Nisa might have been the old name for Larymna, and although this conjecture is totally unsupported, it is at least, so to speak, in the right parish.

Ἀνθηδών (2. 508) MAP 2

REFS. *Gazetteer*, No. 437; Frazer, *Pausanias* v. 92–5; *AJA* 5 (1889), pp. 78 and 443–60; *AJA* 6 (1890), pp. 96–107; *AM* 19 (1894), p. 457; Desborough, *LMTS*, p. 48 n. 6.

There is, fortunately, no doubt about the location of Anthedon: it lay at the foot of Mt. Messapios, at a place now called Mandhraki, near Loukisia (I.9 Khalkis 24 at 163E/037N). Some excavations have been carried out at the site, mainly in the area of the small harbour, and the identification is proved by inscriptions (*IG* vii, p. 642). The acropolis, lying to the south-east of the harbour, is steep on all sides, though nowhere precipitous, except on the south-west, where the modern track passes the site. The top is roughly circular, about 180 metres in diameter.

The American trial trenches on the acropolis revealed only 'two walls, roughly built, of small irregular stones',[68] but some Mycenaean surface-sherds were claimed by Noack,[69] and others have since been found by Hope Simpson (in 1959), together with obsidian and fragments of later pottery ranging from Geometric to Hellenistic: the Mycenaean sherds are attributable to LH IIIB–C:1. Elsewhere on the site some bronze tools were found, including double-axes, which Desborough describes as a bronze-founder's hoard, possibly of early LH IIIC date.[70]

The site is large and impressive, and the little sheltered harbour must have been of considerable importance: it is the only port in Boeotia which is mentioned in the Catalogue, apart from Aulis itself, unless some of the unidentified places were ports, and the omission of Larymna (unless it is Nisa), and of Livadhostro (the ancient Creusis),[71] is surprising.

The names of the places from which the Boeotian contingent is drawn are distributed fairly evenly over the area of historical Boeotia, except for the enclave round Aspledon and Orchomenos, and in many cases they coincide with the historical centres. But such places as Tanagra, Chaeronea, and Lebadeia do not appear, and none of the ports—for example, Larymna or Creusis—unless some of the unidentifiable names conceal references to them. Conversely, there are seven of these unidentifiable names (Schoinos, Skolos, Eteonos, Eilesion, Arne, Mideia, and Nisa), though some of the places appear to have existed in historical times (Schoinos, Skolos, Eteonos), and their approximate location to have been known. The picture of Boeotia which the Catalogue presents thus differs from historical Boeotia.

On the other hand, the Boeotia of the Catalogue does resemble what we know of Mycenaean Boeotia, though we have no means of knowing, for example, whether the boundaries implied by the Catalogue are historically correct. But of the sixteen places mentioned the location of which can be fixed with any certainty, only one—Koroneia—has so far failed to produce evidence of Mycenaean occupation, and there are no important Mycenaean sites which do not appear to be mentioned, with the possible exception of Gla, and as we saw (above, p. 31), there is some reason to think that Gla was not a town in the normal sense. In any case, it may be referred to under one of the unidentifiable names, as indeed may other Mycenaean sites apparently not mentioned.

Whether or not, however, the Boeotia of the Catalogue might equally well be said to resemble Protogeometric or Geometric Boeotia, it is really impossible to say, since without the excavation of all the more certainly locatable towns we cannot be sure whether they were occupied during these periods or not. But at the moment we have no evidence for the occupation at this time of eleven of the sixteen places we can locate, though only in the cases of Eutresis (above, p. 27) and, possibly, Medeon (above, p. 26) is this perhaps significant. On the other hand, the fact that the Catalogue mentions so many places that were unknown in historical times suggests that we are dealing with a very different Boeotia from the historical one, and even though some of the important historical centres which do not appear to be mentioned may be referred to under another name, the very fact that they did undergo a change of name requires some explanation. The most likely period for sites to be deserted and for others to be given a new name is undoubtedly the 12th century B.C., during which Mycenaean civilization came to an end.

The Boeotia of the Catalogue coincides with what little we are told about Boeotia elsewhere in the Homeric poems, and indeed in mythology generally, except perhaps for the omission of Alalkomenai (cf. *Il.* 4. 8, and above on Okalea). Thus, as we saw, the reference to Hypothebai is in accordance with the tradition that Thebes was sacked by the Epignoi *before* the Trojan War, and Eleon, the home of Phoenix,[72] is mentioned.

The reference to Hypothebai in fact appears to provide a *terminus post quem* for this part of the Catalogue, since the excavations on the Cadmeia have shown that the 'first palace' was destroyed early in the LH IIIB period, and the 'second palace' later in the same period.[73] Huxley has argued[74] that the Catalogue must here reflect LH IIIB, but it must be emphasized that the reference to Hypothebai does at best only provide a *terminus post quem*: Thebes was certainly still inhabited in LH IIIC.[75] The difficulty in believing that the Boeotian section of the Catalogue reflects LH IIIB is precisely that the Boeotians are referred to in it (*Il.* 2. 494 and 510), for there was a strong tradition later that the Boeotians only occupied Boeotia *after* the Trojan War, and the archaeological evidence, in so far as it suggests anything, suggests the arrival of a new people in LH IIIC.[76] Huxley accepts Thucydides' view that an advance force of Boeotians arrived in time to take part in the Trojan War, but one wonders whether Thucydides had any other evidence for his view apart from the reference to Boeotians in the Catalogue itself, and apart from the destruction of the Cadmeia, which the tradition did not connect with the arrival of the Boeotians, there is certainly no archaeological evidence for the arrival of a new people before LH IIIC. Thus the reference to Boeotians in the Catalogue suggests an LH IIIC date.

On the other hand, the archaeological evidence from Eutresis and, possibly, Medeon suggests that these places were abandoned at the beginning of LH IIIC at latest, and the destruction of Gla at about the same time[77] probably means that other places mentioned in the Catalogue were destroyed or abandoned as a result of the invasions at the end of LH IIIB.

Thus the reference to Boeotians in the Catalogue seems to reflect LH IIIC, while the reference to Eutresis, Medeon, and possibly other places appears to reflect LH IIIB. We shall see how this may have come about in Part III (see pp. 164–8 below).

NOTES ON THE BOEOTIAN SECTION

1. *Hesperia*, Suppl. viii (1949), pp. 39–42. Blegen noted that the ships resembled the design on a vase from Tragana in Messenia.
2. *Hesperia*, Suppl. viii (1949), pp. 39f.
3. Cf. *Oxyrhynchus Papyri* v. 174–5, No. 842, col. xiii, line 26.
4. Cf. *AM* 19 (1894), p. 405; *Orchomenos*, i, Taf. VII.

5. *NK*, p. 20, No. 4.
6. Thus Burr, *NK*, p. 21 and Karte 4.
7. *Pausanias* v. 21–2.
8. *AJA* 61 (1957), pp. 9–28, and *Studies in Ancient Greek Topography* (Berkeley and Los Angeles 1965), pp. 103–21.
9. Pritchett, op. cit., p. 104.
10. *NK*, p. 21 and Karte 4.
11. Cf. *Oxyrhynchus Papyri* v. 170–1, No. 842, col. xii, lines 12–14, where Skolos, Erythrai, and Skarphe (= Eteonos) are said to have formerly made up one state with Plataea. Strabo (9. 409) records that some said that Skolos, Eteonos, and Erythrai were in the territory of Plataea.
12. Hence in Thucydides 2. 23. 10 the *Περαϊκήν* of the MSS. has been emended to *Γραϊκήν*, but this reading, although adopted by the Oxford Text, may after all be due solely to the antiquarian interests of Stephanus: cf. Frazer, *Pausanias* v. 82.
13. The sherds are now in the museum of the Amphiaraion. We are very grateful to Mr. Petrakos for this information.
14. The vicinity is described by Frazer, *Pausanias* v. 66.
15. Cf. *BSA* 14 (1907/8), pp. 226–318.
16. It is presumably the one referred to in *BSA* 14 (1907/8), p. 229. Cf. *RE*, Suppl. vii. 509.
17. *NK*, pp. 21–2.
18. The sherds were found by Mr. John M. Fossey of the University of Birmingham, to whom we are indebted for this information.
19. Cf. *Oxyrhynchus Papyri* v. 170–1, No. 842, col. xii, lines 8–20.
20. Cf. Frazer, *Pausanias* v. 62–3.
21. *NK*, p. 22, cf. Karte 4. For Mycenaean tombs near Chlembotsari see *JHS Arch* for 1965/6, p. 13.
22. Burr, loc. cit., n. 5.
23. *AJA* 61 (1957), pp. 22–3.
24. Cf. Burr, *NK*, Karte 4.
25. Fimmen, *KMK*, p. 6; *RE* Suppl. vi, p. 609.
26. Cf. the first Greek position at the Battle of Plataea: Herodotus 9. 19.
27. Burr, *NK*, p. 23 and Karte 3.
28. *NK*, p. 23; cf. E. Kirsten, *RE* 19 (1937), pp. 1128f.
29. *CIG* i, Nos. 2859–69. The goddess Athena was reputed to have been born at Alalkomenion (Strabo 9. 413, cf. *Il.* 4. 8).
30. *Pausanias* v. 168–9; Philippson, *GL* i. 740, No. 140; *AA* 1940, pp. 184 and 187.
31. *Gazetteer*, No. 410. The reference to *Ἀλαλκομενηΐς Ἀθήνη* in *Il.* 4. 8 evidently led Strabo to assume that Alalkomenion existed at the time of the Trojan War—as indeed the Mycenaean sherds found at Kato Agoriani confirm, if this is Alalkomenion—and to wonder why the place was not mentioned in the Catalogue: he suggests that the men of Alalkomenion were 'sacred' and were hence excused!
32. Heurtley, *BSA* 26 (1923–5), pp. 38f. and Pl. VII. On a visit in 1961 we found MH and LH sherds at Livadhostro on the slopes of the hill now crowned by the remains of a Turkish tower (*Gazetteer*, No. 422). Cf. Pritchett, *Studies in Ancient Greek Topography*, Part I, pp. 54–6.
33. Goldman, *Excavations at Eutresis in Boeotia*, pp. 236–9.
34. Cf. pp. 153–4 below for a further discussion of the significance of Eutresis.

35. *BSA* 26 (1923–5), p. 44.
36. *BSA*, loc. cit.
37. Frazer, *Pausanias* v. 163–4.
38. *NK*, p. 24 n. 3.
39. See pp. 162–4; cf. also p. 34 above.
40. *BSA* 27 (1925/6), p. 82.
41. *BSA* 28 (1926/7), p. 129, and *BSA* 32 (1931/2), p. 190.
42. Cf. André Kenny, *LAAA* 22 (1935), pp. 189–206; Frazer, *Pausanias* v. 110; Kahrstedt, *JdI* 52 (1937), pp. 1 f.; Wace and Stubbings, *CH*, p. 288.
43. *Oxyrhynchus Papyri* v. 170–1, No. 842, col. xii, lines 17–19.
44. See plan in *RE* 20 (1950), p. 2266.
45. Cf. Frazer, *Pausanias* v, plan on p. 9 and p. 11; Frazer and van Buren, *Graecia Antiqua*, pp. 136f.; cf. also the mining and countermining of the famous siege (Thucydides 2. 75–8).
46. *PAE* 1899, pp. 50–1.
47. Furumark (*Chron. MP*, p. 52) believed that all the pottery from the burnt layer of the 'first palace' on the Cadmeia should be attributed to LH IIIA:1. He dismissed as intrusive *AE* 1909, Pl. 3, Nos. 6 and 10 (which are obviously LH IIIA:2/B), and classed all the big false-necked jars (his Type 64) as LH IIIA:1. But an LH IIIA:2 date is possibly more consistent with the style of the vases, and more probable for the great quantity of plain wares, and especially for the false-necked jars. But, in any case, the destruction of the 'first palace' has now been dated to *c.* 1300 B.C. by the burnt floors with early LH IIIB pottery. In the 'second palace' (on a different alignment), the burnt layer where the cylinders and jewellery were found contained *developed* LH IIIB pottery.
48. Blegen (*Troy* iv. 8–10) thought that the destruction of Troy VIIa took place well before the end of LH IIIB, and has since shown a tendency to push the date further back (cf., for example, *Troy and the Trojans*, pp. 160–3). But some scholars think that some of the sherds are LH IIIC rather than LH IIIB: e.g. Nylander, *Antiquity* 37 (1963), p. 7 (quoting Furumark's opinion). Mylonas (*Hesperia* 33 (1964), pp. 363–4) puts the destruction 'towards the very end of the LH IIIB ceramic phase'.
49. Cf. Miss Gray's remarks (*HHC*, p. 259): '. . . it is noticeable that the description suits Troy VI and the events suit Troy VIIa; the real city had lost its prosperity even before the enemy came to destroy it. It looks as though tradition had again concentrated history.'
50. Cf. Desborough, *LMTS*, p. 121.
51. See p. 34 above, and p. 162 below.
52. Cf. Nilsson, *The Minoan–Mycenaean Religion* (2nd edn. 1950), pp. 262f.
53. *AM* 19 (1894), pp. 405f.
54. *Essays Presented to William Ridgeway* (1913), pp. 116–23.
55. For recent work at the site see *Ergon* for 1955 and following years.
56. *Ergon* for 1961, pp. 47–8.
57. *BCH* 18 (1894), pp. 297–301.
58. Or 'megara'? There seem to be two hearths!
59. That the garrison had chariots is suggested by the traces of roads leading to the south and south-east gates.
60. *LMTS*, p. 121.
61. *LAAA* 22 (1935), pp. 189f.
62. See below, p. 39.
63. Burr *NK*, p. 27, suggests the neighbourhood of Stroviki and Tourloyanni.

64. *HCS*, pp. 57–8. Strabo 9. 405 quotes as variants *Ἶσον*, *Κρεῦσαν*, and *Νῦσαν*.

65. Cf. Allen, *HCS*, p. 58.

66. *HHI*, p. 157 n. 10.

67. *AJA* 20 (1916), pp. 44–5, cf. *Gazetteer*, No. 413. In 1964 we discovered that the site at Bazaraki (Upper Larymna) near which Oldfather (op. cit., pp. 41 f. and fig. 3) traced part of an ancient road was occupied in the Mycenaean (LH III) period, and perhaps earlier.

68. *AJA* 6 (1890), p. 99.

69. *AM* 19 (1894), p. 457.

70. *AJA* 6 (1890), pp. 104f. and Pl. xv; Desborough, *LMTS*, p. 48 and nn. 6 and 8.

71. Cf. p. 27 above on Eutresis, and note 32.

72. Cf. *Il.* 9. 448 and 10. 266, and below, p. 129. Presumably this Eleon is the one in Boeotia.

73. Cf. above, n. 47.

74. *BICS* 3 (1956), p. 22.

75. Desborough, *LMTS*, pp. 121–2.

76. Desborough, op. cit., p. 251.

77. Desborough, op. cit., p. 121.

THE MINYANS

Ἀσπληδών (2. 511) MAP 2

REFS. *Gazetteer*, No. 399; Bulle, *Orchomenos* i. 116 and 119–20, Abb. 31–2; Wace and Thompson, *PT*, pp. 196–7; Philippson, *GL* i. 742, No. 158.

Burr[1] is probably right to locate Aspledon at Pyrgos (T.8 Atalandi 803E/077N): the village was formerly known as Xeropyrgo, a name which calls to mind the tradition recorded by Pausanias (9. 38. 9) that Aspledon was abandoned by its inhabitants because of a shortage of water. The hill is imposing[2] and forms a landmark similar to the ridge of Orchomenos opposite. Trial excavations have revealed MH and Mycenaean occupation, and there are traces of what appear to have been Cyclopean circuit-walls on the lower southern slopes, about thirty metres from the edge of the plain, together with an inner ring around the little medieval tower in the centre. The site is a large one (about 250 by 150 metres) and the Mycenaean settlement extended over terraces below to the east. The pottery was of excellent quality, especially the *Minyan* ware, and the LH IIIA–B, and there was also some *Matt-painted* and *Yellow Minyan*. This settlement was undoubtedly important in the LH III period, and, perhaps in contrast to the fortresses on the north-east side of the lake, it seems to have held a fair population. There was no evidence of occupation in the Early Iron Age.

The excavators located the classical Tegyra here, but it is more likely that this should be identified with the small site at Polyira.[3]

Ὀρχομενός (2. 511) MAP 2

REFS. *Gazetteer*, No. 396; Schliemann, *Orchomenos* (1881), and translation in *JHS* 2 (1881), pp. 122–63; Bulle, *Orchomenos* i (1907); Kunze, *Orchomenos* ii and iii (1931 and 1934); *BCH* 19 (1895), pp. 137f., *AM* 30 (1905), pp. 129–32; *AA* 1915, pp. 204f.; *ADelt.* 1 (1915), parart., pp. 51–3; *MV*, p. 42, Pl. 19: 135; Furumark, *MP*, p. 651, etc.; Frazer, *Pausanias* v. 180–7, 191–2; Wace and Thompson, *PT*, pp. 193–6; Desborough, *LMTS*, p. 120; Ålin, *EMF*, pp. 121f.

Orchomenos was clearly one of the major Mycenaean capitals. The tholos-tomb (PLATE 1), named in the time of Pausanias (9. 38. 2) 'The Treasury of Minyas', closely resembles the 'Treasury of Atreus' at Mycenae: it must certainly belong to the same period,[4] and was perhaps built by the same architect. Moreover, the fact that the German excavations were focused on the area of the tomb has somewhat obscured the extent of the Mycenaean city and the richness of the material finds.[5] Orchomenos was also inhabited in the Early Iron Age.

The *floruit* of Orchomenos was probably the LH IIIB period, as was that of Gla and most Mycenaean centres, except possibly Thebes, and it can be assumed that at that time she controlled the system of fortified settlements around the northern shores of Lake Copais at least (in particular the fortress of Gla), and the magnificent drainage works which must surely be associated with them (PLATE 2).[6] Yet in the Catalogue Orchomenos appears to control hardly any part of the lake, as is shown by the fact that Kopai is in Boeotian hands—and Arne and Mideia, for that matter, if these are really to be sought in the region of the lake: even a port for her ships is denied her, if Nisa is Larymna.[7]

In short, it is very difficult to believe that the Catalogue here accurately reflects the LH IIIB period—the date to which it ostensibly refers—though perhaps when Achilles mentions the wealth of Orchomenos (*Il.* 9. 381) we catch a glimpse of the Orchomenos that once had been. The Orchomenos of the Catalogue would rather appear to reflect LH IIIC, when, to judge by the destruction and desertion of Gla, the drainage works, for which Orchomenos was traditionally responsible (cf. Strabo 9. 415 and Pausanias 9. 38. 7), fell into neglect.

NOTES ON THE MINYAN SECTION

1. *NK*, pp. 29–30.
2. Cf. the photograph in *AA* 1940, p. 187, Abb. 40.
3. *Gazetteer*, No. 397: T.8 Atalandi 738E/103N.
4. LH IIIB according to Mylonas, *Ancient Mycenae*, pp. 87–8; LH IIIA according to Wace, *Mycenae*, pp. 119–31.
5. For the topography cf. Frazer, *Pausanias* v. 191 f. Ålin (*EMF*, pp. 121 f.) notes that much of the Mycenaean pottery lies unpublished in the Chaeronea Museum. The painted wall-plaster, especially from the area of the 'Friedhof' and the 'Kloster' (*Orchomenos* i, Taf. I), indicates that there was a palace here.
6. André Kenny, *LAAA* 22 (1935), pp. 189–206; cf. Kahrstedt *JdI* 52 (1937), pp. 1 f.; Frazer, *Pausanias* v. 110; Wace and Stubbings, *CH*, p. 288.
7. See p. 32 above, and cf. Miss Gray, *HHC*, p. 274. Larymna would presumably have been the port of Orchomenos.

THE PHOCIANS

Κυπάρισσος (2. 519) MAP 2

Pausanias (10. 36. 5) records a tradition (presumably local) that Kyparissos was the ancient name for Antikyra, and that the sons of Iphitos were buried there after their return from Troy (10. 36. 10). But this tradition had to be harmonized (cf. Pausanias, loc. cit.) with the typical 'oecist' myth that Antikyra was named after Antikyreus, a contemporary of Herakles, for this implied that it was already called Antikyra in Homer's day.

It would be convenient to have a Catalogue town in the region of the bay of Antikyra, and thus to give the Phocians another port besides Krisa, and Mycenaean finds have been made both in the vicinity of Antikyra[1] and in that of ancient Medeon opposite.[2] But one is always suspicious of such claims, and it would be unwise to assume too readily the identification of Kyparissos with Antikyra.

Πυθών (2. 519) MAP 2

REFS. *Gazetteer*, No. 446; for other refs. and full discussion see Ålin, *EMF*, pp. 129f.; cf. also Desborough, *LMTS*, pp. 122f., and Index, s.v. 'Delphi'.

The Mycenaean settlement at Delphi appears to have centred on the area north and east of the Temple of Apollo. It probably belongs exclusively to LH III, flourishing in LH IIIB, but continuing for at least some time into LH IIIC.[3] Thereafter there is little evidence for occupation of the site until the Late Geometric period, Protogeometric sherds being particularly rare.[4]

Nilsson[5] argues for a continuity of cult at Delphi from Mycenaean times, but although the numerous votive objects found in the region of the Archaic sanctuary of Athena Pronaia[6] probably indicate that there was some sort of Mycenaean cult at Delphi, there is certainly a considerable gap in the archaeological evidence for its continuity into historical times, and it is, perhaps, unwise to build too heavily on the supposed Cretan connections of Delphi, or on any possible connections between the Python-shooting myth and Minoan snake-cults. In fact, as Forrest has pointed out,[7] it appears that the real importance of Delphi as a religious centre dates only from its connections with the trading and colonizing ventures of Chalcis, Corinth, and their allies in the 8th century.

The tradition of the old name—*Πυθώ* or *Πυθών*—is strong, being twice referred to elsewhere in Homer, together with Phoibos Apollo and his stone threshold (*Il.* 9. 405; *Od.* 8. 80), and once (*Od.* 11. 581) in connection with the story of Tityos' molestation of Leto. The epithet *πετρήεσσα* (repeated in the

Ionic form in *Il.* 9. 405) is, of course, apt, especially to anyone approaching from Krisa below.

Κρῖσα (2. 520) MAP 2

REFS. *Gazetteer*, No. 447; Frazer, *Pausanias* v. 459–62; *RA*, Ser. 6, 8 (1936), pp. 129f.; *RA*, Ser. 6, 31 (1948), pp. 621f.; *BCH* 61 (1937), pp. 299f.; *BCH* 62 (1938), pp. 110f.; Ålin, *EMF*, pp. 130f.; Desborough, *LMTS*, p. 125.

The acropolis of Krisa (now called Ayios Georgios after the chapel at its eastern end) occupies the tip of a long rocky spur projecting southwards from Mt. Parnassos, and overhanging the northern valley of the Pleistos in great precipices (I.7 Xilokastron 310E/061N). The *Hymn to Apollo* describes it perfectly (282–5):

> *ὑπὸ Παρνησὸν νιφόεντα,*
> *κνημὸν πρὸς ζέφυρον τετραμμένον, αὐτὰρ ὕπερθεν*
> *πέτρη ἐπικρέμαται, κοίλη δ' ὑποδέδρομε βῆσσα,*
> *τρηχεῖ . . .*

(cf. line 438 and Pindar *Pyth.* 5. 34f.). It completely dominates the Gulf of Krisa and the routes up the Pleistos valley, both the upper one via Delphi and the lower one on the valley floor.

Fortifications were unnecessary on the southern and eastern sides, but on the north and west there are remains of extensive Cyclopean circuit-walls, built of very massive blocks—one was recorded by Frazer as 9 ft. long by 5 ft. high! The area of the acropolis thus enclosed is about 350 metres north to south by 300 metres, not including the western spur, on which is a little chapel of Ayios Elias. Less than a kilometre to the north is the village of Khryso, past which winds the road to Delphi.

The earliest buildings on the site belong to the MH period, and in LH I a small megaron was constructed, but although some of the earlier pottery is particularly fine, especially the MH/LH I *Yellow Minyan*, the fortifications date from LH III only. The settlement appears to have been destroyed by fire at the end of the LH IIIB period, or at the very beginning of LH IIIC, and to have been completely deserted thereafter.[8]

According to the French excavators, the settlement at Kirrha below, near the modern harbour of Itea, declined after the early part of the Mycenaean period, while the acropolis site at Khryso became correspondingly more important, until, at the end of the Mycenaean period, Kirrha had become no more than a harbour-town.[9] As a result, Lerat argues[10] that Krisa was probably at first the name of the bay and the port at Kirrha, and only later the name of the settlement at Khryso. This hypothesis, however, seems somewhat overcomplicated, and there is no real reason to doubt that the site near Khryso was always called Krisa, since it was inhabited from the MH period, and it is almost certain that the Krisa of the Catalogue is the upper site. If this is right, there can be no question but that the mention of Krisa in the Catalogue reflects the Mycenaean period.

Δαυλίς (2. 520) MAP 2

REFS. *Gazetteer*, No. 441; Furtwängler and Loeschke, *MV*, pp. 34 f.; Wace and Thompson, *PT*, p. 201; Furumark, *MP*, pp. 638–9; Frazer, *Pausanias* v. 222–5; Åalin, *EMF*, pp. 134f.

Daulis (the later Daulia, and the modern Dhavlia: T.8 Atalandi 539E/086N) is known to have been a Mycenaean site. The acropolis is a massive rounded hill, one of the foothills of Parnassos, to which it is connected by a narrow ridge on the north-west, where there are the remains of a gateway. The Hellenic fortifications are fine, though not so well preserved as those of Panopeus. The top (extending for about 250 metres north to south, by 200 metres) is covered for the most part in dense scrub, with a few trees, and both Strabo (9. 423) and Pausanias (10. 4. 7) say that the name Daulis was derived from the 'thickets' (δαυλοί), though Pausanias also reports a rival derivation from the nymph Daulis, daughter of the Kephisos.

In 1881 Stamatakis cleared out a well on the acropolis, containing mainly MH *Matt-painted* pottery, but some LH III sherds, together with obsidian blades and small stone whorls,[11] and in 1959 Hope Simpson found some worn LH III sherds on the surface, and a rim fragment of a *Stemmed Bowl* of *Yellow Minyan* ware (MH/LH I). There is no evidence so far that the site was occupied during the Protogeometric or Geometric periods.

Daulis controls an entrance to the σχιστὴ ὁδός,[12] where Oedipus slew Laius (cf. Pausanias 10. 5. 4), and a pass north into the Kephisos valley via the modern village of Dhavlia. There is a copious spring at the north foot of the acropolis and the remains of many ancient mills.

Πανοπεύς (2. 520) MAP 2

REFS. *Gazetteer*, No. 440; Frazer, *Pausanias* v. 215–19; *JHS Arch.* for 1961/2, p. 31.

The acropolis of Panopeus (I.8 Levadhia 598E/071N) towers above the hamlet of Ayios Vlasis (PLATE 3*a*), on the southern edge of a broad valley bounded on the west by the foothills of Mt. Parnassos. It dominates the routes to the north and east, and also a small pass through the hills on the south. The Hellenic fortifications are among the finest in Greece, being particularly well preserved on the south side, but there are also traces of what appears to have been a Cyclopean wall, in one place three courses high, running round the south-eastern slopes about 40 metres below the later walls (PLATE 3*b*). In this area, in 1961, we picked up some Mycenaean sherds, including LH IIIA–B from *Deep Bowls* and *Kylikes*, a flat base from a MH/LH I *Yellow Minyan* goblet, and chips of obsidian. The Cyclopean wall could be traced for some distance to the south-east, and at the eastern end of the hill it turned to the north, thus at all points following the line of the later walls, but outside them. It would appear that it once encircled the whole of the rocky summit (about 250 metres east to west by 80 metres), and much of the upper slopes on the east side.

Since Schedios, one of the two brothers who led the Phocians, is said elsewhere (*Il.* 17. 307–8) to have had his home at Panopeus, it may be that this was traditionally the capital of heroic Phocis, and the site certainly conforms to this pre-eminence, while the epithet *καλλιχόρος* which is given to it by the *Odyssey* (11. 581) is amply justified by the wide sweep of good agricultural land which it commands. It was also celebrated in legend as the place where Prometheus made the first men, and Pausanias (10. 4. 4) saw there two huge stones, of the colour of clay, and smelling like the skin of a man, which were supposed to be the remains of the clay he used!

Ἀνεμώρεια (2. 521) MAP 2

Kirsten[13] placed Anemoreia at the site of Kastrouli in the Pleistos valley, to the south-east of Delphi and to the south-west of Arakhova,[14] but the excavators of the site wisely do not follow the identification, since, as they say,[15] the site is not important and the Mycenaean pottery found is of poor quality. Frazer[16] thought that the modern village of Arakhova itself might occupy the site of Anemoreia ('the windy town'), since at this point the storms sweep down from the outlying precipices of Parnassos. Moreover, when Delphi was made independent of Phocis (*c.* 457 B.C.), Anemoreia became the boundary between the territory of Delphi and that of Phocis (cf. Strabo 9. 423), and Arakhova, standing as it does on the crest between the eastern and western slopes of the valley, is a natural frontier marker. Bursian[17] noted ancient walls here, but the modern village must have obliterated most of the traces.

Ὑάμπολις (2. 521) MAP 2

REFS. *Gazetteer*, No. 455; Frazer, *Pausanias* v. 442–6; *JHS* 16 (1896), pp. 291 f.

The location of Hyampolis is well established by inscriptions.[18] It lay on a flat tableland with steep slopes, rising about 30 metres from the level of the plain, some 2 kilometres west of the village of Exarchos (T.8 Atalandi 698E/176N), in a valley enclosed on all sides by rugged hills. The natural acropolis was fortified in classical times with walls of excellent isodomic masonry, enclosing an area about 200 metres north-east to south-west by 150 metres. On the eroded slopes outside the walls, where classical and Hellenistic pottery was less obtrusive, Hope Simpson found in 1959 a sherd of LH IIIB date, several other probably Bronze Age sherds, and a few chips of obsidian. This is probably sufficient to prove that the place was inhabited in Mycenaean times, when taken with its similarity to other Mycenaean sites, and the fact that it lies on the easiest route from Orchomenos to the sea at the plain of Atalante.

The situation of Hyampolis was strategically important: it was in this pass that the Phocians met and defeated the invading Thessalian cavalry in the 6th century B.C. (Herodotus 8. 28; cf. Pausanias 10. 1. 3); Jason of Pherae captured part of the city on his march from Phocis to Herakleia in 371 B.C. (Xenophon, *Hellenica* 6. 4. 27); and in the Sacred War the Boeotians defeated the Phocians here in 347 B.C. (Diodorus 16. 56).

"*πάρ ποταμὸν Κηφισὸν δῖον*" (*Il.* 2. 522) MAP 2

Burr[19] tacitly assumes that this refers to the town of Parapotamioi. It lay on a broad hill (now called Levendi), connected on the east to the ridge bounding the plain of Chaeronea on the north and extending eastwards to Orchomenos, and dominated the defile (called 'stena') between the plain of Chaeronea and the broader plain of the main Kephisos valley to the west.[20] Some Bronze Age sherds have in fact been found here (by Hope Simpson in 1959), though the majority of the sherds on the surface were classical or Hellenistic.

It is more natural, however, to take the Homeric phrase "*πὰρ ποταμὸν Κηφισόν*" to refer not merely to the later town of Parapotamioi, but to *all* those who dwelt beside the river Kephisos—a view which Pausanias records (10. 33. 7–8), but which he dismisses as conflicting with Herodotus' mention (8. 33) of a place called Parapotamioi. Other prehistoric sites in the valley which might be referred to in the phrase in question are Ayia Marina,[21] Dhrachmani,[22] Modion,[23] and Palaiokastro.[24]

Λίλαια (2. 523) MAP 2

REFS. *Gazetteer*, No. 463; Frazer, *Pausanias* v. 410–14; *BSA* 17 (1910/11), pp. 60–4.

The historic Lilaia is firmly located just east of the small village of Kato Agoriani (T.7 Lamia 349E/243N). The city walls climb up from the plain on to a long, thin, and jagged ridge, precipitous on its east side, with the lower town in the flat ground at the foot of this acropolis. The dedications at the spring[25] confirm the ancient testimony which unanimously places the sources of the river Kephisos here—(cf. the Homeric phrase *πηγῇς ἔπι Κηφισοῖο* in *Il.* 2. 523)—though in fact the spring is only one of the sources of the river.

There is as yet no evidence that the site of the historic Lilaia was inhabited in the Mycenaean period (or in the Early Iron Age for that matter), and it is perhaps not the sort of site which the Mycenaeans normally seem to have chosen. But a little to the west, above and 400 metres south-east of the modern village, there is a small conical hill which looks more like a Mycenaean site, and upon which Hope Simpson found (in 1959) sherds of coarse Bronze Age pottery (including the handles of EH vessels), and one piece which might be from an LH III *Deep Bowl*.[26] This may well be the Lilaia referred to in the Catalogue. Further search and, still more, excavation would probably produce more LH III pottery, though at Glunista, near the site of the historic Drymaia, excavation has revealed what appears to be Late Bronze Age occupation of a provincial 'un-Mycenaeanized' nature.[27]

The political division implied by the towns listed in the Phocian section of the Catalogue does not differ materially from historical Phocis, except that some of the later centres (notably Amphissa and Elatea) are absent, and one place (Kyparissos) does not appear to have existed in historical times, at least under that name. On the other hand, the distribution-pattern of the Homeric towns agrees well with the distribution of Mycenaean settlements, particularly in the area of Delphi and in the Kephisos valley, and the destruction of Krisa and the apparent desertion of Delphi at the end of LH IIIB or the beginning of LH IIIC suggest that this may have been the time when Kyparissos disappeared, while the obvious time for the establishment of the new centres would be the Early Iron Age. In other words, the Catalogue's picture of Phocis seems to fit Mycenaean Phocis rather better than that of any later period, although our present knowledge of the Protogeometric and Geometric periods in this area is, as so often, too slight for any certainty.

NOTES ON THE PHOCIAN SECTION

1. At 'Kastro tou Stenou' (I.7 Xilokastron △ 220 at 433E/945N): *Gazetteer*, No. 444; *AM* 14 (1889), pp. 267–9; *AE* 1956, parart., pp. 24–5 and fig. 6; cf. *AJA* 59 (1956), p. 227.
2. At Ayios Theodoros (I.7 Xilokastron 'Ay. Theodoroi' ♁ at 489E/938N): *Gazetteer*, No. 443; *PAE* 1907, p. 111; *AE* 1908, p. 65; Furumark, *MP*, p. 648; *JHS Arch.* for 1962/3, pp. 21 f.; *BCH* 87 (1963), pp. 839 f.; Ålin, *EMF*, p. 132.
3. Desborough, *LMTS*, p. 123.
4. Desborough, loc. cit. and p. 44.
5. *The Minoan–Mycenaean Religion* (2nd edn. 1950), pp. 466 f. and 576 f.
6. Lerat has suggested (*BCH* 81 (1957), pp. 708 f.), since no walls were found here in association with Mycenaean pottery and the stratification had obviously been disturbed, that the builders of the Archaic sanctuary collected these Mycenaean objects from elsewhere and deposited them here. Desborough (*LMTS*, p. 124) suggests they came from the Mycenaean settlement north-east of the Temple of Apollo, but is of the opinion that the spot from which they came, wherever it was, must have been used for cult purposes.
7. *Historia* 6 (1957), pp. 160–75.
8. Desborough, *LMTS*, p. 125.
9. *Kirrha*, p. 33. The imported Middle Minoan pottery found at Kirrha (op. cit., p. 29) provides some corroboration for the legend of Cretan connections with Delphi (cf. *Hymn to Apollo* 388 f., and Pindar *Pyth.* 5. 34 f.).
10. *RA*, Ser. 6. 31 (1948), pp. 621–32.
11. *MV*, pp. 34 f.
12. A prehistoric settlement has been found on the small rocky hill at the 'Schiste Odos', where the road from Daulis to Delphi met the road from Levadhia: *Gazetteer*, No. 442.
13. *RE* 21. 1, col. 215.
14. *Gazetteer*, No. 445: I.7 Xilokastron in square 370E/050N.
15. Dor, Jannoray, and van Effentere, *Kirrha* (1960), p. 20.
16. *Pausanias* v. 233.
17. *Geographie von Griechenland* (1852), i. 170.
18. *JHS*, 16 (1896), pp. 291 f.; *BCH* 37 (1913), pp. 444 f.; *AJA* 19 (1915), p. 334; *ADelt.* 2 (1916), pp. 263 f.
19. *NK*, p. 33.
20. *Gazetteer*, No. 454: T.8 Atalandi 609E/134N.
21. *Gazetteer*, No. 456.
22. *Gazetteer*, No. 457.

23. *Gazetteer*, No. 460.

24. *Gazetteer*, No. 461.

25. *CIG* iii, No. 232. Cf. *Hymn to Apollo* 240f.; Strabo 9. 407 and 424; Pliny, *NH* 4. 8; Statius, *Theb*. 7. 348 f.; Pausanias 9. 24. 1.

26. Cf. *Gazetteer*, No. 463.

27. *Gazetteer*, No. 462; *PAE* 1909, p. 130; 1910, p. 166; *Rev. Ét. Gr.* 25 (1912), p. 259.

THE LOCRIANS

Κῦνος (2. 531) MAP 2

REFS. *Gazetteer*, No. 466; Leake, *Travels in Northern Greece* ii. 175; *RE* 12 (1st edn. 1925), pp. 29f.; especially p. 31; Philippson, *GL*, p. 740, No. 31.

The site of Kynos (PLATE 4*a*) is marked by a hill now called Pyrgos (after the remains of a small square tower towards its northern end), about 2 kilometres north-east of the village of Livanates, and some 30 metres from the shore (T.8 Atalandi ⍿ at 843E/311N). The hill is a conspicuous 'high mound' site, measuring 130 metres north to north-west by 90 metres, with steep slopes rising about 15 metres above sea level. The harbour lay a little to the north near the chapels of Ayios Nikolaos and Ayios Theodoros.

The fields inland to the west and south, like the hill, are strewn with ancient sherds, amongst which Mycenaean (fine quality LH IIIA–B) and classical predominate, and on the hill itself Hope Simpson has found (1958 and 1959) obsidian, a sherd of *MH Grey Minyan*, a large number of Mycenaean sherds (including a *Krater* fragment with a panel-style pattern, attributable to LH IIIC:1), several late Geometric and Archaic, and many classical and Hellenistic pieces.

Strabo (9. 425) describes Kynos as the seaport of Opous, and it thus furnishes a valuable fixed-point, especially for the location of Opous. He also says it was the home of Deucalion.

'Οπόεις (2. 531) MAP 2

Opous later became the Locrian metropolis, and since Opoeis was the home of Menoitios and Patroklos (*Il.* 23. 83f.), it may have been regarded as the heroic capital. Unfortunately, it is still uncertain whether it should be located at Kyparissi or at Atalante:[1] both agree more or less with the 60 stades given by Strabo (9. 425) as the distance between Kynos and Opous, and Kynos could have served as a port for either, since the shore at Kyparissi is not very suitable for a harbour.

Blegen[2] investigated the citadel of Kastraki or Kokkinovrachos at Kyparissi, which may have been the citadel of historic Opous, but there is as yet no evidence that it was occupied in Mycenaean times, and being some 300 metres above the coastal plain, it is not a very suitable site for a Mycenaean settlement.

On the lower slopes, however, about 1·5 kilometres to the south of the village of Kyparissi, there are signs of a considerable ancient settlement, mainly in the area to the south of the chapel of Ayios Ioannis. At one point, south of a small ravine and about 300 metres west of the chapel, Hope Simpson found a deposit revealed by erosion, from which came LH IIIB–C sherds, together with late Protogeometric or Geometric, large numbers of Archaic (including Corinthian), and some classical pieces.[3]

But since the modern town of Atalante has destroyed most of the traces there, judgement cannot be final.

Καλλίαρος (2. 531) MAP 2

We have no guide to the position of this town. The text of Strabo is unfortunately deficient at the vital point (9. 426), though it does state that Kalliaros *οὐκέτι οἰκεῖται*. The conjecture of Oldfather,[4] welcomed by Burr,[5] that it lay in the vicinity of Opous, is no more than a guess.

Βῆσσα (2. 532) MAP 2

Strabo (9. 426) tells us (if we are prepared to take the name for granted in what is in fact a lacuna in his text) that Bessa, like Kalliaros, *οὐκ ἔστι* and that it was *δρυμώδης τις τόπος*. If this can be taken seriously, it should indicate some inland valley, and the vicinity of the village of Kallidromon has been suggested,[6] but presumably Strabo's information is, in fact, no more than a guess based on the name itself.

Σκάρφη (2. 532) MAP 2

This is presumably the same place as the historic Skarpheia, and if this is so, its position is fairly precisely fixed—ten stades from the sea and thirty from Thronion (Strabo 9. 426). From Pausanias (7. 15. 3) it appears, further, that Skarpheia lay on the route from Elateia to Thermopylae via Thronion (cf. Livy 33. 3. 6), and this places it between the villages of Kainourion and Molos.

Some remains have in fact been found at Trochala between these two places[7] which may represent Skarpheia, but there is as yet no evidence for prehistoric occupation.

Αὐγειαί (2. 532) MAP 2

The name *Αὐγειαί*, like Bessa, has to be supplied in a lacuna in Strabo's text (9. 426), and even if this can be accepted, it seems to tell us little about it, save that it no longer existed, unless we further accept Meineke's suggestion for the rest of the lacuna: *οὐδ' [αἱ Αὐγειαί, τὴν δὲ χώ]ραν ἔχουσι Σκαρφιεῖς*. If this can be believed, we should look for Augeiai near Skarpheia. However, since *Αὐγειαὶ ἐρατειναί* also appears in Menelaus' kingdom (*Il.* 2. 583), one or other may be due to some very early corruption in the text of the *Iliad*.

Τάρφη (2. 533) MAP 2

REFS. *Gazetteer*, No. 469; Leake, *Travels in Northern Greece* ii. 179; *JHS* 28 (1908), pp. 234–49; *BCH* 61 (1937), pp. 148–63, esp. Pl. xv.

Leake conjectured that the medieval castle of Boudonitza (or Bodonitza or Pundonitza), above the village of Mendhenitsa (T.7 Lamia 460E/367N), stood on the site of classical Pharygai and of Homeric Tarphe (cf. Strabo 9. 426). The site is a superb one (PLATE 4*b*), commanding a fine view of the Gulf of Malis and of Euboea, and controlling an important pass (the Klisoura) through the hills to the south from Molos in Locris to Dhrimaia in Phocis.

The walls of the castle follow the line of ancient Hellenic walls in many places, and several portions of the older masonry have been noted, either in position or reused.[8] Some of the work is of isodomic ashlar masonry and the black-glazed sherds suggest a 4th-century date.

We could find no evidence of prehistoric occupation here (in 1958), but the site is certainly suitable, and as Leake says, the territory of Mendhenitsa 'perfectly corresponds to the well-wooded and productive district which Strabo ascribes to Tarphe'.[9] The classical name—'Pharygai'—might be derived from *φάρυγξ* meaning a defile or pass (cf. the Latin *fauces*), and refer to the Klisoura pass.

Θρόνιον (2. 533) MAP 2

The Homeric description of Thronion as *Βοαγρίου ἀμφὶ ῥέεθρα* is compared by Oldfather[10] with *Il.* 2. 522 (*πὰρ ποταμὸν Κηφισὸν δῖον*), but the present phrase is a local description confined to Thronion, whereas the previous one, as we saw,[11] is more naturally taken as referring to a whole district. A better comparison is with the descriptions of Lilaia (*πηγῇς ἔπι Κηφισοῖο* in *Il.* 2. 523) or Pherai (*παραὶ Βοιβηΐδα λίμνην* in *Il.* 2. 711).

The location of the historic Thronion was established by the discovery of an inscription set up by the council and people of the Thronienses, near the hamlet of Pikraki.[12] The site, now called *Παλαιόκαστρο εἰς τὰ μάρμαρα*, is a long plateau-like ridge of little height, on the south side of the coastal plain and a short distance from where the river Boagrios issues into it (T.7 Lamia 543E/383N). Traces of ancient occupation (the sherds being mainly Hellenistic or Roman) extend over an area measuring about 300 by 200 metres, and although the ridge is not very defensible, and does not look much like a Mycenaean site, the position is a good one, as befits the capital of the Epicnemidian Locrians, and it is possible that excavations would reveal that it was inhabited in prehistoric times. We were unable to find any prehistoric sherds on the surface in 1961, but it is unlikely that this fertile coastal plain would have been overlooked, though we should possibly look elsewhere for prehistoric—and for Homeric—Thronion.

The Catalogue only recognizes the *eastern* Locris, which is described as being opposite Euboea. The boundaries implied by the names listed agree more or less with those of the historical state, in so far as these are known, except that

Larymna and the other (later) towns on the Aetolimni peninsula, Halae and Corsea, are omitted.[13] But the emphasis is placed on the north-western region and it is clear from Strabo's discussion that many of the places named were either completely or almost unknown in historical times.[14]

In fact, few identifications are possible, but the area has never been properly explored, particularly for prehistoric settlements, and it seems likely that the low hill-country in the interior would repay investigation.

The omission of *western* Locris should not be surprising, since it was always very much of a backwater even in classical times.[15] Occupation in the Mycenaean period was probably confined mainly to the thin coastal strip.[16]

NOTES ON THE LOCRIAN SECTION

1. Cf. Blegen, *AJA* 30 (1926), pp. 401–4.
2. Loc. cit.; cf. *Gazetteer*, No. 465.
3. *Gazetteer*, No. 465: T.8 Atalandi 851E/204N.
4. *RE* 10 (1919), pp. 1613f.
5. *NK*, p. 35.
6. Philippson, *GL* i. 344 and 689.
7. Oldfather, *RE* 3a (1929), pp. 460f.; Philippson, *GL* i. 344, 696, 703, and 728.
8. *JHS* 28 (1908), pp. 245–6, figs. 3–4; *BCH* 61 (1937), pp. 154–6, esp. fig. 9.
9. But once again Strabo's description may derive simply from the name 'Tarphe', which was given he says ἀπὸ τοῦ δάσους.
10. *AJA* 20 (1916), p. 43.
11. Above, p. 44.
12. *CIL* ii. 533; Oldfather, *RE* 6a (1937), pp. 609f.
13. Oldfather, *AJA* 20 (1916), pp. 32–61, esp. pp. 43f.
14. As Oldfather (op. cit., p. 43) says: '. . . the Locrian villages to the northwest, especially between Thermopylae and Cynus, are so elaborately enumerated, considering their utter insignificance, that it was a puzzle for later geographers to identify all the names with known sites.'
15. Cf. P. M. Fraser, *Gnomon* 26 (1954), reviewing Lerat, *Les Locriens de l'Ouest*, p. 255: 'We know of practically no writers or sculptors who can definitely be assigned to this Locris, and the area remains one of the most undistinguished in Greece.'
16. Cf. *Gazetteer*, Nos. 451, 452, and 453, and Desborough, *LMTS*, p. 125 and nn. 8–12.

EUBOEA

Χαλκίς (2. 537) MAP 2

There is plenty of evidence for Mycenaean and Early Iron Age occupation here, but the exact position of the central site in prehistoric times is still in doubt. Chamber tombs at Trypa and Vromousa[1] were excavated by Papavasileiou in 1910,[2] and the pottery, published in 1952,[3] ranged from LH I to LH IIIC 'Granary Style'. But most of the vases were LH IIIB–C:1, and it was remarked that 'the closing stage of the Mycenaean period is sketchily represented'.

Theochares thought[4] that the centre of Mycenaean Khalkis should be looked for near the springs of Arethusa, where the centre apparently was in the Archaic period. He found some EH pottery near the spring,[5] and there are also some Protogeometric vases from here.[6]

Neolithic, EH, and LH sherds have also been found on a little chersonese known as Kaki Kephali, on the northern edge of the modern town,[7] while Protogeometric burials and pottery of the Geometric and Archaic periods have turned up on Yiftika hill, about 1 kilometre east of the town, near the Venetian aqueduct.[8]

Εἰρέτρια (2. 537) MAP 2

REFS. *Gazetteer*, No. 562; *AA* 1922, p. 316; *BSA* 52 (1957), pp. 14f.; *JHS Arch.* for 1964/5, p. 18.

We would still adhere to the opinion that Homeric Eretria is to be located at the site of the historic city, near Nea Psara. Strabo (9. 403 and 10. 448) is our only authority for the existence of an 'Old Eretria' near by, and this could not in fact have been the city sacked by the Persians in 490 B.C., as he says, since the Eretrians had been living on the site at Nea Psara since at least the 8th century B.C.[9]

Boardman, however, maintains[10] that 'if the Eretrians held that their earliest city lay elsewhere, the least we can do is to try to believe them, even when Strabo records an impossible occasion for the destruction of that city'. But we cannot be sure of the basis of the tradition recorded by Strabo: it may merely have been local gossip which, for example, fancifully gave the name 'Old Eretria' to some well-known ruin in the neighbourhood. A confusing number of candidates have now been proposed: the late Dr. Papademetriou found Mycenaean pottery at a point about 2 kilometres east of Eretria;[11] the Swiss expedition propose a hill about 4 kilometres to the east, 'where walls of Mycenaean style and prehistoric sherds are to be found on the surface'.[12] Lastly, the site of Xeropolis, near the harbour of Lefkandi, has been suggested.[13]

The position of this last site, to the *west* of Eretria, and indeed on the edge of the Lelantine plain, seems, however, to conflict with Strabo's directions, such as they are. One wonders whether it might, perhaps, be Strabo's *Οἰχαλία κώμη τῆς Ἐρετρικῆς*, reputed to have been destroyed by Herakles.[14]

The acropolis of Eretria (I.10 Nea Psara 'Kastelli' △125 at 460E/914N) is exactly the sort of site we should have expected for Mycenaean Eretria, and would have effectively dominated both harbour and plain. Boardman's argument that 'neither Mycenaean nor Protogeometric Greeks would readily have faced the difficulties involved in combining acropolis and harbour in one township'[15] is hard to understand: the acropolis is, admittedly, 2 kilometres from the sea, but Nestor's Pylos is 5 kilometres from its harbour, and the Mycenaean Eretrians may simply have used the harbour, without bothering to build permanent dwellings there. Boardman dismissed as uncertain the report of Mycenaean sherds on the acropolis,[16] but in 1959 Hope Simpson found four sherds there which are certainly Mycenaean (from LH IIIB–C:1 *Kylikes* and *Deep Bowls*), some obsidian, and two pieces of *Grey Minyan* ware. There is thus no doubt that the acropolis was occupied in Mycenaean times, though whether it was also occupied in the Protogeometric period is still uncertain.[17]

Ἱστίαια (2. 537) MAP 2

REFS. *Gazetteer*, No. 561; *AEM* 2 (1959), pp. 307, 310–11, and 313; Philippson, *GL* i. 742, No. 8; Pernier, *Ann.* 3 (1916–20), pp. 276f.

The site at Oreos must surely be that of both the Homeric and the historical Histiaia.[18] The acropolis, now inevitably called 'kastro', is a typical 'high mound' site of natural defensive strength, near the sea and on the edge of a wide, fertile plain (T.8 Atalandi △40 at 889E/558N).[19] The top is large (150 metres north-east to south-west by 110 metres are the maximum dimensions), and there is a considerable westwards extension along the continuation of the ridge, with signs of occupation on the slopes where they are not too steep.

Trial excavations have established that the site was occupied from EH to LH, though no details were given in the report.[20] In 1959 Hope Simpson found some sherds of MH *Grey Minyan*, pieces of LH IIIB *Kylikes*, and obsidian, as well as Geometric, classical, and Hellenistic sherds.

Κήρινθος (2. 538) MAP 2

REFS. *Gazetteer*, No. 558; Philippson, *GL* i. 742, No. 19; Pernier, *Ann.* 3 (1916–20), pp. 273–6; *BSA* 52 (1957), p. 2 and n. 8; *AEM* 2 (1959), pp. 281 and 312.

The Homeric epithet ἔφαλος indicates that Kerinthos was on the sea, and Strabo (10. 446) says that it was near the river Boudoros. It should almost certainly be located at the hill now called Kastri, about 4 kilometres north of the village of Mantoudhi, and on the south-east side of the mouth of the Boudoros stream (T.9 Psakhna 206E/407N).

The hill is a long ridge (about 800 metres long by 150 metres wide), rising abruptly from the shore to a height of 30 metres, though the ancient settlement seems to have been mainly confined to the western end of the ridge, and the gentler western and south-western slopes on the landward side. On the top of this western part of the site are the foundations of a long oblong enclosure, and the remains of foundations of Archaic and (?) classical circuit-walls can also be seen.

Neolithic celts, EH and MH sherds, and obsidian, have been found on the top, and in 1959 Hope Simpson picked up some LH IIIB sherds about half-way down the western slope, near the remains of one or two courses of rough walling resembling Cyclopean. The wall appears to have been some 3 metres wide, with small stones characteristically packed into the interstices between the larger.

Sherds of the Archaic and classical periods are plentiful on the slopes, and Boardman also records Geometric pottery from the site.[21]

Δῖον (2. 538) MAP 2

REFS. *Gazetteer*, No. 560; Philippson, *GL* i. 570; *PAE* 1912, pp. 119 f., esp. p. 140.

We should probably locate Dion at the flat-topped hill about 2 kilometres west of the modern village of Lichas,[22] near the tip of the Kenaion promontory (cf. Strabo 10. 446). The site (T.8 Atalandi 668E/470N) is now called 'Kastri', presumably from the remains of what appears to be a medieval tower, though partly composed of ancient blocks. Sherds of all periods from at least MH to Hellenistic have been found here.[23]

The site near Gialtra[24] is possibly that of Athena Diades mentioned with Dion by Strabo (loc. cit.).

Κάρυστος (2. 539) MAP 2

The historic town of Karystos was centred on the area known as Palaiochora, about 20 minutes to the north of modern Karystos, and extended down to the sea. But most, if not all, of the traces have been destroyed by the new settlement since 1833, the ancient material being largely absorbed into the modern houses. A Frankish kastro, rising 300 metres above sea level, dominates the town on the north-east, and it is possible that the ancient acropolis lay somewhere on the ridge which projects southwards from the kastro, where there are signs of ancient walling. Sporadic prehistoric finds have been made in the vicinity,[25] but no Mycenaean or other prehistoric settlement has yet been found.

Στύρα (2. 539) MAP 2

REFS. *AM* 16 (1891), p. 54; *AEM* 2 (1959), pp. 309–10.

The acropolis of historical Styra lies a little to the south of the small modern port of Nea Styra (I.10 Nea Psara 805E/640N approx.), and it is presumably to a town on this site that the Catalogue refers. EH and MH sherds and obsidian have been found near here, but so far no evidence for occupation in the

LH period, or the Early Iron Age. The area is, however, eminently suitable for a Mycenaean centre, and it seems likely that some evidence for Mycenaean occupation will eventually turn up here.

It is not possible to determine whether the Catalogue's picture of Euboea is best seen as a reflection of the Mycenaean period or of the Early Iron Age. Admittedly the view that Euboea was not thickly inhabited in the Mycenaean period[26] now requires considerable modification:[27] indeed, if we are to suppose that the Catalogue reflects Mycenaean Euboea, we should perhaps have expected a reference to at least Amarynthos and Dystos,[28] and to one or two places unknown in the historical period.[29] But the Catalogue is not, and does not purport to be, a complete list of all the settlements of any period, and not much weight should be placed on what it omits. Certainly it is not plausible to argue that it fits the Protogeometric or Geometric periods any better, since apart from Karystos and Styra, from which there is as yet no evidence for either Mycenaean or Early Iron Age occupation, all the places mentioned were inhabited throughout the periods concerned.[30]

NOTES ON THE EUBOEAN SECTION

1. *Gazetteer*, No. 553: I.9 Khalkis 330E/999N approx.
2. *PAE* 1910, pp. 265 f.; 1911, pp. 237 f.; Ålin, *EMF*, p. 126.
3. *BSA* 47 (1952), pp. 49–95; cf. Desborough, *LMTS*, p. 122.
4. *AEM* 2 (1959), p. 282.
5. Op. cit., pp. 308–9.
6. Desborough, *PG*, p. 199.
7. *Gazetteer*, No. 555: I.9 Khalkis 293E/000N; cf. Philippson, *GL* i. 686; Theochares *AEM* 2 (1959), pp. 282, 308, 311.
8. I.9 Khalkis 300E/987N; cf. *JHS Arch.* for 1958, p. 11; *BSA* 52 (1957), pp. 1 f.
9. Boardman, *BSA* 52 (1957), p. 22.
10. Ibid.
11. *BSA* 52 (1957), pp. 22 and 24.
12. *AJA* 69 (1965), p. 355 (Strabo 9. 403 is, however, misquoted here).
13. *Gazetteer*, No. 554: I.9 Khalkis 353E/930N (Hope Simpson regrets that a wrong map reference was given for this site in the *Gazetteer*, and that its position was erroneously marked on the map there). M. R. Popham and L. H. Sackett are currently excavating here under the auspices of the British School of Archaeology at Athens: cf. *BSA* 61 (1966), pp. 60 f. The new finds, including 'evidence of a MH or LH fortification wall', together with arguments concerning the strategic position of the site, go some way towards strengthening the conjecture that it may be the site of Strabo's 'Old Eretria', despite the fact that he appears to place it *east* of Eretria. But it still seems questionable whether 'Old Eretria' ever really existed.

    The importance of Lefkandi in the LH IIIC period is of great interest (see pp. 161 f. below).
14. Strabo 10. 448.
15. *BSA* 52 (1957), p. 23.
16. Ibid. and n. 145.

17. It is possible that excavation on the acropolis would produce evidence of Protogeometric and Geometric occupation, though it may have been abandoned at the end of the Mycenaean period. Later the focus of settlement seems to have shifted to the plain below. The Swiss excavations in the Sanctuary of Apollo revealed a level with structural remains of the Geometric period (*JHS Arch.* for 1964/5, p. 18), and Protogeometric sherds have also been found (*BSA* 61 (1966), pp. 57f., 106f.).

18. Cf. Pausanias' statement (7. 26. 4) that there were still some who called Oreos by its old name in his day.

19. Cf. the Homeric epithet *πολυστάφυλος*.

20. *AEM* 2 (1959), pp. 307f. See now *BSA* 61 (1966), pp. 39f.

21. *BSA* 52 (1957), p. 2. Protogeometric sherds have also now been found on the site (*BSA* 61 (1966), pp. 43f.).

22. Wrongly named 'Lithada' by Burr (*NK*, p. 39).

23. *BSA* 61 (1966), p. 37.

24. *Gazetteer*, No. 559: T.8 Atalandi 788E/471N.

25. *AEM* 2 (1959), p. 284 and pp. 309f.

26. Wace and Stubbings, *CH*, p. 289.

27. See the 'Survey of Prehistoric Euboea' by L. H. Sackett and others in *BSA* 61 (1966), pp. 33–112.

28. For Amarynthos cf. *Gazetteer*, No. 564; for Dystos, *Gazetteer*, No. 573, and Åלin, *EMF*, p. 127.

29. With the exception of the Aetolian section (see pp. 107–10 below), the Euboean section is the only one relating to the mainland which mentions no places unknown in the historical period.

30. We note that in the south-east part of Euboea (*BSA* 61 (1966), pp. 77–83, 'The Karystos Area') no remains of the Protogeometric or Geometric periods have yet been found, and only one site (*BSA* 61 (1966), p. 80, no. 89, Philagra) has so far produced Mycenaean sherds.

ATHENS

Ἀθῆναι (2. 546) MAP 3

REFS. *Gazetteer*, No. 348; Iakovides, *Ἡ Μυκηναϊκὴ Ἀκρόπολις τῶν Ἀθηνῶν*; Ålin, *EMF*, pp. 99f.; Desborough, *LMTS*, p. 113; *JHS Arch.* for 1964/5, p. 4; for 1965/6, pp. 3–4.

The difficulty with this entry lies not so much in what it contains as in what it omits, for although the mention of Athens itself need excite no surprise whatever period the Catalogue is thought to reflect, we should, on the analogy of other entries, have expected at least some other places in Attica to be mentioned. Page's argument[1] that 'we have no reason to believe that any place except the great fortress of Athens was worth mentioning in the Catalogue' is not a sufficient explanation: the Catalogue elsewhere refers to plenty of places which can hardly be regarded as more worthy of mention than, for example, Eleusis, Aphidna, Marathon, or Thorikos.[2]

Some scholars have sought an explanation in the tradition that the synoecism of Attica was effected by Theseus,[3] and so *before* the Trojan War, and Huxley[4] has argued that the archaeological evidence supports the belief that the synoecism had in fact taken place by LH IIIB. But whether or not the synoecism had taken place so early is, surely, largely irrelevant to the problem we are considering: whenever the synoecism took place, it did not result in the other settlements' in Attica ceasing to exist,[5] and, however tightly they were controlled from Athens, we should still have expected the Catalogue to refer to some of them.

We must at least admit the possibility that lines referring to some of the other places in Attica which have strong mythological associations either dropped out accidentally in the course of transmission,[6] or were deliberately omitted at some point in order to project the synoecism back into the heroic past. For Page's remark[7]—'once more the self-control of the Athenian editors is to be admired: not one single Attic place did they interpolate into the Catalogue or elsewhere'—surely misses the point: it may have been precisely Athenian editors who deliberately omitted reference to other places in Attica.

On the other hand, as Allen and Page have pointed out,[8] the very obscurity of Menestheus, son of Peteos, strongly suggests that the reference to him is ancient, since the temptation to smuggle the sons of Theseus into the *Iliad* must have been enormous, and to some extent the mention of Menestheus, as it were, protects the rest of the Athenian entry. Where so much is obscure about the origins of the Catalogue and the factors which governed the inclusion or omission of places,[9] we certainly should not assume that Athens alone was not mentioned from the first.

But the doubts about this entry are at least sufficient to make it an unreliable guide to the period reflected by the Catalogue.

(AGAMEMNON)
(BOEOTIANS)
(ARCADIANS)
(DIOMEDES)
Aigion
Helike?
Aigialos
Hyperesia
Pellene
Sikyon
MT. KYLLENE
Gonoessa?
Stymphelos
Pheneos
Araithyrea
Orneai
Orchomenos
Mantinea
Tegea
+Rhipe
Stratie
Enispe
Parrhasia?
MT. PARNON
Thisbe
Thespeia
Eutresis
Plataia
Erythrai?
Skolos?
MT. KAITHAIRON
MT. PARNES
Aphidna
Marathon
Styra
Karystos
Eleusis
Megara
Athenai
Salamis
Korinthos
Kleonai
Nemea
Mykenai
Argos
Lerna
Midea
Tiryns
Asine
Eiones?
Epidauros
Aigina
Thorikos
Sounion
Keos
Troizen
Mases?
Hermione
Place names in the Catalogue
(a) Location established
(b) Location not certain
(c) Location unknown
Districts etc. in the Catalogue
Other ancient place names
(including some not Homeric)
Asine
Mases?
Rhipe
Parrhasia?
Thorikos
0
10
20
30
40 Miles

MAP 3

NOTES ON THE ATHENIAN SECTION

1. *HHI*, n. 72 on p. 171.

2. For Eleusis cf. *Hymn to Demeter* (lines 97, 318, 356, and 490) and Allen and Halliday, *The Homeric Hymns*, pp. 111–14. For Aphidna cf. Herodotus 9. 73. For Marathon cf. *Od.* 7. 80, Strabo 8. 383 (the Tetrapolis): the Marathon Tetrapolis still retained special representation in Athenian embassies to Delphi in historical times (Boëthius, *Die Pythais*, ch. 3, esp. pp. 43 f.; *SIG* ii. 541, no. 1). For Thorikos cf. *Hymn to Demeter* 126; Apollodoros 1. 9. 4, 2. 4. 7, 3. 15. 1.

3. Cf. Thucydides 2. 15. 1–2; Plutarch, *Theseus* 24; etc. The references in the *Odyssey* to Sounion as *ἄκρον Ἀθηνέων* (3. 278), and to Marathon (7. 80), may imply an acceptance of the tradition of the synoecism by Theseus.

4. *BICS* 3 (1956), pp. 22–3. It is perhaps worth noting that 'if tholoi indicate independent dynasties' (op. cit., p. 22), the LH IIIB pottery from the Menidhi tholos (Furumark, *Chron. MP*, p. 66) invalidates Huxley's conclusion (loc. cit.) that 'these ceased much earlier', even if we accept his explanation of the 'late Marathon tholos'.

5. As Hignett (*A History of the Athenian Constitution*, pp. 34–5) points out, Thucydides probably used the word *ξυνοικίζω* because the Athenian festival which commemorated the event was called *συνοίκια*, although he himself clearly did not believe that the entire population of Attica was gathered into a single city by Theseus, since the whole point of the passage is in fact that the majority still lived outside the city at the beginning of the Peloponnesian War. A more correct technical term for a number of communities becoming associated in political rights is *συμπολιτεύω*.

6. Cf. Allen, *HCS*, p. 172.

7. *HHI*, n. 72 on p. 171.

8. Allen, *HCS*, pp. 24, 55–6; Page, *HHI*, pp. 145–6, and nn. 78 and 79 on pp. 172–5.

9. See pp. 154–5 below.

SALAMIS

Σαλαμίς (2. 557) MAP 3

REFS. *The Arsenal*: *Gazetteer*, No. 387; Furumark, *Chron. MP*, pp. 77–8; Fimmen, *KMK*, p. 9; Ålin, *EMF*, p. 114; Desborough, *LMTS*, index, s.v. 'Salamis'.

Kamini near Ambelaki: *Gazetteer*, No. 388; *JHS Arch.* for 1961/2, p. 7, records Sub-Mycenaean tombs here.

Magoula near Kamatero: Frazer, *Pausanias* ii. 478. (Some Neolithic, EH, MH *Grey Minyan*, and LH IIIB–C sherds in the British School at Athens collection may be from this site, but cf. Pritchett, *Studies in Ancient Greek Topography*, Part I, pp. 95 f.)

A group of vases said to have been found in a tomb in Salamis was published by Robinson, *AJA* 54 (1950), pp. 1–9, Pls. I–VII (cf. Ålin, *EMF*, pp. 113 f.). For more LH III chamber-tombs see *JHS Arch.* for 1963/4, p. 5, and for 1964/5, p. 6.

The reference to Salamis in the Catalogue has often been unjustly suspected, partly on the ground that Ajax is too important a hero to be relegated to so comparatively insignificant a kingdom, partly because of the line (*Il.* 2. 558) which has him station his forces near those of the Athenians. But, firstly, the insignificance of Ajax' kingdom is, surely, in fact its own best protection: no one would have *invented* such a kingdom for him once his role in the story of the Trojan War had assumed the importance it did.[1] Secondly, as Allen pointed out,[2] even the line στῆσε δ' ἄγων ἵν' Ἀθηναίων ἵσταντο φάλαγγες does not necessarily imply what the Athenians claimed it implied: inherently, it is no different from other 'battle-station' passages in the Catalogue (e.g. *Il.* 2. 526 and 587).

More recently, Page has argued that Ajax 'cannot have been included in a Mycenaean list of commanders in the Trojan War' because he 'belongs to a generation much earlier than Agamemnon'.[3] But although some of the things that are said about Ajax elsewhere in the *Iliad* seem to hint at a hero of the days when a warrior's main defence was his great body-shield,[4] we simply do not know whether these passages were originally connected with Ajax or not.

There is thus no compelling reason to suspect that either of the lines referring to Ajax is 'late'. But the mention of Salamis is no more help than the mention of Athens in determining the period reflected by the Catalogue, since the island was certainly inhabited from Neolithic times onwards.

Strabo (9. 393) says that the ancient town of Salamis, deserted in his day, faced towards Aegina and the south, whereas the city of his own times lay on a peninsula-like place opposite Attica.[5] Unfortunately, Salamis as a whole, and particularly the southern part, has not yet been thoroughly explored, but all the *Mycenaean* finds have so far been made in the north-east of the island, and if the wall Fimmen records[6] was really Cyclopean, it may be that the main centre in the Mycenaean period lay near the Arsenal.[7]

NOTES ON SALAMIS

1. It is noticeable that three of the greatest heroes of the Trojan War—Ajax, Odysseus, and Achilles—are all assigned to comparatively unimportant kingdoms in the Catalogue (see below, pp. 103–6 and 127–31), and that even Agamemnon himself is apparently cut off from the Argive plain. After discussing the cases of the others, Page (*HHI*, p. 132) concludes: 'The picture drawn by the Catalogue may very well be early and true: as a late fiction, created in contradiction of the *Iliad*, it would be so absurd as to be inconceivable.' But surely this is true of Ajax' Salamis too?
2. *HCS*, p. 57. Allen himself says (ibid.) that the line 'was meant to eke out the Catalogue at a weak point'. But if either this or the desire to link Salamis to Athens had been the motive for the alleged 'interpolation', the interpolator could surely have made a better job of it!
3. *HHI*, p. 147.
4. Cf. p. 9 above and p. 165 below.
5. Near modern Kamatero: *JHS* 76 (1956), p. 34 n. 3.
6. *KMK*, p. 9. The modern naval base makes any search in the area difficult.
7. The pottery from the tombs near the Arsenal (cf. Furtwängler and Loeschke, *MV*, pp. 41 and 83) is classed by Furumark (*Chron. MP*, pp. 77–8) as mainly LH IIIC:2, though some as LH IIIC:1: a Cyclopean wall would, presumably, antedate this period. Some LH IIIB sherds are included in the British School at Athens collection, and there are LH IIIB vases among those published by Robinson, and in the tomb-group reported in *JHS Arch.* for 1964/5, p. 6.

THE KINGDOM OF DIOMEDES

Ἄργος (2. 559) MAP 3

REFS. *The Larissa*: *Gazetteer*, No. 12; Volgraff, *Mnemosyne* 56 (1928), pp. 313f., and *Mededeelingen der K. Akad. van Wetenschappen*, Letterkunde 66 (1928), Ser. B, No. 4; *BCH* 54 (1930), p. 480; *JHS Arch.* for 1954, p. 9, for 1963/4, p. 8, for 1964/5, pp. 11–12, for 1965/6, p. 8.

The Aspis: *BCH* 30 (1906), pp. 5f.; *BCH* 31 (1907), pp. 137f.; Furumark, *MP*, p. 645; Desborough, *LMTS*, pp. 80f.

The Deiras Cemetery: Åkin, *EMF*, pp. 42f. (esp. p. 42 and refs. in n. 222); Desborough, *LMTS*, pp. 80f., Index, s.v. 'Argos', and Addenda, p. 278.

This was presumably Diomedes' capital, with its citadel on the Larissa and a town extending at least as far to the south and east as the area of the museum, though there is evidence that the Aspis was also fortified in Mycenaean times. It is interesting that there does not seem to be any evidence for a destruction here at the end of LH IIIB. Argos also appears to have been important and prosperous in the Protogeometric and, especially, the Geometric era.

The citadel was said to have been founded by Danaos (Strabo 8. 371), and his alleged tomb was preserved in the middle of the Agora, but Pausanias says that the citadel got its name from the daughter of Pelasgos (2. 24. 1).

Τίρυνς (2. 559) MAP 3

REFS. *Gazetteer*, No. 8; Frickenhaus, Müller, and Rodenwaldt, *Tiryns*; Åkin, *EMF*, pp. 25–36; Desborough, *LMTS*, p. 79 and Index s.v. 'Tiryns'; *AE* 1956, Parart., pp. 5f.; *JHS Arch.* for 1962/3, pp. 15f.; *BCH* 87 (1963), pp. 751f.; *AJA* 67 (1963), p. 281 and Pl. 63, fig. 10; *JHS Arch.* for 1963/4, p. 8, and for 1964/5, p. 11.

Lower Town: *AA* 1909, p. 122.

Tholos Tomb: *AM* 38 (1913), pp. 347f.; *JHS Arch.* for 1938/9, p. 30 (? second tholos).

The epithet τειχιόεσσα, which is, of course, particularly appropriate to Tiryns, is also, however, applied to Gortyn in Crete (*Il.* 2. 646). The walls of Tiryns were supposed to have been built for King Proitos by the Cyclopes (Strabo 8. 372; Pausanias 2. 25. 8), sent from Lycia according to Strabo. Pausanias comments upon the Cyclopean technique, particularly the use of small stones in the interstices.

Tiryns, like Mycenae, was inhabited from the earliest times right down to the historical period, though undoubtedly its greatness belongs to the Mycenaean era. Desborough[1] thought that after the destruction at the end of LH IIIB there was a break in occupation, the re-occupation being marked by the LH IIIC (or Sub-Mycenaean) graves built within the ruined houses. But the pottery from the recent excavations at the site suggests that it was inhabited throughout LH IIIC.[2]

Ἑρμιόνη (2. 560) MAP 3

REFS. *Gazetteer*, No. 31; *PAE* 1909, pp. 175–6; Fimmen, *KMK*, p. 13; *AM* 36 (1911), p. 37; Burr, *NK*, p. 45; Åin, *EMF*, p. 52.

There is a Mycenaean settlement of moderate size (127 metres by 55 on the top) on a hillock now called 'kastri' or 'magoula', about 500 metres west of the modern town of Hermione, and to the south of the hill of *Πρών* where lay the necropolis of classical Hermione, and the city of Pausanias' time (2. 34. 11) (L.9 Idhra 896E/813N). To the south and west of the site is a fertile plain, growing corn, olives, oranges, and vines. Frickenhaus and Müller thought that the site was that of the Mycenaean cemetery,[3] but Mrs. Hope Simpson and Miss Burford, who visited it in 1959, found sherds of EH, MH, LH I, and LH IIIA–C:1 pottery, and it seems clear that the site was a settlement rather than a cemetery.

Classical Hermione lay on the promontory,[4] but the name in the Catalogue may refer to the earlier site.

Ἀσίνη (2. 560) MAP 3

REFS. *Gazetteer*, No. 19; Frödin and Persson, *Asine* (1938); Ålin, *EMF*, pp. 47 f.; Desborough, *LMTS*, pp. 82 f. and Index, s.v. 'Asine'.

There is no need to repeat the conclusions of the excavators of Asine,[5] except to emphasize the excellence of the citadel and of the harbour, with its wide beaches for the drawing up of ancient ships.[6] It is also worth noting the degree of continuity here: Asine seems to have escaped the destructions at the end of LH IIIB and, to judge from the tombs, to have been a flourishing place in LH IIIC.[7]

Τροιζήν (2. 561) MAP 3

Mycenaean settlements have been found on the borders of Troizen,[8] but not in the immediate vicinity of the historical town, though there are EH remains on the plateau of the Asklepieion.[9] It is difficult to believe that there was not a Mycenaean settlement somewhere on the edge of the fertile plain of Troizen, and it would be unwise to make very much of the present lack of evidence: Troizen is rich in mythology (cf. Pausanias 2. 30. 5–32. 6), although it seems that the connections with Theseus are secondary to his connections with Athens.[10]

The 'Mycenaean tombs' reported from the 'garden of Paspati'[11] are in fact Geometric,[12] which indicates that the site of the historical Troizen was occupied in the Geometric period.

Ἠϊόνες (2. 561) MAP 3

Strabo's note on Eiones (8. 373) looks suspiciously like pure invention, but there is a possibility that the interesting Mycenaean site at Kandia[13] may be

Eiones, although it is unlikely to have been of much importance, and the suggestion is only a guess.

Ἐπίδαυρος (2. 561) MAP 3

The historical *town* of Epidauros, as opposed to the sanctuary of Asklepios, lay on the promontory to the south of the modern port of Palaia Epidhavros (K.8 Korinthos △ 63 at 853E/097N).[14] Mycenaean tombs have been found a short distance to north of the promontory, on the south-west outskirts of the village,[15] and the promontory was probably also the site of the Mycenaean settlement, particularly the steep-sided hill on which stands the chapel of the Panayia. So far no evidence for Mycenaean or Early Iron Age occupation has been found here, but in 1961 we found a few *Grey Minyan* sherds and some chips of obsidian, near the chapel.

Αἴγινα (2. 562) MAP 3

This must presumably refer to the island of Aegina, although Strabo (8. 375) has a curious note that there was a place called 'Aegina' in Epidauria.

Evidence for Mycenaean habitation on the island has been found on the sites of the temples of Aphrodite[16] and Aphaia,[17] and on the top of Mt. Oros,[18] but little of it is later than LH IIIB.[19] There is also Protogeometric from the temple of Aphrodite and Geometric from the temple of Aphaia.

Μάσης (2. 562) MAP 3

The directions given by Pausanias (2. 36. 1–3) show that Mases (in his day a harbour used by the people of Hermione) lay in the vicinity of the bay of Koiladia. A Mycenaean settlement has been found here, on a small, low, rocky promontory, about 2 kilometres north of Koiladia, and 2·5 kilometres west of the main road from Kranidhion to Nauplion (L.8 Leonidhion ⍏ at 810E/872N).[20] The settlement is small, and the recognizable sherds belong to LH IIIB,[21] but this may have been Mases.

The political division implied by the list of places in Diomedes' kingdom will be discussed after the section on Agamemnon's kingdom (see pp. 70–2 below).

NOTES ON DIOMEDES' KINGDOM

1. *LMTS*, p. 79.
2. Cf. Mylonas, *Hesperia* 33 (1964), p. 376 n. 70.
3. *AM* 36 (1911), p. 37.
4. Cf. Pausanias 2. 34. 9–10, and *AM* 36 (1911), Taf. 1.
5. Cf. especially *Asine*, pp. 103, 151 f., and 339 f.

6. Cf. George Seferis, *The King of Asine* (translated by Rex Warner, 1960), line 10.
7. Desborough, *LMTS*, pp. 82–4, esp. 83.
8. Cf. *Gazetteer*, No. 37: Welter, *Troizen und Kalauria*, p. 10 and Taf. 1, cf. also p. 50; *AM* 36 (1911), p. 33; Fimmen, *KMK*, p. 13. A new site was discovered by Mrs. Hope Simpson and Miss Burford in 1959, on an isolated hill crowned by a chapel of Ayios Georgios, at the south end of the plain of Lessia: *Gazetteer*, No. 39.
9. Welter, op. cit., p. 10 and Taf. 1.
10. Cf. Nilsson, *The Mycenaean Origin of Greek Mythology*, p. 166.
11. *ADelt.* 5 (1889), pp. 163f.
12. *AM* 36 (1911), p. 33; cf. Nilsson, op. cit., pp. 18 f.; Burr, *NK*, pp. 46–7.
13. *Gazetteer*, No. 26: K.8 Korinthos 669E/095N. Cf. Burr, *NK*, pp. 47–8.
14. Cf. Pausanias 2. 26–29. 1, and Frazer, *Pausanias* iii. 260 f.
15. *ADelt.* 4 (1888), pp. 155 f.; Ålin, *EMF*, pp. 51 f.
16. *Gazetteer*, No. 392; Ålin, *EMF*, pp. 114f.; Desborough, *LMTS*, p. 119.
17. *Gazetteer*, No. 393; Ålin, *EMF*, p. 115; Desborough, *LMTS*, loc. cit.
18. *Gazetteer*, No. 394; Ålin, *EMF*, p. 115; Furtwängler, *Aigina*, p. 473; Fimmen, *KMK*, p. 9.
19. Desborough, *LMTS*, pp. 119–20.
20. *Gazetteer*, No. 29: *RE*, Suppl. vi (1935), p. 606; cf. Burr, *NK*, pp. 48–9; Ålin, *EMF*, p. 52, s.v. 'Keladi'.
21. Hope Simpson visited the site in 1959 with his wife.

THE KINGDOM OF AGAMEMNON

Μυκῆναι (2. 569) MAP 3

REFS. *Gazetteer*, No. 1; A. J. B. Wace, *Mycenae* (1949); G. E. Mylonas, *Ancient Mycenae* (1957) and *Mycenae and the Mycenaean Age* (1966); *BSA* 56 (1961), pp. 81–9; *BSA* 57 (1962), pp. 193–223; *JHS Arch.* for 1964/5, pp. 9–11, for 1965/6, pp. 7–8; Ålin, *EMF*, pp. 10 f.; Desborough, *LMTS*, pp. 73 f.

The description of Mycenae as ἐϋκτίμενον πτολίεθρον is, of course, amply justified by the Mycenaean remains, but the phrase is in fact a rather commonplace metrical expedient, used often enough in the Catalogue (cf. *Il.* 2. 501, 505, 546). Elsewhere in the poems Mycenae is εὐρυάγυια (*Il.* 4. 52) or πολύχρυσος (*Il.* 7. 180, 11. 46; *Od.* 3. 304).

Mylonas has now shown that the Lion Gate was constructed and the circuit-walls considerably strengthened in the middle of LH IIIB,[1] and the roads radiating out from the citadel also probably belong to this period (PLATE 5).[2] The citadel itself appears to have been sacked twice in the Mycenaean period, once at the end of LH IIIB, and again at the end of LH IIIC: 2, while recent excavation suggests that there was considerable occupation within the walls in LH IIIC.[3]

As in the case of Tiryns, the Catalogue's mention of Mycenae *could* refer to the Early Iron Age town, but there can be no doubt that by then the days of its greatest glory were long past.

Κόρινθος (2. 570) MAP 3

REFS. *Gazetteer*, No. 56; *Hesperia* 18 (1949), pp. 148–57 and Pls. 13–24; *Hesperia* 20 (1951), pp. 291–300; Ålin, *EMF*, p. 55; Desborough, *LMTS*, p. 85.

It was unfortunate that the news of Weinberg's discoveries at Old Corinth did not appear in time for Dunbabin to have the opportunity of altering his conclusion[4] that 'the reference to ἀφνειὸς Κόρινθος fits the 8th century, and, *as we judge by the remains*, no earlier period'. Yet even before the definite proof of a Mycenaean *settlement* at Old Corinth had appeared, the abundant Mycenaean remains in Corinthia as a whole should have warned adherents of the '8th century' view, as was seen long ago by Allen:[5] as he said, 'the conditions which made the historical Corinth the principal port of Greece, acted in the heroic period also'. As for Leaf's argument that the district is infertile,[6] the facts have always been against him.[7] Dunbabin correctly remarked on the commercial and strategic importance of Corinthia;[8] and the agricultural wealth of the district, and its importance in the Mycenaean period, is shown not only by the Mycenaean settlements, but by the wall near Isthmia,[9] the evidence of trade with southern Boeotia,[10] and the traces of Mycenaean highways for wheeled traffic leading from Mycenae in the direction of Corinth and the Isthmus.[11]

In short, the reference to ἀφνειὸς Κόρινθος in the Catalogue *might* be to the district rather than to a town on the site of the historical city, but the recent discoveries make this hypothesis unnecessary whether we suppose the reference is to a Mycenaean town or to a later one.

It appears, however, that the later Corinthians were dissatisfied with being put under Agamemnon's rule in the Catalogue, and that they, or the literary gentlemen campaigning on their behalf,[12] tried to identify their city with the Homeric Ephyre, home of Sisyphos and Bellerophon (*Il.* 6. 152 and 210).

Κλεωναί (2. 570) MAP 3

REFS. *Gazetteer*, No. 47; Gebauer, *AA* 1939, pp. 271–2; *RE*, Suppl. vi. 606; *AA* 1913, p. 114; Frazer, *Pausanias* iii. 82–3.

The site of the historical Kleonai lies about 4 kilometres north-west of the modern village of Ayios Vasilios (K.8 Korinthos 525E/332N), commanding an important pass down the river Longopotamos to Corinthia, through which one of the Mycenaean roads from Mycenae probably ran.[13]

The highest and westernmost of the hills which formed the acropolis of the historical city was the centre of an important Mycenaean settlement. Indeed, to judge from the sherds we picked up when we visited the place in 1960, the Mycenaean phase was the most important in this area, the settlement apparently extending for about 300 metres north to south by about 250 metres east to west. The hill is steep on the west and north-west, gentle on the south, while it connects with another, lower, hill on the east. The sherds we found in 1960 included MH–LH *Yellow Minyan* and *Ephyrean* wares, and fragments from LH IIIA–B *Kylikes* and *Deep Bowls*, of the finest quality.

'Ορνειαί (2. 571) MAP 3

REFS. *Gazetteer*, No. 18; *JHS Arch.* for 1961/2, p. 31.

The exact location of the historical Orneai has never been properly ascertained, but it must presumably lie in the valley of Leondi.[14] The site is probably in the vicinity of the village of Gymno, to south of Leondi, in the widest part of the valley. The village lies on a slope above the valley to the west, with a fine spring above its uppermost houses, at the foot of a knoll which forms the summit of the hill on which the village lies. This knoll bears some traces of ancient settlement, and tombs are reported in the vicinity.

We visited this site in the summer of 1961, but could not find any evidence for occupation earlier than the classical period. About 3 kilometres south-south-east of Gymno, however, just off the track to Sterna and Argos, there is a steep and rocky hill (PLATE 6*a*), known locally as 'kastro' (K.7 Tripolis 349E/243N), presumably because of the ancient tower which stands upon it. The hill lies on the east side of the road, exactly at the highest point of the narrow pass between the Inachos valley and the routes to ancient Phlious and Stymphalos.

On the summit of the hill, which measures some 170 metres east to west by 55 metres north to south, there are the remains of a classical or Hellenistic watch-tower (3 metres by 3 metres in plan), of which three courses of isodomic masonry are preserved. This tower is a good indication of the strategic importance of the site. Around it and extending over the whole summit and the upper slopes to south and east—the northern slopes are much steeper—we found a considerable number of Mycenaean sherds of a 'provincial' nature, ranging from LH II to LH IIIB (mainly the latter), together with five sherds of *Grey Minyan* ware, some obsidian, and a few pieces of classical pottery.

This site must now clearly be considered in connection with the location of Homeric Orneai, especially if it should in fact turn out that there are no prehistoric remains in the vicinity of Gymno.

Ἀραιθυρέη (2. 571) MAP 3

REFS. *Gazetteer*, No. 44; *JHS Arch.* for 1961–2, p. 31.

The statements of Strabo (8. 382) and Pausanias (2. 12. 4–6) about Araithyrea, clearly indicate that it was held to have been the forerunner of Phlious, and some lines of Apollonius Rhodius (*Argonautica* 1. 115–17) confirm that it lay near the springs of the Asopos, i.e. on the south side of the plain of Phlious. Pausanias says that it lay on a 'mound' or 'hillock' (*βουνός*), not far from Phlious, called the 'Arantine mound', while Strabo states that it was beside Mt. Kelossa (the modern Polyphengo) and thirty stades from the later city of Phlious. Thus it appears that we have to look for a low hill, near Polyphengo and the Asopos, and a little over three miles from the site of the historical Phlious.

In 1961 we discovered a small settlement on the west bank of the Asopos (here only a small stream), at a place called Ayia Eirene, immediately south of the road from modern Nemea (Ayios Georgios) to Stymphalos, and about 2·5 kilometres west-north-west of the former (K.7 Tripolis 404E/329N). The site is a small, low, heavily eroded hillock, at the foot of the higher hills bounding the southern side of the plain of Phlious. The sherds were scrappy and worn, but LH IIIA–B *Kylikes* and *Deep Bowls* were represented, and there did not appear to be any diagnostic later sherds. The total area of the settlement did not appear to exceed 150 by 100 metres.

This site conforms more or less with what we are told about the location of Araithyrea, except that it is not quite as far from Phlious as Strabo said Araithyrea was, and although the traditions about Araithyrea may represent no more than the claims of the people of Phlious, they are at least consistent.

Σικυών (2. 572) MAP 3

REFS. *Gazetteer*, No. 77; Blegen, *AJA* 24 (1920), pp. 10–11 and fig. 8 (the site is marked No. 12 on fig. 1); *AA* 1939, p. 272; Frazer, *Pausanias* iii. 41–6; Skalet, *Ancient Sicyon* (1928), pp. 1 f., 40 f.

Strabo (8. 382) says that Sicyon was formerly called 'Mekone' and, still earlier, 'Aigialoi', and that it was an *ἐπινειὸν . . . ἔχον λιμένα*, but the harbour-town in fact seems to have been separate from the classical city,[15] and both

Diodorus (20. 102) and Pausanias (2. 5. 6) make it clear that the acropolis of the old city lay on the plateau where the modern village of Vasiliko stands.[16] It is presumably, then, to a town here that the Catalogue refers, and not to one nearer the sea.

A prehistoric site has been found on the eastern end of the spur jutting out from the plateau just east of Vasiliko (K.8 Korinthos 498E/505N). Its centre was the small hillock at the end of the spur, but the Mycenaean settlement extended for at least 100 metres down the slopes to north and north-west, to judge from the sherds on the surface. The site is a fine one, overlooking the plain of Sicyon to the north and north-east and a fertile valley to the north-west.

In 303 B.C. Demetrios Poliorcetes razed much of the old city in the plain and transferred the population to the plateau on which the acropolis of the old city had been situated (Diodorus 20. 102; Pausanias 2. 7. 1).

Ὑπερησίη (2. 573) MAP 3

REFS. *Gazetteer*, No. 82; O. Walter, *ÖJh.* 19/20 (1919), Beiblatt, cols. 5–42; Frazer, *Pausanias* iv. 176–8; *JHS Arch.* for 1960/1, p. 31.

Pausanias (7. 26. 2) says that Hyperesia was the old name for the historical city of Aigeira, and that the new name, although adopted while the Ionians were still living there (i.e. before the Dorian invasion), did not supersede Hyperesia at once, just as in Pausanias' day there were still some who called Oreos in Euboea by its ancient name, Histiaia.

In 1960 we found a quantity of fine-quality LH IIIA–C sherds on the acropolis of Aigeira (I.7 Xilokastron 416 at 197E/689N). In fact there did not seem to be any pottery of any other period on the surface here, and the foundations of walls also appeared to be Mycenaean. The acropolis measures about 140 metres, north to south, by 120 metres, but the Mycenaean settlement does not appear to have extended far down the seaward slopes to the north, where the classical town of Aigeira lay. This was partially excavated and planned by Walter,[17] who discusses the historical city and particularly the Temple of Zeus and the Theatre. Of especial interest are the remains of a harbour at Mavra Litharia at the southern foot of the long ridge of Aigeira.[18]

A Mycenaean tomb was excavated by Verdelis at Psila Alonia, 1·5 kilometres to the east-south-east of the acropolis.[19]

Γονόεσσα (2. 573) MAP 3

REFS. *Gazetteer*, No. 80.

A town called 'Donoussa' which once stood between Aigeira and Pellene, according to Pausanias (7. 26. 13), laid claim to being Gonoessa by the simple expedient of altering the *Γονόεσσαν* of the Catalogue to *Δονόεσσαν*! Another candidate is, presumably, the *Γονοῦσσα ἡ ὑπὲρ Σικυῶνος* of Pausanias 2. 4. 4 and 5. 18. 7, and this has been identified with Titane,[20] although Pausanias does not mention the question in his descriptions of Titane.

Titane is probably to be located at the chapel of Ayios Tryphon, a few minutes' walk to the north of the village which has now been given the name Titane—it used to be called Voivonda—and about a kilometre to the south of the modern village of Gonoussa (old Lopesi). The chapel stands on the eastern tip of a spur projecting from the west into the valley of the Asopos, and surrounded by fine isodomic walls (K.7 Tripolis 398E/448N). The site thus occupies a strategic position on the route from Phlious to Sicyon, and that it was inhabited in the Mycenaean period is indicated by the discovery of an LH IIIB *Tall Kylix* stem here by Mrs. Hope Simpson and Miss Burford in 1959.

Πελλήνη (2. 574) MAP 3

The site of the historical Pellene is certainly established: it occupied the top of a high ridge extending to the north-east of and above the little modern village of Pellene, formerly called Zougra (I.7 Xilokastron 804 at 327E/588N). It was well situated on the one hand to control the routes south into Arcadia, and on the other to afford a commanding view over the Gulf of Corinth. There are easy routes (via Trikkala) to Stymphalos, Pheneos, and Orchomenos, and a relatively easy one to Sicyon.

We visited the site in 1960, and, although we could find no prehistoric sherds, the possibility of Mycenaean occupation cannot be ruled out, despite the height and remoteness of the site. But it is possible that the name Pellene in the Catalogue referred to some other place.

Αἴγιον (2. 574) MAP 3

REFS. *Gazetteer*, No. 304; *JHS Arch.* for 1954, p. 11; *Ergon* for 1954, p. 39; *LAAA* 4 (1912), p. 131; *OpAth.* 5, s.v. 'Aigion'; Frazer, *Pausanias* v. 159 f.; Ålin, *EMF*, p. 63.

The Homeric Aigion should presumably be located at the site of the historical and modern town. It stands on a high bluff overlooking the sea (I.6 Patrai 959E/847N), and controls not only the coastal route, but the fertile terraces and plains to the east and west.

A Mycenaean (LH III) cemetery discovered at the square of Psila Alonia, on the seaward slopes of the town near the hospital, shows that the site was inhabited in the Mycenaean period.

"*Αἰγιαλόν τ' ἀνὰ πάντα*" (2. 575) MAP 3

Pausanias (7. 1. 1) says that the whole coastland between Elis and Sicyonia was formerly called Aigialos, Strabo (3. 383) that it was called Aigialeia. There may be some confusion here with the town Aigialeia (Pausanias 2. 5. 6–8) or Aigialoi (Strabo 3. 382), but Herodotus (7. 94, cf. 5. 68) uses the term *Αἰγιαλεῖς* of the inhabitants of this coast. However, it is really impossible to decide whether the word *αἰγιαλόν* in the Catalogue is a proper name, or simply means 'shore'.

It is thus difficult to be certain where the Catalogue places the western boundary of Agamemnon's dominions, and we cannot assume that it does not mention the coast west of Aigion.[21]

Ἑλίκη (2. 575) MAP 3

According to the contemporary Heracleides Ponticus, the earthquake which destroyed the historical city of Helike took place on a winter's night in 373 B.C.: the old city was twelve stades from the sea, and all this intervening space and the city itself vanished beneath the waves (Strabo 8. 384–5, Pausanias 7. 24. 5–13). The Homeric epithet *εὐρεῖα* presumably refers to the broad coastal plain which existed before the earthquake, but if the sites of Hyperesia and Aigion may be taken as examples (to say nothing of all the classical towns of Achaea), Helike must have had a citadel. Now recent investigations have shown that the ancient Keryneia, formerly placed at a site near Gardena, above Rizomylo and the plain of Helike,[22] should be located instead at Mamousia, on the saddle between the Bouphasia (ancient Kerynites) and the Kalavryta (ancient Buraikos) rivers.[23] Thus Bura, which had previously been located at Mamousia, is now placed east of the Kalavryta.[24]

This shuffle to the east has therefore left the site at Gardena without an ancient name, and since it directly overlooks the coastal plain where the historical town of Helike was situated until the disaster, it is possible that this was its acropolis. The site lies on a high spur north-east of and above the modern village of Kerinia, about 8 kilometres south-east of Aigion and in the foothills of Mt. Klokos (I.6 Patrai 015E/792N). Mycenaean occupation is indicated by the bronze double-axe shown to Professor W. A. McDonald and Hope Simpson in 1962.[25]

Neither the kingdom of Diomedes nor that of Agamemnon corresponds with any known historical state, and the strangeness of the latter in particular has prompted the opinion that no such state ever really existed.[26] Elsewhere in the *Iliad*, moreover, there are passages which suggest not only that Agamemnon ruled at least the Argive plain, but also that he exercized some sort of authority over a wider area. Thus, in a famous passage in Book 2, he is said to have possessed a sceptre given to his ancestor, Pelops, by Hermes, which entitled him *πολλῇσιν νήσοισι καὶ Ἄργεϊ παντὶ ἀνάσσειν* (2. 108), and in Book 9 Diomedes recognizes that his sceptre gave him the right *τετιμῆσθαι περὶ πάντων* (9. 38). Similarly, in Book 1 Calchas declares that he fears the anger of a man *ὃς μέγα πάντων Ἀργείων κρατέει καί οἱ πείθονται Ἀχαιοί* (1. 78–9; cf. 10. 32–3), while in Book 9 not only does Nestor say to Agamemnon: *Ἀτρεΐδη, σὺ μὲν ἄρχε· σὺ γὰρ βασιλεύτατός ἐσσι* (9. 69), but it appears that Agamemnon is in a position to give Achilles seven cities bordering on Nestor's own realm (9. 149–53, cf. 291–5).

Unfortunately, unless and until, for example, more Linear B tablets are found at Mycenae, the evidence of archaeology will not be sufficient to determine just how far the control exercised from the palace extended, and even if a horde of tablets were to turn up, they would, presumably, only relate to the time immediately prior to one or other of the destructions, and might not, therefore, strictly speaking, be relevant to the question of Agamemnon's kingdom in the Catalogue.

The very strangeness of the kingdom, however, far from indicating that it never really existed, in fact provides the best ground for believing that it does correspond to reality, and the inconsistencies between it and the authority ascribed to Agamemnon elsewhere should not be exaggerated. When Nestor, for example, describes Agamemnon as βασιλεύτατος, the context suggests that he really means no more than that Agamemnon is the richest and most powerful king, and this interpretation is borne out by such passages as *Il.* 1. 281, where Nestor says that Agamemnon φέρτερός ἐστιν ἐπεὶ πλεόνεσσιν ἀνάσσει, just as in the Catalogue itself he is said to be ἄριστος because he πολὺ δὲ πλείστους ἄγε λαούς (2. 580).

Moreover, the whole plot of the *Iliad* turns on the refusal of one of the heroes to fight under Agamemnon's leadership any longer, and no one suggests that Achilles be threatened with a θωή as was Euchenor of Corinth (*Il.* 13. 663 f.). This seems to imply a distinction between such cities as Corinth and Sicyon (cf. *Il.* 23. 296 f.) over which Agamemnon actually ruled, and whose princes were bound to follow him in war, and the other states whose princes followed him simply because he was the most powerful king. Admittedly many of them refer to the oath they had sworn, not to return home before they had taken Troy,[27] but the taking of the oath itself indicates that they were not *constitutionally* bound to follow Agamemnon when he went to war.

Even the independence of Argos is recognized elsewhere: we are told, for example, that the commissioners sent round Greece by Adrastos, king of Argos, to raise an army against Thebes in the generation before Agamemnon, called without success at Mycenae (*Il.* 4. 372 f.), and as Allen says,[28] 'you do not send ambassadors to your own country'. Indeed, for what it is worth, Strabo (8. 372) records that Argos was more powerful than Mycenae until the time of the Pelopidai.

Finally, although Agamemnon's apparent ability to dispose of cities in Messenia may suggest that his authority extended more widely than the Catalogue implies, there is no direct conflict with the Catalogue here, since the Seven Cities are never mentioned in it. Moreover, although the suspicions attaching to the Embassy episode[29] may be largely the result of hypercriticism, it would clearly be unwise to base any far-reaching conclusions on Agamemnon's offer of the Seven Cities to Achilles: the poet who first composed the Embassy episode may have lifted the lines about them from some 'little catalogue',[30] which originally had nothing to do with the Trojan War, without much regard to the implications of what he was saying.[31]

Nevertheless, Agamemnon's control over the Seven Cities, and still more the other references to some sort of overriding authority exercised by him, may well reflect a real situation, for the evident cultural unity of Greece during LH IIIB, and the contemporary Hittite references to a powerful state called 'Aḫḫijavā', suggest that there was some sort of political unity in Greece at the time,[32] and if this is so, there can hardly be any doubt that Mycenae was the capital. But the Catalogue itself certainly does *not* reflect such a state of affairs: there is no suggestion in it that any of the other heroes owed Agamemnon any sort of allegiance, and he himself is cut off from the Argive plain by Diomedes' fortresses at Argos and Tiryns—a situation which is hardly conceivable in LH IIIB.

On the other hand, the picture of the northern Peloponnese which the Catalogue presents to us probably does reflect the Mycenaean rather than any subsequent period. For, although most of the towns mentioned in both Diomedes' and Agamemnon's kingdoms continued to exist in historical times, Eiones seems to have vanished, Mases to have become merely the harbour-town of Hermione, Araithyrea to have given place to Phlious, and Hyperesia to have changed its name to Aigeira, while the two kingdoms themselves had certainly ceased to exist. We cannot be certain that places like Eiones and Araithyrea did not exist in the Early Iron Age, or that states with something like the boundaries of Agamemnon's and Diomedes' kingdoms did not linger on, but the changes are most likely to have occurred when Mycenaean civilization passed away.

As we have said, we cannot tell whether there were real Mycenaean states corresponding to the kingdoms of Diomedes and Agamemnon, but the individual town-names in both kingdoms coincide well with the chief Mycenaean settlements: now that Corinth has been vindicated, there are few names which cannot be associated with a Mycenaean site, and there is only one major Mycenaean site—Dendra (Midea)—which is not mentioned in the Catalogue. But Midea, like Lerna and Nemea, despite their importance in mythology, is never mentioned elsewhere in the Homeric poems, and too much should not be made of its omission from the Catalogue.

In short, as in the Catalogue's account of Boeotia, so in that of the kingdoms of Diomedes and Agamemnon, we appear to find a reflection not so much of the great days of LH IIIB, as of the succeeding period when, as Desborough has shown,[33] the cultural unity of LH IIIB had disintegrated, but the Mycenaean way of life still went on.

NOTES ON THE KINGDOM OF AGAMEMNON

1. *Ancient Mycenae*, pp. 20–40.
2. Cf. Steffen, *Karten von Mykenai* (1884), and Text, pp. 8 f.; Mylonas, *Mycenae and the Mycenaean Age* (1966), pp. 86–8. In 1961 we examined the ancient bridge at Kasarma and are convinced that Wace was wrong to dismiss it as 'classical' (*Mycenae*, p. 27; cf. fig. 38*b*, where the bridge is, however, wrongly described as 'Mycenaean culvert on road to Berbati'). The bridge is of typical 'Cyclopean' construction (PLATE 5 *a* and *b*, cf. 5*c*), and its V-shaped 'false arch' closely resembles those of the culverts on the road eastwards from Mycenae to Berbati along the slopes of Agrilovouno.
3. Cf. *JHS Arch.* for 1962/3, pp. 12–15, *BCH* 87 (1963), pp. 739–42, *BCH* 89 (1965), pp. 708–17, *JHS Arch.* for 1966/7, pp. 8–9.
4. *JHS* 68 (1948), p. 59.
5. *HCS*, pp. 64–6.
6. *AJA* 26 (1922), pp. 151 f.
7. Cf. *AJA* 24 (1920), pp. 1–13, and *AJA* 27 (1923), pp. 156 f.
8. Loc. cit.
9. *Antiquity* 32 (1958), pp. 80–8 and refs. there; Desborough, *LMTS*, p. 221; *Hesperia* 35 (1966), pp. 346–62.

10. *BSA* 26 (1923–5), pp. 38–48.

11. Cf. Steffen, op. cit.

12. Cf. Allen, *HCS*, p. 65 n. 2. Other scholars have sought Ephyre elsewhere: e.g. at Korakou (Blegen, *Korakou*, p. 54; Burr, *NK*, p. 50) or at Aietopetra (Dunbabin, op. cit., p. 60 n. 18).

13. Cf. Wace, *Mycenae*, fig. 7 and p. 47.

14. Cf. Pausanias 2. 25. 5–6 and Frazer ad loc.

15. Skalet, *Ancient Sicyon*, p. 7.

16. Cf. Skalet, op. cit., pp. 2 and 25.

17. *ÖJh.* 19/20 (1919), Abb. 12 (Plan of Acropolis), cf. Abb. 7 on cols. 15–16.

18. Op. cit., col. 9.

19. *AE* 1956, parart., pp. 11–12; cf. *BCH* 82 (1958), pp. 726–7, and *JHS Arch.* for 1957, pp. 7–8. Its contents included 'vases of the last Mycenaean period'.

20. E. Meyer, *Peloponnesische Wanderungen* (1939), p. 11.

21. J. K. Anderson (*BSA* 49 (1954), p. 72) concludes that Agamemnon's kingdom did not extend 'west of Helike' (which is presumably a slip for 'west of Aigion'), and argues that this does not agree with the later political divisions of Achaea. But, since we cannot be sure precisely what is meant by αἰγιαλός, it is unwise to resort to negative, and thus vulnerable, archaeological arguments about the *lateness* of the Mycenaean remains found in the historical Achaea (cf. *CH*, p. 291; E. T. Vermeule, *AJA* 64 (1960), pp. 1 f.).

22. Frazer, *Pausanias* iv. 168.

23. *BSA* 48 (1953), pp. 154 f.

24. Frazer (*Pausanias* iv. 168–9) located Bura at Mamousia.

25. Cf. *Gazetteer*, No. 306.

26. e. g. J. K. Anderson, *BSA* 49 (1954), p. 72. The boundaries of the kingdom of Agamemnon are no stranger than many a frontier in the world today.

27. Cf. *Il.* 2. 284–8, 339 f., 4. 266–7.

28. *HCS*, p. 66.

29. Cf., for example, Page, *HHI*, pp. 297–315.

30. Cf. *Il.* 13. 685–700 for another 'little catalogue', and see pp. 165–6 below.

31. As Page (op. cit., p. 166 n. 42) says, 'the poet of the Embassy cares nothing about Mycenaean geography'.

32. Huxley, *Achaeans and Hittites*, esp. pp. 25 f.; Desborough, *LMTS*, pp. 218–19.

33. *LMTS*, pp. 225–30. For a further discussion of the possibility that the Catalogue reflects LH IIIC see pp. 161–4 below.

THE KINGDOM OF MENELAUS

Λακεδαίμων (2. 581) — MAP 4

Huxley follows Toynbee in taking the name *Λακεδαίμων* to refer to a city 'probably in the neighbourhood of Therapnai',[1] but *κοίλη* and *κητώεσσα* are hardly appropriate epithets for a town, and although it has been alleged[2] that in Homer *Λακεδαίμων* only twice refers to the *kingdom* of Menelaus—here in the Catalogue and in *Od.* 21. 13—there can be no certainty about this: it must mean the country at least once (*Od.* 21. 13), and it does not necessarily ever mean a city. It is usually used simply to refer to the home of Menelaus and Helen,[3] just as Phthia—which is probably also not a city[4]—is used for the home of Achilles.

It is thus perhaps better to take *Λακεδαίμων* as referring to the whole kingdom.

Φᾶρις (2. 582) — MAP 4

REFS. *Gazetteer*, No. 99; *BSA* 51 (1956), p. 170; *BSA* 55 (1960), pp. 79–81, and Pl. 17*a*; *BSA* 56 (1961), pp. 164, 169–73.

Frazer[5] located Pharis at Vaphio, but Pausanias (3. 20. 3) speaks of going past Amyklai and heading straight for the sea, and this must surely indicate that Pharis lay on the road to Gythion and not some distance off it as Vaphio does. It is therefore better to place it at Ayios Vasilios (M.7 Yithion 197E/412N).

The site lies on a hill south-east of the junction between the main Sparta–Gythion road and the branch road to Xerokambi. The hill is not very high, steep on the north and sloping gently to the south and west. Abundant Mycenaean (LH IIIB) sherds are to be found here and on the lower hills to the south-west, while a few EH and MH sherds have been found near the chapel, where there is also some classical and Hellenistic pottery. So far there is no evidence for Protogeometric or Geometric occupation of the site.

Σπάρτη (2. 582) — MAP 4

REFS. *Classical Sparta*: *Gazetteer*, No. 94; *BSA* 55 (1960), p. 70; *BSA* 56 (1961), p. 164; *JHS Arch.* for 1957, p. 10; Desborough, *LMTS*, p. 88; Ålin, *EMF*, p. 92.

The Menelaion: *Gazetteer*, No. 95; Tsountas, *AE* 1881, pp. 130–1; *BSA* 15 (1908/9), pp. 108–57 (the shrine); *BSA* 16 (1909/10), pp. 4–11 (the Mycenaean house); *BSA* 55 (1960), pp. 72–3; *BSA* 56 (1961), pp. 164, 170 n. 312, 173; Desborough, *LMTS*, pp. 88 and 90.

The site of the historical Sparta (L.7 Sparti 157E/531N) was inhabited from at least LH III onwards, and it is, perhaps, simplest to take the Homeric

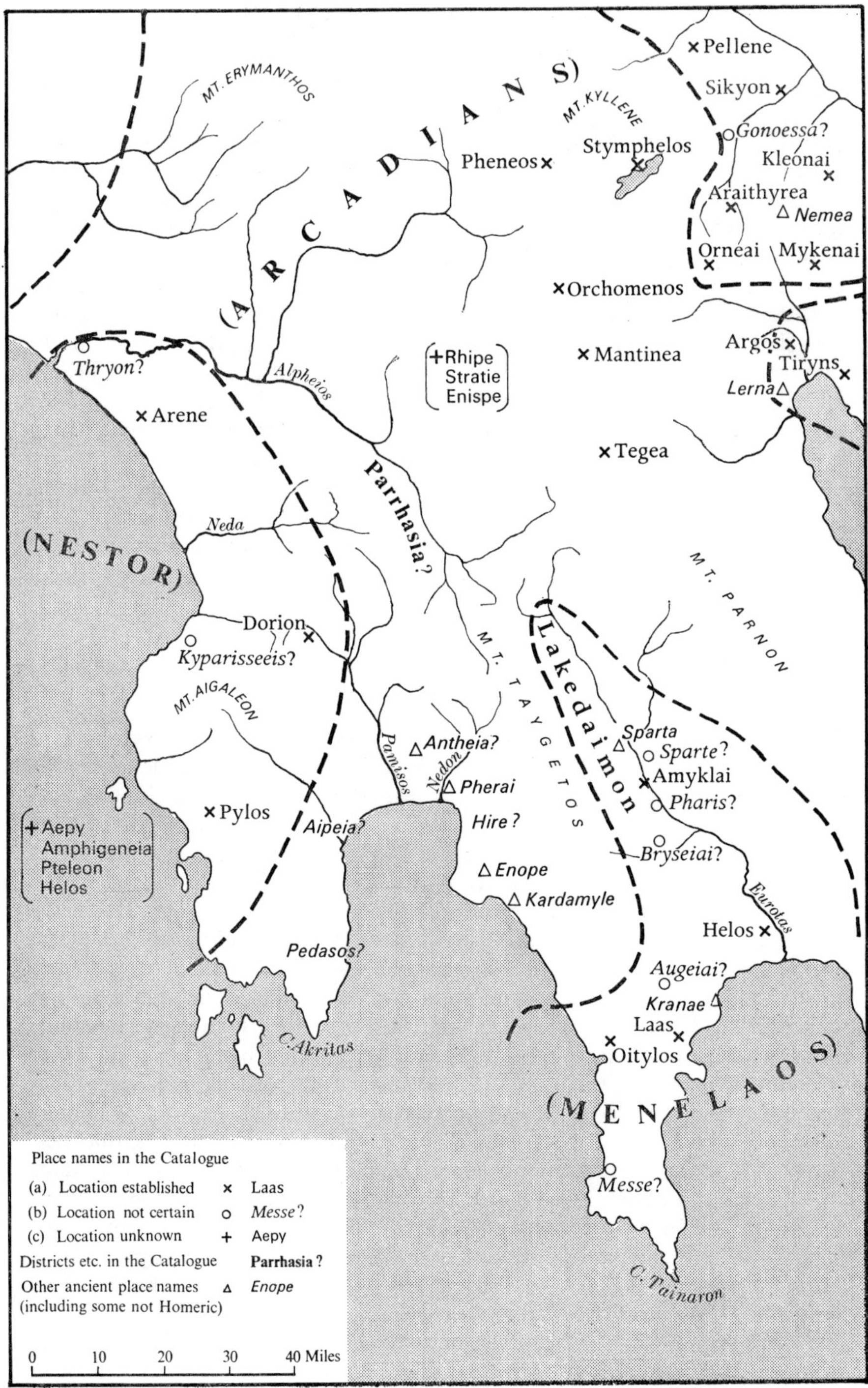

Pellene
Sikyon
Gonoessa?
Kleonai
(ARCADIANS)
MT. ERYMANTHOS
MT. KYLLENE
Pheneos
Stymphelos
Araithyrea
Nemea
Orneai
Mykenai
Orchomenos
Argos
Tiryns
Lerna
Mantinea
Rhipe
Stratie
Enispe
Thryon?
Arene
Alpheios
Tegea
Parrhasia?
Neda
(NESTOR)
MT. PARNON
Dorion
Kyparisseeis?
MT. TAYGETOS
Lakedaimon
MT. AIGALEON
Sparta
Sparte?
Amyklai
Pharis?
Antheia?
Pamisos
Nedon
Pherai
Hire?
Bryseiai?
Pylos
Aipeia?
Aepy
Amphigeneia
Pteleon
Helos
Enope
Kardamyle
Eurotas
Helos
Pedasos?
Augeiai?
Kranae
Laas
Oitylos
C. Akritas
(MENELAOS)
Messe?
C. Tainaron
Place names in the Catalogue
(a) Location established × Laas
(b) Location not certain o Messe?
(c) Location unknown + Aepy
Districts etc. in the Catalogue Parrhasia?
Other ancient place names Δ Enope
(including some not Homeric)
0 10 20 30 40 Miles

Map 4

Σπάρτη as referring to a city on this site. But the more important settlement in Mycenaean times seems to have lain across the Eurotas at the site of the later Menelaion (L.7 Sparti ♁ at 182E/510N), and if this is not Lakedaimon (see above), it is possible that the *Σπάρτη* of the Catalogue refers to this place.

In either case, if *Λακεδαίμων* refers to the country, Sparte was presumably thought of as Menelaus' capital: the name is usually used, like Lakedaimon, to refer simply to the home of Helen and Menelaus, but at least once—*Il.* 4. 52—it must mean a city. It has been argued[6] that when, in the *Odyssey*, Telemachos finds Menelaus at home, celebrating a marriage-feast for his daughter and son, the fact that the son's bride comes *Σπάρτηθεν* (*Od.* 4. 10) means that Menelaus' home was not thought of as being *at* Sparte. But the point is, surely, that whereas he was giving his daughter to a foreigner (Achilles' son), he had found a wife 'from Sparte' for his son. It would be difficult to explain why the name *Σπάρτη* should be used for the home of Helen and Menelaus unless it was regarded as the place where they normally lived.

Sparte is possibly referred to after Pharis for metrical reasons,[7] but the Catalogue does not by any means invariably refer to the most important town in a kingdom first: Iolkos does not come first in Eumelos' kingdom, for example (*Il.* 2. 711–12), nor Panopeus in Phocis (*Il.* 2. 519–23).[8]

Μέσση (2. 582) MAP 4

REFS. *Gazetteer*, No. 131; *BSA* 56 (1961), pp. 122–3 and 174 and Pl. 20 *a–c*.

Strabo (8. 364) says that some regarded Messe as unknown, others as a shortened form for *Μεσσήνη*(!), but despite this, it seems reasonable to identify it with Pausanias' 'Messa' (3. 25. 9–10), which he describes as a city and harbour a little north of the city of Hippola. The historical Messa lies in the region south of Mezzapo,[9] and Homeric Messe has been placed at the site of the medieval castle of Maina, built in 1248 by William II de Villehardouin, the fourth Frankish Prince of the Morea.[10] The fortress (PLATE 6*b*) lies at the end of the promontory of Tigani, south of Mezzapo (M.7 Yithion 061E/939N).

One might suppose that this barren and waterless headland would have been rather unsuitable as a habitation site, but there is no doubt that it makes an excellent fortress, walls being necessary on the landward side alone. A cross-wall on the south-west is definitely ancient, being prior to other (?Frankish) walls built against it,[11] and towards its western end, where it is reasonably well preserved, it can be seen to be constructed of two lines of roughly dressed blocks with a filling of smaller stones in between. The thickness of the wall here is two metres or more. The projecting towers and walls have an outer facing of fairly large rough limestone blocks, the largest being about 1·20 by 0·70 metres, with small stones in the interstices: this looks much like 'Cyclopean' masonry of Mycenaean date. In view of this, it is a pity that it has so far proved impossible to discover any unquestionably ancient sherds on the surface because of the intense weathering on the site.

If these remains are in fact those of a Mycenaean fortress, there would be an interesting parallel here with the fortress on the promontory of Araxos in

Elis,[12] since we would have two fortresses set at the two extremities of the Peloponnese, at ports of call on the route to the west. The identification of Messe with the site at Tigani receives some support from the constant din created by the 'pigeons and seafowl'[13] in the cliffs of the Thyrides to the south, which calls to mind the Homeric epithet *πολυτρήρων*.

Βρυσειαί (2. 583) MAP 4

Pausanias gives us little help in the quest for Bryseai. In his commentary (3. 20. 2 f.), he hops in and out of Taÿgetos at will, and the only fixed point is the sanctuary of Eleusinian Demeter at 'Kalyvia tis Sokhas', partially excavated by the British School.[14] But at this point there is a lacuna in the text (3. 20. 5), and the only clues that remain are that Taleton, a peak of Taÿgetos, rises above Bryseai and was sacred to Helios, and the implication that Bryseai lay near an exit from Taÿgetos (. . . *ἀπιοῦσιν ἐκ τοῦ Ταϋγέτου*). A third and more tenuous clue is provided by the name 'Bryseai' itself, which suggests copious springs.

J. M. Cook[15] rightly dismissed von Prott's location of Bryseai at 'Kalyvia tis Sokhas', but his own suggestion, that it lay at Kefalari a mile to the north, ignores the clue of Mt. Taleton. Frazer[16] and others have identified this peak with the one now called Prophitis Elias, and if this is right, it appears to rise, not above 'Kalyvia tis Sokhas', but directly behind Xerokambi.[17] The location of Bryseai at Ayios Vasilios, formerly proposed by Mrs. Waterhouse and Hope Simpson, also fails to take account of all the clues, in that Ayios Vasilios is some way from the foot of Taÿgetos, and does not abound in springs. In any case, Ayios Vasilios is probably Pharis, as we have seen. In fact Bryseai probably lies somewhere in the region of Xerokambi, or perhaps even below Koumousta, where there are springs of great size and beauty.

A possible location is the Mycenaean site discovered by the Ephor of Lakonia, Dr. Christou, near the village of Anthochorion (formerly Katsouleika), about two kilometres south of Xerokambi on the road to Goranoi, near a place called Kaminia and the church of Analipsis (M.7 Yithion ⛪ at 177E/377N). Here Christou found several Mycenaean tall-stemmed *Kylikes* of good quality.[18]

Αὐγειαί (2. 583) MAP 4

It is still uncertain whether Augeiai should be located at the site of the classical Aigiai, though Strabo (8. 364) regards the two places as identical.[19] It is also not possible to decide as yet whether the burial mounds at Koutoumou (M.7 Yithion 213E/209N), near classical Aigiai, known locally as the 'tombs of the kings', are Mycenaean or Hellenistic/Roman, but no surface indications of a Mycenaean site have yet been found.

In view of the recurrence of *Αὐγειὰς ἐρατεινάς* in the Locrian section (*Il.* 2. 532), a Homeric 'diplography' cannot be ruled out, although the Locrian Augeiai might be the likelier candidate for removal. On the other hand,

Stephanus of Byzantium remarks (s.v. *Αὔγεια*), *ἔστι καὶ Λακωνικὴ πόλις με . . . . . . πνῶν. τὸ ἐθνικὸν Αὐγεάτης*, and Meineke suggests that the name *Θεραπνῶν* may be concealed in '. . . *πνῶν*'. If neither Lakedaimon nor Sparte is to be located at the Menelaion site (=Therapnai), this could conceivably be Augeiai, but on the whole it is perhaps better to equate Augeiai with Aigiai, assuming that nothing is wrong with the text of the Catalogue at this point.

Ἀμύκλαι (2. 584) MAP 4

REFS. *The Amyklaion*: *Gazetteer*, No. 97; Tsountas *AE* 1892, pp. 1 f.; Fiechter *JdI* 33 (1918), pp. 107 f.; Buschor and von Massow, *AM* 52 (1927), pp. 1 f.; *BSA* 55 (1960), pp. 74–6; *BSA* 56 (1961), pp. 164, 170, 173–4; Desborough, *LMTS*, p. 88.

Vaphio: *Gazetteer*, No. 98; *AE* 1888, pp. 197 f.; *AE* 1889, pp. 129 f.; *BSA* 37 (1936/7), pp. 187–91; *BSA* 55 (1960), pp. 76–8 and Pl. 19; *BSA* 56 (1961), pp. 164, 168–75.

If Pharis is in fact to be located at Ayios Vasilios (see above), it seems likely that Allen[20] was right to consider the prehistoric sites at the Amyklaion and at Vaphio as going together, particularly since the classical Amyklai seems to have occupied much of the same area.[21] The site at Vaphio (L.7 Sparti 193E/464N) is the largest Mycenaean site yet discovered in Laconia, and the famous gold cups from the tholos tomb near by are sufficient evidence of its wealth and importance.

Ἕλος (2. 584) MAP 4

REFS. *Gazetteer*, No. 120; *BSA* 55 (1960), pp. 97–103 and Pl. 21; *BSA* 56 (1961), pp. 165, 168–74; *JHS Arch.* for 1959/60; pp. 9–10 and figs. 9 and 10; *JHS Arch.* for 1960/1, pp. 32–3 and figs. 34 and 35; *JHS Arch.* for 1963–4, pp. 9–10 (a fortification-wall in association with LH IIIB pottery); Desborough, *LMTS*, p. 88.

The Mycenaean settlement at Ayios Stephanos (M.7 Yithion △39 at 320E/234N) is the most important of the numerous Mycenaean sites now known round the Helos plain, and despite the fact that Pausanias' distances (3. 22. 3) would place the Helos which he *saw* on the eastern side of the plain,[22] Ayios Stephanos is the most likely to have been the *ἔφαλον πτολίεθρον* of Homer: it was probably closer to the sea, if not actually on it, in Mycenaean times.[23] The abundant classical, Hellenistic, and Roman remains in the district between Vlakhioti and Vezani, on the eastern side of the plain, do in fact indicate that classical Helos lay in this region,[24] but the remains are nowhere sufficient to suggest a city or even a large town, and it is more likely that classical Helos was a synoikismos of scattered villages and farms. With the exception of the recently developed rice and cotton industries in the marsh itself, which are centred on Skala and modern Helos, the modern agricultural economy follows exactly the same pattern.

The settlement at Ayios Stephanos has been excavated by Lord William Taylour. Pottery ranging from EH to LH IIIC has been found, and the Mycenaean settlement was apparently walled in LH IIIB.

Λάας (2. 585) MAP 4

REFS. *Gazetteer*, No. 127; *BSA* 12 (1905/6), pp. 274–5; *BSA* 13 (1906/7), pp. 232–4.

Classical Las has been securely located at the hill of Passava (M.7 Yithion 109 at 202E/131N), but the 'polygonal' masonry (better described as 'ashlar') which was said to rise to a height of two-thirds of the medieval castle wall on the east side,[25] is in fact mostly out of its original position, and the tell-tale mortar is, of course, medieval.[26] There is not sufficient evidence to warrant the attribution of the large blocks—some are 1·50 metres by 0·80 metres—to the Mycenaean period, and so far the only object which could be said to be prehistoric, found on the hill, is a solitary chip of obsidian.[27] Classical and Hellenistic sherds, however, abound. Thus, although the site would have made a magnificent Mycenaean fortress, the evidence for Mycenaean occupation is still lacking.

The traditions attaching to Kranai[28] and to classical Las,[29] however, as well as the important Mycenaean settlement at Mavrovouni,[30] all testify to the early importance of this district. Strabo (8. 364) says that the Dioskouri were called 'Lapersai' because they sacked Las,[31] and that the Heraklidai used it as a naval station because of the excellence of its harbour.[32]

Οἴτυλος (2. 585) MAP 4

REFS. *Gazetteer*, No. 132; *BSA* 56 (1961), pp. 121, 174, Pl. 19*d*; cf. *JHS Arch.* for 1957, p. 10.

The village of Oitylos (M.7 Yithion 95E/115N), with its harbour at Limeni, occupies a strategic point, well suited to command both the north–south route along the west coast of the Mani, and also the western end of the pass from Gythion to Areopolis.[33] There is no doubt that the classical and later Oitylos (Pausanias 3. 25. 10) lay on the seaward slopes of the hill occupied by the modern village, and that its acropolis lay on the summit.[34] There is, as yet, no evidence for Mycenaean or Early Iron Age occupation, but the combination of the literary evidence and the continuity of the name ('Vitylo' during the Turkish occupation) are strong arguments for believing that the Homeric Oitylos also lay here.

The names in Menelaus' kingdom cover only a part of the historical Laconia—the whole of the Malea peninsula and of Kynouria are absent—but the distribution of the names over the main Eurotas valley and the Tainaron peninsula makes sense geographically. Unfortunately, despite the fact that the approximate locations of the individual towns are in most cases well attested, there is only one (Amyklai) which can be certainly identified, though it is highly probable that Oitylos occupied much the same site as the village which still bears the name. It is thus not really possible to determine how far the distribution of the places mentioned in the Catalogue coincides with the distribution of the Mycenaean sites, though they appear to follow much the same pattern, except perhaps in the Tainaron peninsula, where the Catalogue puts four towns (Messe, ? Augeiai, Laas, and Oitylos), but where the only

Mycenaean sites so far known are those at Kranai and at Mavrovouni near Gythion. However, evidence for Mycenaean occupation will probably be forthcoming from some of these places, and at least none of the important Mycenaean sites in Laconia seems to be missing, assuming that Vaphio is Amyklai and that Ayios Stephanos is Helos.

The pattern of Early Iron Age settlement is, as usual, too little known for comparison with Homeric Laconia to be profitable, but Sparta seems to have controlled much the same area as Menelaus in the 8th century B.C., after the conquest of Helos and before the First Messenian War,[35] and the Catalogue could be held to reflect this period here at least as well as the Mycenaean.

Apart from the Catalogue, Kranai and Kythera both appear in the *Iliad*,[36] and there are pre-Dorian traditions connected with other Mycenaean settlements in Laconia, particularly Pellana, the home of the Tyndareus legend,[37] and Geronthrai[38]—the latter, together with Amyklai, Pharis, and Helos, was traditionally associated with the Dorian conquest.[39] Both Pellana and Geronthrai might have been expected to figure in the Catalogue, whatever period it is held to reflect.

NOTES ON THE KINGDOM OF MENELAUS

1. Toynbee, *JHS* 33 (1913), pp. 246–7; Huxley, *Early Sparta*, p. 13 and n. 6 on p. 97; cf. Burr, *NK*, pp. 53–8, and Schol. ad *Il.* 2. 581.
2. *RE* iiiA (2nd edn. 1929), pp. 1271–2.
3. Cf. *Il.* 3. 239, 244, 387, 443; *Od.* 4. 1 (where the epithets are the same as in the Catalogue), 313, 702; 5. 20; 13. 414; 15. 1; 17. 121. On the origin of the name 'Lakedaimon' see *Glotta* 38 (1959), pp. 14–17.
4. See below, pp. 128–9; cf. *Il.* 1. 155, 9. 363, 395; *Od.* 11. 496.
5. *Pausanias* iii. 363–4, cf. p. 134.
6. Huxley, *Early Sparta*, p. 97 n. 7.
7. Burr, *NK*, p. 54.
8. That Panopeus was thought of as the capital of Phocis is indicated by *Il.* 17. 307–8 (see above, pp. 42–3).
9. *BSA* 56 (1961), p. 123.
10. *BSA* 13 (1906/7), p. 243.
11. For a full discussion see *BSA* 56 (1961), p. 122 and fig. 6.
12. See below, p. 98, on Myrsinos in Elis (*Il.* 2. 616).
13. *BSA* 13 (1906/7), loc. cit.
14. For refs. see *BSA* 55 (1960), p. 82.
15. *BSA* 45 (1950), p. 261, discussing the Eleusinion at 'Kalyvia tis Sokhas'.
16. *Pausanias* iii. 264.
17. Cf. *BSA* 55 (1960), p. 81.
18. *JHS Arch.* for 1962/3, p. 17; *Ergon* for 1962, pp. 134f.; *BCH* 87 (1963), p. 764.
19. Cf. *BSA* 56 (1961), pp. 114f.

20. *HCS*, p. 24.

21. *BSA* 55 (1960), p. 82, under 'Slavochori'.

22. Perhaps in the region of Ayios Strategos: cf. *Gazetteer*, No. 110 (M. 8 Molaoi 431E/213N).

23. For ἔφαλον πτολίεθρον cf. Κήρινθος ἔφαλος (*Il.* 2. 538), Χαλκὶς ἀγχίαλος (*Il.* 2. 640), and ἀγχίαλος Ἄντρων (*Il.* 2. 697).

24. *BSA* 24 (1919/20, 1920/1), p. 150.

25. *BSA* 12 (1905/6), p. 275. For the identification with Las see *BSA* 13 (1906–7), pp. 232–4.

26. *BSA* 12 (1905/6), pp. 274–5, Pl. 3 and fig. 3.

27. On closer examination the 'LH III' sherds mentioned in *BSA* 51 (1956), p. 170, prove to be enigmatic.

28. *Gazetteer*, No. 124: M. 7 Yithion 280E/203N. Cf. *Il.* 3. 445; Pausanias 3. 22. 1–2.

29. Pausanias 3. 24. 6–8, 10–11; Strabo 8. 364.

30. *Gazetteer*, No. 125: M. 7 Yithion 234E/135N.

31. Cf. Schol. ad Lycophron, *Alex.* 1369 Ζηνὶ τῷ Λαπερσίῳ ὁμώνυμος Ζεύς.

32. The Spartans still used it as a naval station in 411 B.C.: cf. Thucydides 8. 91. 2, 92. 3.

33. Cf. *BSA* 13 (1906/7), p. 239.

34. *JHS Arch.* for 1957, p. 10.

35. Cf. G. L. Huxley, *Early Sparta*, pp. 26–33.

36. For Kranai cf. *Il.* 3. 445, but Allen's suggestion (*HCS*, p. 67 n. 2) that Agamemnon's Corinthian forces might have gathered here is geographically absurd. For Kythera cf. *Il.* 10. 268 and 15. 430 f. Andron (*FGrH* 10 F 11) conjectured from *Od.* 4. 514–18 that the home of Thyestes and Aigisthos was on Kythera (cf. Tzetzes, *Chil.* 1. 461; Allen *HCS*, pp. 67–8; Wace and Stubbings, *CH*, p. 292). We may compare Elaphonisi (Onugnathos) where Agamemnon was said to have set up a sanctuary of Athena, and where, it was claimed, lay the tomb of Kinados, the pilot of Menelaus' ship (Pausanias 3. 22. 10).

37. *BSA* 56 (1961), pp. 125–7, 166, 170–2, 174; Pl. 21 *b* and *c*.

38. *BSA* 11 (1904/5), pp. 91 f.; *BSA* 16 (1909/10), pp. 72 f.; *BSA* 55 (1960), pp. 85–6 and Pl. 17*b*; *BSA* 56 (1961), pp. 164, 168–73; Pausanias 3. 2. 6 and 3. 22. 6.

39. Strabo 8. 364–5; Pausanias 3. 1. 5–6; 3. 2. 6–7; 3. 19. 6; 3. 20. 6; 3. 22. 6.

THE KINGDOM OF NESTOR

Πύλος (2. 591) MAP 4

REFS. *Gazetteer*, No. 197; *AJA* 65 (1961), No. 42; Ålin, *EMF*, pp. 82 f.; Desborough, *LMTS*, Index, s.v. 'Pylos'; for latest reports see *AJA* 64 (1960) and subsequent volumes.

The controversies both ancient and modern about the location of Nestor's Pylos are perhaps best summed up in the riddle which Strabo records (8. 339): *ἔστι Πύλος πρὸ Πύλοιο. Πύλος γε μέν ἐστι καὶ ἄλλος*. But the discovery of the great Mycenaean palace and town at Ano Englianos, and the decipherment of the Linear B tablets, in which the name 'Pu-ro' frequently occurs, have at least made it virtually certain that this was the original Pylos of the legends. This accords with 'the vulgar Greek opinion'[1] that Nestor's Pylos was the Messenian, and with Strabo's statement (8. 359) that *ἡ παλαιὰ Πύλος ἡ Μεσσηνιακή* lay under Mt. Aigaleon.[2]

Strabo himself argued that Nestor's Pylos was the Triphylian one, mainly on the basis of the description of Telemachos' voyage home from Pylos to Ithaka in the *Odyssey* (15. 296–300),[3] and of Nestor's reminiscences of the war between the Pylians and the Epeians, in the *Iliad* (11. 670–761).[4] It must be admitted that a Pylos near the Alpheios fits Nestor's account of the cattle-rustling which sparked the war off, and of the preliminaries to the battle near Thryoessa, better than a Pylos in Messenia,[5] but Nestor's claim that he pursued the routed Epeians as far as Bouprasion suggests that we should not press the details of the saga too far, and his description of Thryoessa as *τηλοῦ ἐπ' Ἀλφειῷ, νεάτη Πύλου ἠμαθόεντος* (*Il.* 11. 712) in fact fits the Messenian Pylos better than the Triphylian. In any case, if Nestor's tale perhaps points rather to Kakovatos, it must equally be admitted that the description of Telemachos' journey by chariot from Pylos to Pherai (Kalamata), points to Ano Englianos.[6] Perhaps the most plausible solution to the difficulties, however, is that although the real Pylos which lay behind the legends, was the Messenian, later poets thought of it as being much nearer the Alpheios.

Recent excavations have revealed an extensive lower-town below the palace at Ano Englianos, which flourished in the LH IIIA–B period, but which was inhabited *continuously* from late in the MH period to the very end of LH IIIB. There is thus no need, on *archaeological* grounds at least, to look for a 'Matropylos' in a different place, earlier than the building of the LH IIIA–B palace at Ano Englianos.[7]

After the destruction of the 'Old Messenian Pylos', according to Strabo (8. 359), some of its inhabitants moved down to Koryphasion. This is probably just a much-telescoped, traditional explanation of the process by which the *classical* Pylos came to be located at Koryphasion, and if this is so, we do not have to look for yet another *Mycenaean* Pylos at Koryphasion itself.[8] The Mycenaean site there[9] may be connected with the port for Ano Englianos.

Ἀρήνη (2. 591) MAP 4

REFS. *Gazetteer*, No. 257; *AJA* 65 (1961), No. 19.

Strabo (8. 346) says that the usual identification of Arene was with Samikon, and both he and Pausanias (5. 6. 2–3) agree that the *ποταμὸς Μινυήϊος* which Nestor says flowed into the sea near Arene (*Il.* 11. 722–3), was the Anigros. This location for Arene accords well with the topographical indications of Nestor's tale (cf. *Il.* 11. 722–6, especially), and is probably correct.

An important Mycenaean walled settlement has been found at Klidhi, below the acropolis of Samikon (K.5 Pirgos in square 470E/110N), and Yalouris has recently published the finds from the Mycenaean burial mound at the site.[10] He also identifies the settlement with Homeric Arene, and believes that the tomb is the one pointed out to later travellers as the Tomb of Iardanos.

Θρύον (2. 592) MAP 4

The description of Thryon as *Ἀλφειοῖο πόρον* in the Catalogue suggests that it is the same place as the *Θρυόεσσα πόλις . . . τηλοῦ ἐπ' Ἀλφειῷ* of Nestor's tale in *Iliad* 11 (lines 711–12), and in this case we have to look for a steep hill (cf. the *αἰπεῖα κολώνη* of *Il.* 11. 711) at a ford over the Alpheios. Following a too literal interpretation of *Il.* 5. 545, however, which describes the Alpheios as flowing *Πυλίων διὰ γαίης*, Dörpfeld and Bölte (followed by Burr) thought that Thryon must necessarily be placed north of the Alpheios, and consequently Bölte picked on the heights near Strephi,[11] and Burr on the site near Salmone.[12] But neither of these places is of any strategic value, and neither lies either on the Alpheios or near a ford over it; furthermore, neither has yet produced any Mycenaean remains.

Strabo provides a good clue to the location of Thryon: he says (8. 349) that Thryon or Thryoessa was thought to be the Epitalion of his day because the whole place was *θρυώδης* ('full of rushes'), especially the *fords over the river*. Epitalion is probably to be placed at Dardiza, near the modern Epitalion (formerly Agoulinitsa: K.5 Pirgos in square 370E/410N): Meyer speaks of the location as 'certain',[13] and the extensive spread of surface pottery, including a fine Archaic terracotta perirrhanterion,[14] and the position of the site are strong grounds for accepting the identification. It is even, perhaps, significant that the modern toponym for the site at Dardiza—'Samakia'—has the same connotation as the Homeric name Thryon or Thryoessa (i.e. 'reedy').[15]

Proof of Mycenaean occupation has recently been found at Ayios Georgios near by, confirming the evidence from the Mycenaean cemetery there.[16]

Αἰπύ (2. 592) MAP 4

It is obvious from Strabo's discussion (8. 349) that there was no clear tradition about the location of Aipy. He says that there was even disagreement as to whether *ἐΰκτιτον* was the epithet and *Αἰπύ* the name or vice versa, and hence whether a place which was naturally or artificially defended should be sought.

Of the positive claims which he records, the identification with Margalai in Amphidolia can probably be ruled out, since this would put Aipy north of Thryon/Thryoessa which Nestor describes as *νεάτη Πύλου ἠμαθόεντος* (*Il.* 11. 712).[17] The identification with Epitalion on the other hand, involves the assumption that Thryon refers merely to the ford, and makes nonsense of Nestor's reference to Thryoessa as a *πόλις*, assuming Thryon and Thryoessa to be the same place.

In view of this, and the absence of any other traditions about it, it does not seem worth while to guess at the location of Aipy,[18] and this is a pity since there is a slight possibility that the name occurs in the Linear B tablets from Pylos.[19]

Κυπαρισσήεις (2. 593) MAP 4

REFS. *Gazetteer*, No. 234; *AJA* 65 (1961), No. 22.

Strabo (8. 349) distinguishes clearly between the Kyparissia on the Messenian coast and the Homeric Kyparisseeis, which, he says, lay in Makistia 'when Makistia extended beyond the Neda', and this should be a warning against a too ready assumption that Kyparisseeis was the same place as the historical Kyparissia. Yet, as Strabo himself goes on to say, the river near the latter was called the Kyparisseeis, and Pausanias (4. 36. 7) spells Kyparissia *Κυπαρισσιαί*. The probability is, then, that the Homeric name does refer to a town on this site, though the modern name cannot be used to strengthen the argument since in medieval times, and up to the War of Independence, the place was called Arkadia.[20]

The site (PLATE 7*a*) is of considerable importance (L.5 Kiparissia 518E/761N), commanding the coastal route to Triphylia and the pass westwards via Dorion to the upper Pamisos. It was certainly inhabited in Mycenaean times,[21] though so far there is no evidence that it was also inhabited in the Early Iron Age.

Ἀμφιγένεια (2. 593) MAP 4

Strabo's information about the location of Amphigeneia (8. 349) is precise, but unfortunately completely enigmatic. According to him, Amphigeneia, like Kyparisseeis, lay in Makistia, in the neighbourhood of the river Hypsoeis, where there was a shrine of Leto. It should, therefore, be sought in north-western Messenia, and it is thus strange to find the suggestion that it should be identified with the later Ampheia, for that lay in *north-eastern* Messenia.[22] Allen's suggestion, on the other hand, that the *Ἀμφιγένειαν* of the Catalogue is a corruption of *ἂμ Φιγαλείαν*,[23] is a drastic resort.

Professor Marinatos' conjecture that Amphigeneia might have been the ancient name for his fine Mycenaean site at Mouriatadha[24] has no support.

Πτελεόν (2. 594) MAP 4

Strabo's sources are here (8. 349–50) worse than useless: of course we know that there was another Pteleon in Thessaly (*Il.* 2. 697), but we can hardly believe the claim that the Pteleon in Messenia was a colony from the Thessalian Pteleon. As for 'Pteleasion', 'a woody and uninhabited place', we have met this sort of thing before, in the Locrian section,[25] and we begin to scent guesswork. In short, we really have no evidence for locating Nestor's Pteleon.

Ἕλος (2. 594) MAP 4

Pliny the Elder (*NH* 4. 5. 15) placed Helos between Methone and Cape Akritas, but Strabo (8. 350) says that some maintained that it was a place near the Alpheios, others a city, while others again claimed that it lay in the region of the 'Alorion marsh', wherever that might be. It is thus at least clear that there was no certainty about its location, and Professor Marinatos' conjecture that it might be the site near Moira[26] is again unsupported.

Δώριον (2. 594) MAP 4

REFS. *Gazetteer*, No. 242; N. Valmin, *The Swedish Messenian Expedition* (1938); *Op.Ath.* I (1953), pp. 29–46; *AJA* 65 (1961), No. 27; Ålin, *EMF*, pp. 76 f.; Desborough, *LMTS*, p. 94.

The excavations at Malthi (L.6 Kalamai 694E/773N) and the extensive exploration of this region by Valmin have together demonstrated that Malthi is almost certainly the Homeric Dorion.[27] Pausanias (4. 33. 6–7) followed the pass to Kyparissia, and on the way, after Andania Polichne, and the springs Elektra and Koios, came across a spring called Achaia and the ruins of Dorion. The crucial identification here is that of the spring Achaia with the spring at the modern village of Kokla.[28] Kokla was a famous Khan or resting-place for travellers until the twentieth century and the advent of the railway, and one can imagine Pausanias resting there, and perhaps trying to decide whether or not to undertake the climb up to the ridge at Malthi. Strabo (8. 350) tells us that 'some say Dorion is a mountain, some a plain', and Valmin recalls an interesting inscription[29] regulating the frontiers between Messenia and Megalopolis, which mentions a district called Doris, apparently to be assigned to Messenia: he plausibly connects this with the Soulima Plain, in which Malthi is the dominating centre, and he points[30] out an interesting parallel for Doris–Dorion in Bouprasis–Bouprasion.[31]

After mentioning Dorion, the Catalogue goes on to describe it as the place where the Muses met Thamyris the Thracian coming from Oichalie and put an end to his singing (*Il.* 2. 594–600). According to the Catalogue itself, this Oichalie, the home of Eurytos (*Il.* 2. 596), lay in the kingdom of the Asklepiadai, in Thessaly (*Il.* 2. 730), but it appears that the Messenians later claimed that there was a place called Oichalia in or near their own country,[32] and it must be admitted that this claim is supported by the story of Odysseus' meeting with Eurytos' son, Iphitos, *ἐν Μεσσήνῃ* (*Od.* 21. 11 f.).[33] It is also perhaps significant that this particular 'expansion' of the Catalogue, dealing with Thamyris, begins in the middle of a line, whereas elsewhere such 'expansions' always begin a new line: one is tempted to conjecture that *Il.* 2. 594 once read *καὶ Πτελεὸν καὶ Ἕλος καὶ Δώριον Οἰχαλίην τε.*

At first sight, all the indications seem to point to Nestor's kingdom's being a reflection of a Mycenaean kingdom. Three of the nine places listed in it in the Catalogue—Aipy, Pteleon, and Helos—were evidently unknown in historical times, and the whereabouts of a fourth—Amphigeneia—was dubious. On the other hand, of the remaining five places, Pylos, Arene, Kyparisseeis, and Dorion were all inhabited in the Mycenaean period, while Thryon was also, if correctly located. Moreover, neither Pylos nor Dorion was subsequently inhabited, assuming that they are to be identified with Ano Englianos and Malthi respectively.

The Linear B tablets, however, although they refer to a number of places in Messenia, do not appear to refer to any of the places mentioned in the Catalogue, except Pylos itself and Kyparisseeis, unless we are to accept that 'Tu-ru-w-u' is Thryon, 'A-pu$_2$' is Aipy, 'A-pi-ke-ne-a' is Amphigeneia, and 'E-re-i' is Helos.[34] Furthermore, although our inability to locate Aipy, Amphigeneia, Pteleon, and Helos makes it impossible to be certain where the boundaries of Nestor's realm were thought of as being, it does seem to lie in *western* Messenia, and certainly does not seem to have been thought of as including the lower part of the Pamisos valley. For, wherever precisely the Seven Cities offered by Agamemnon to Achilles (*Il.* 9. 149–56 = 291–8) were supposed to be situated,[35] they clearly lay somewhere around the Gulf of Messenia, and although they are described as *νέαται Πύλου ἠμαθόεντος* (*Il.* 9. 153 = 295), which, on the analogy of *Θρυόεσσα . . . νεάτη Πύλου ἠμαθόεντος* (*Il.* 11. 711–12), should mean 'the last cities *in* sandy Pylos',[36] the Catalogue clearly knows nothing of them.[37] Indeed, the *context* of the passage in *Iliad* 9 itself is against taking *νέαται Πύλου ἠμαθόεντος* there to mean that the cities were *in* Nestor's kingdom, for in that case we should surely have expected at least some explanation of how Agamemnon was able to dispose of them without reference to Nestor.[38] Moreover, when in the *Odyssey* Telemachos and Peisistratos break their journey at Pherai, there is no suggestion that they were still in the realm of Peisistratos' father, and the implication is that they have passed outside it.[39]

The state ruled from the palace at Ano Englianos, on the other hand, probably did include the lower Pamisos valley. The tablets appear to reveal an administrative division into two provinces, 'De-we-ro-ai-ko-ra-i-ja' and 'Pe-ra$_3$-ko-ra-i-ja', which are taken to mean 'this side of (δεῦρο) Ai-ko-ra-i-ja' and 'beyond (πέραν) Ai-ko-ra-i-ja' respectively,[40] and if, as seems probable, 'Ai-ko-ra-i-ja' is the mountain range of Aigaleon (modern Ayia Varvara),[41] the dividing-line indicated would be, roughly speaking, the line of hills between the Pylos-region of western Messenia and the Pamisos valley. In this case, the eastern border of the Pylos of the tablets is likely to have been formed by Mt. Taÿgetos.[42]

Thus neither the names of the places in nor the boundaries of Nestor's kingdom in the Catalogue, appear to coincide very well with those of the tablets. But although this is disturbing, it does not by any means prove that the Catalogue does not here reflect the Mycenaean period. The difficulties of deciphering the tablets are notorious and preclude any certainty as to what is or is not mentioned in them, and we should also remember that they form only a part of the administrative records of Ano Englianos for probably a single year. We should not, therefore, assume that the places listed in the Catalogue are not Mycenaean towns, just because they are not certainly mentioned in the tablets. Nor should we conclude that Nestor's kingdom does not reflect a real Mycenaean kingdom, simply because it appears to be different in extent from the state ruled from Ano Englianos *c.* 1200 B.C. The Catalogue, after all, ostensibly refers to the time of the Trojan War, at least some time earlier than the period of the tablets.[43] Alternatively, it may be that the Catalogue reflects a period *after* the date of the tablets, but still within the Mycenaean period.[44]

It is difficult to determine what period, if any, is reflected by Nestor's tales of border wars with the Epeians (*Il.* 11. 670–761) and Arcadians (*Il.* 7. 132–56), and of Herakles' attack on Pylos itself (*Il.* 11. 689–93). If we accept that the geographical background to these stories is Mycenaean,[45] there is no reason why we should not accept the date given by the dramatic context—two generations earlier than the Trojan War—rather than a later one, in the sub-Mycenaea nor Protogeometric period.[46] The visitation of Herakles may have nothing to do with the struggles of Achaeans against Dorian invaders:[47] it is just as likely that the reason for the location of a Herakles myth at Pylos was that Pylos was one of the gates of the underworld.[48]

Most of the place-names in Nestor's tales are identical with those of the Catalogue, and there is some additional information, for example that Bouprasion is *πολυπύρον*, that Alision is also *Ἀλισίου κολώνη*,[49] and that there is a river *Μινυήϊος* near Arene. The description of Thryoessa as *τηλοῦ ἐπ' Ἀλφειῷ* (*Il.* 11. 712), not only confirms the description *Ἀλφειοῖο πόρον* applied to Thryon in the Catalogue (*Il.* 2. 592), but should also give pause to those who follow Strabo's pedantic arguments for believing that the Pylos of Nestor's tale cannot be the Messenian Pylos.[50]

NOTES ON NESTOR'S KINGDOM

1. Allen, *HCS*, p. 77.
2. As Strabo saw (8. 337, cf. Pausanias 4. 36. 5), *Πύλος* in Homer sometimes means the city of Nestor, sometimes the whole country.
3. 8. 351. Strabo's argument that if Telemachos had sailed from the *Messenian* Pylos to Pheai, the poet would not have mentioned Krounoi and Chalcis, but the Neda, Acidon, and the Alpheios, is made more dubious by the fact that the line *βὰν δὲ παρὰ Κρουνοὺς καὶ Χαλκίδα καλλιρέεθρον* (*Od.* 15. 295) does not appear in any MS. of the *Odyssey*: cf. Monro, *Homer's Odyssey XIII–XXIV*, pp. 57–8.
4. Cf. *RE* 23. 2 (1959), cols. 2113–61 for a recent exposition of these arguments.
5. Strabo 8. 351. But see McDonald *AJA* 46 (1942), pp. 538–45, especially n. 44 on p. 544.
6. For an ancient (and probably Mycenaean) high road on the main route from Pylos to Kalamata (Pherai) see *AJA* 65 (1961), p. 257 n. 14, and *AJA* 68 (1964), pp. 240f.
7. As do, for example, Huxley *BICS* 3 (1956), p. 21, and Marinatos, *La Parola del Passato* 78 (1961), p. 220.
8. As Marinatos, for example, does: op. cit., pp. 223f.

9. *Gazetteer*, Nos. 217 and 218; *AJA* 65 (1961), No. 61; Marinatos, op. cit., pp. 225–6.

10. *ADelt.* 20 (1965), pp. 6–40 and 185–6.

11. *RhM* N.F. 83 (1934), p. 328. It is surely not allowing too much to 'poetic licence' to suppose that a river which in fact forms the frontier of the *Πυλίων γαίη*, should be said to flow through it.

12. *NK*, p. 65 and Abb. 27; cf. *Gazetteer*, No. 262, *BCH* 85 (1961), p. 273. *JHS Arch.* for 1961/2, p. 12 reports vases 'assigned to the intermediary period between Sub-Mycenaean and Protogeometric' from a tomb 1 km. west of Salmone.

13. *Neue Peloponnesische Wanderungen* (1957), p. 60.

14. *JHS Arch.* for 1961/2, p. 14.

15. Cf. *AJA* 65 (1961), p. 228.

16. *Gazetteer*, No. 270; *AJA* 65 (1961), No. 12; cf. now *ADelt.* 21 (1966), pp. 171–2, *ADelt.* 22 (1967), pp. 210–11.

17. Margalai (or Marganeis) lay north of the Alpheios, near Olympia: cf. *RE* 14, cols. 1680–2, and *RE* 1, col. 1901.

18. *Hymn to Apollo* 423 merely repeats the line; cf. Burr, *NK*, p. 65 and n. 6, for a selection of unsupported conjectures.

19. Cf. L. R. Palmer, *Mycenaeans and Minoans*, pp. 86–7. William F. Wyatt, *CPh.* 59 (1964), pp. 184f., suggests that *Αἰπύ* in *Il.* 2. 592 is a misunderstanding of *Πύλου αἰπὺ πτολίεθρον* in *Od.* 15. 193, and that therefore *Αἰπύ* never existed. But his conception of the singer's psychology seems too elaborate, and it seems likely that both *Il.* 2. 592f. and *Od.* 3. 7f. were ultimately based on an earlier poetic tradition of nine towns in the Pylian kingdom.

20. Frazer, *Pausanias* iii. 463.

21. Cf. *AJA* 65 (1961), No. 22.

22. Cf. Hirschfeld, *RE*, s.v. 'Amphigeneia'; Valmin, *La Messénie ancienne*, p. 77 n. 13. For the location of Ampheia see Frazer, *Pausanias* iii. 410.

23. *JHS* 30 (1910), p. 302.

24. *Gazetteer*, No. 236; Marinatos, *La Parola del Passato* 78 (1961), p. 226; *Ergon* for 1960, p. 152.

25. Strabo 9. 246; cf. p. 48 above.

26. *Gazetteer*, No. 235; Marinatos, *La Parola del Passato* 78 (1961), pp. 226–32; *Ergon* for 1960, pp. 157–8.

27. Valmin, *La Messénie ancienne*, pp. 11–14, etc.

28. Valmin, op. cit., p. 13.

29. *Inschriften von Olympia*, No. 46; cf. *IG* v. 2, pp. xxvii, 100f.

30. Op. cit., p. 106 n. 25.

31. Cf. Strabo 8. 340 and 345.

32. Strabo (8. 339 and 350; cf. 8. 360 and 10. 448) identified this Oichalia with Andania in Arcadia, Pausanias (4. 2. 2) with Karnasion, or a ruined village called Eurytion (4. 2. 3; 4. 3. 10; 4. 33. 5).

33. The passage appears to imply that *Μεσσήνη* was part of Lakedaimon, and Strabo (8. 367) used it to show that Ortilochos' city, Pherai (cf. *Od.* 3. 488–9), along with the other six offered by Agamemnon to Achilles (*Il.* 9. 149–53), were part of the realm of Menelaus (cf. above, p. 86, and n. 35 below).

34. Cf. Page, *HHI*, p. 199 and n. 101 on p. 216; Webster, *MH*, p. 119; Palmer, *Mycenaeans and Minoans*, pp. 86–9.

35. Cf. *BSA* 52 (1957), pp. 231–59, and a more recent article by Hope Simpson in *BSA* 61

(1966), pp. 113–31. Palmer (*Mycenaeans and Minoans*, p. 80) regards the localization by Strabo (8. 359–61) and Pausanias (4. 31. 1, 34–5) of Antheia, Aipeia, and Pedasos on the *west* side of the Messenian Gulf, between Korone and Methone, as 'sheer guesswork', but perhaps we should not dismiss such traditions so cavalierly.

36. The Epeian attack on Thryoessa in revenge for Nestor's cattle-raid clearly indicates that νεάτη Πύλου ἠμαθόεντος in *Il.* 11. 712 must mean 'the last city *in* sandy Pylos', and this is, of course, proved by *Il.* 2. 592 if Thryon and Θρυόεσσα πόλις were the same place.

37. It has been suggested that *Il.* 9. 149f. (= 291 f.) originally formed part of the Catalogue (Burr, *NK*, pp. 60–1; Wad-eGery, *PI*, pp. 55–6; cf. Strabo 8. 368), but if so, it is difficult to see why they were subsequently omitted, since, as Page says (*HHI*, n. 41 on pp. 165–6), 'the poets never, so far as we know, deleted a passage of this type in one place merely because they wished to use it again in another'. It is more likely that the Seven Cities passage derived from Mycenaean tradition, but from one independent of the Catalogue-tradition, like Nestor's tale—cf. the variant there of Θρυόεσσα πόλις for the Θρύον of the Catalogue: there may have been many such 'little catalogues' floating about in the tradition (cf., for example, *Il.* 13. 685–700).

Yet it is odd to find Diocles of Pherai's sons at Troy (*Il.* 5. 541 f.), unless we are to suppose that the comment that they were there τιμὴν Ἀτρεΐδῃς, Ἀγαμέμνονι καὶ Μενελάῳ, ἀρνυμένω shows an awareness that they came from a place which did not figure in the Catalogue, and was intended to imply that they went as a personal favour to the Atreidai.

38. Cf. Nilsson, *The Mycenaean Origin of Greek Mythology*, pp. 84–5; Ventris and Chadwick, *DMG*, p. 145. Page, however, argues (*HHI*, n. 42 on p. 166, cf. *CR* N.S. 10 (1960), p. 106) that 'the poet of the Embassy cares nothing about Mycenaean geography' and 'had no idea whom the places belonged to'. Nevertheless, it seems more likely that the poet who originally brought in the offer of the Seven Cities improperly used the phrase νέαται Πύλου ἠμαθόεντος to locate them '*on the borders of* sandy Pylos', than that he was ignorant of or deliberately ignored the fact that the Catalogue did not list them as cities in Nestor's kingdom. He must, however, have thought that they belonged to Agamemnon in some sense, and this idea may have arisen from a misunderstanding of *Il.* 5. 551–3 (cf. n. 37 above).

39. Cf. n. 6 above for the possibly Mycenaean road between Pylos and Pherai (Kalamata).

40. L. R. Palmer, *Minos* iv (1956), p. 140; Ventris and Chadwick, *DMG* p. 144; cf. Palmer, *Mycenaeans and Minoans*, pp. 82 f.

41. *DMG*, pp. 141–5. Palmer, however, argues (*Minos* iv (1956), pp. 120–45) that the point of division was Cape Akritas, and McDonald (*Minos* vi. (1960), pp. 149–55) accepted this identification. But, as McDonald now agrees, a division in terms of sailing land-marks is less likely than one based on land-routes.

42. This is perhaps suggested by the occurrence in An 661 of the word 'Ne-do-wo-ta-de' which is possibly connected with the Nedon (Palmer, *Minos* iv (1956), pp. 140f.; but cf. also Ventris and Chadwick, *DMG*, pp. 144 and 194). It is interesting to note that the eastern boundary of Messenia was set at Mt. Taÿgetos by a Panhellenic commission after the battle of Chaeronea in 338 B.C. (Polybius 9. 33. 12, 28. 7; Strabo 8. 361; Tacitus, *Annals* 4. 43).

There is no good evidence for determining the northern border of the state ruled from Ano Englianos: Professor Palmer equates 'Pi-jai' with 'Phea(i)' and 'Me-ta-pa' with the place of that name near Olympia, which would mean that the 'Hither Province' extended beyond the Alpheios (*Mycenaeans and Minoans*, pp. 83f.), whereas the Alpheios seems to have formed the northern frontier of Nestor's realm (cf. *Il.* 11. 711–12 and 2. 592); but all is quite uncertain. The Panhellenic commission referred to above set the northern boundary of Messenia at the River Neda, and this appears to have marked the frontier in Strabo's day (8. 348; cf. Pausanias 4. 20. 2).

43. Cf. Huxley, *BICS* 3 (1956), pp. 21–2.

44. See pp. 161–4 below.
45. Wade-Gery, *AJA* 52 (1948), pp. 115–18, but cf. Page, *HHI*, pp. 254–5 and n. 116 on pp. 295–6.
46. Wade-Gery, loc. cit., and *PI*, p. 56 and n. 117.
47. Page, *HHI*, n. 116 on pp. 295–6.
48. Cf. *Il.* 5. 395–7; Nilsson, *The Mycenaean Origin of Greek Mythology*, pp. 88–9.
49. Cf. *Il.* 11. 711: *Θρυόεσσα πόλις, αἰπεῖα κολώνη.*
50. Cf. McDonald, *AJA* 46 (1942), pp. 538–45, especially n. 44 on p. 544.

ARCADIA

Φενεός (2. 605) MAP 4

REFS. *Gazetteer*, No. 83; *JHS Arch.* for 1959/60, p. 10; *AJA* 63 (1959), pp. 280–1, figs. 12 and 13 on Pl. 76; *JHS Arch.* for 1961/2, p. 6; *JHS Arch.* for 1962/3, p. 17; *JHS Arch.* for 1965/6, p. 8.

There had previously been some doubt as to the whereabouts of the acropolis of Pheneos,[1] but the recent excavations have firmly located it at the hill of Pyrgos, less than a kilometre east of the modern hamlet of Pheneos or Kalyvia (K. 7 Tripolis 130E/476N approx.).

The site lies on the north-western edge of Lake Pheneos, on a conspicuous knoll which projects from higher hills on the west (PLATE 7*b*). In 1958 Hope Simpson and his wife collected many fragments of prehistoric pottery on the south-east slopes of the acropolis, including one apparently Neolithic sherd,[2] some MH coarse ware, and several sherds from 'provincial' Mycenaean *Kylikes*, *Angular Bowls*,[3] and *Deep Bowls*, ranging in date from LH IIIA to LH IIIC: a deep sounding has subsequently revealed MH and LH remains.[4] The surface-sherds were spread over an area of about 250 metres north to south by 150 metres, and they represent a considerable settlement. There were, in addition, many chips of obsidian, and later sherds included good 5th-century B.C. black-glazed ware, and one fragment from the base of a Geometric *Skyphos*.

'Ορχομενός (2. 605) MAP 4

REFS. *Gazetteer*, No. 85; Frazer, *Pausanias* iv. 223f.; E. Hiller von Gaertringen and H. Lattermann, *Arkadische Forschungen* (1911), pp. 18f., and plan, Abb. 4, Taf. 1f.; C. Callmer, *Studien zur Geschichte Arkadiens* (1943), p. 24; Fimmen, *KMK*, p. 10; *RE*, Suppl. vi. 608.

There is no doubt about the location of the historical Orchomenos. It occupied the summit of a high conical hill, on the eastern tip of the range of hills which border Lake Pedhias Khotoussis on its south side (K.7 Tripolis 119E/249N). The little hamlet of Kalpaki lies on the south-east foot of the hill, near a fine spring, in much the same way as in Pausanias' day (8. 13. 2–6) the people of Orchomenos lived below the old walls, having deserted the hill-top city.

Fimmen[5] records *Matt-painted* MH sherds from Orchomenos, but although Karo[6] records Mycenaean, he refers only to Fimmen. However, in 1958 Hope Simpson and his wife found a fragment from the foot of an LH IIIB *Kylix*, near the summit of the hill, within the north-east part of the enceinte. There is thus not much doubt that the place was inhabited in Mycenaean times, though so far there is no evidence for continuity of occupation into the Early Iron Age.

Ῥίπη τε Στρατίη τε καὶ ἠνεμόεσσα Ἐνίσπη (2. 606) MAP 4

Neither Strabo (8. 388) nor Pausanias (8. 25. 12) has any constructive comment to make about these places, and Strabo remarks that 'it is difficult to find these places and you would be no better off if you did find them, because nobody lives there'.[7] By elimination, western or north-western Arcadia would seem to be indicated.

Τεγέη (2. 607) MAP 4

REFS. *BCH* 45 (1921), p. 247 fig. 59, p. 248 fig. 61, p. 424 fig. 63, no. 315; Fimmen, *KMK*, p. 10; *BSA* 56 (1961), p. 130 and n. 119; Desborough, *LMTS*, p. 87.

The few Mycenaean finds (LH IIIB–C) from the excavations at the temple of Athena Alea (*Gazetteer*, No. 89: L.7 Sparti 186E/944N) may indicate a continuity of cult, since they were found in proximity to Geometric, or even late Geometric,[8] pottery, but it seems unlikely that the main Mycenaean settlement would have been in this exposed position on the plain of Tegea.

Some late Mycenaean tholos-tombs of diminutive size were excavated by Rhomaios on the east bank of the Sarandapotamos river, and in 1957 a party from the British School at Athens[9] located a Mycenaean settlement on the plateau above the river-gorge, about 500 metres north-east of the tombs (*Gazetteer*, No. 90: L.7 Sparti 194E/931N approx.). The site is about 300 metres in diameter, and dominates the southern edge of the plain: it may be that Homeric Tegea should be located here.

Μαντινέη (2. 607) MAP 4

REFS. *Gazetteer*, No. 87; Frazer, *Pausanias* iv. 201 and 221; *JHS Arch.* for 1961/2, p. 31; *BCH* 87 (1963), pp. 766 f.; *JHS Arch.* for 1963/4, p. 8.

The hill of Gourtsouli (PLATE 8*a*), rising abruptly from the plain a short distance to the north of classical Mantinea (K.7 Tripolis ⸸ Panayia at 168E/144N), should probably be identified with the *Πτόλις* or 'Old Mantinea' of Pausanias. Leake and Loring[10] were misled by Pausanias' description of *Πτόλις* as lying in a small plain, which the context (Pausanias 8. 12. 5–7) appeared to indicate as distinct from the plain of Mantinea. But one must remember that in Pausanias' day the walls of Mantinea would still have been standing, and it would not necessarily have seemed to him that Mantinea and the hill of Gourtsouli were in the same plain, since the view southward at this point would have been obstructed by the walls themselves. As for the spring of Alalkomeneia (Pausanias 8. 12. 7), the fact that there is a copious spring now called Tripechi, just opposite to and east of Gourtsouli,[11] is an added confirmation. If Pausanias regarded the route to Orchomenos as lying to the east, and the mountains on the east side of the plain (i.e. Mt. Alesios) as lying to the north, he might easily have thought of the spring as being to the *north* of Gourtsouli. In any case, in 1961 we examined the hill to the north favoured by Leake, and could find no trace of any ancient remains upon it.

We did, however, find evidence of both Mycenaean and Archaic occupation on Gourtsouli. The top of this rounded, rocky hill is now occupied by the chapel of Panayia and its enclosure, near which is a small spring (dry in summer). On the upper, eastern flank of the hill there are remains of what appear to be Cyclopean walls (PLATE 8*b*), which can be traced for a considerable distance to southwards along this side. In the vicinity of the chapel enclosure we found four Mycenaean (LH IIIB) sherds from *Deep Bowls* and *Kylikes*, and five chips of obsidian, together with the handle of an Archaic *Skyphos* and some classical black-glazed pieces. The recent excavations have revealed evidence for occupation from Late Geometric to early classical times, but were not sufficient in scope to test the extent of Mycenaean occupation.

In view of these recent discoveries on Gourtsouli, and the tradition recorded by Pausanias, Homeric Mantinea may now be located here with some certainty.

Στύμφηλος (2. 608) MAP 4

REFS. *Gazetteer*, No. 84; F. Bölte, *RE* ivA (1932), pp. 436f.; *AM* 40 (1915), Taf. XII; Burr, *NK*, p. 69.

The historic city of Stymphalos lay on the western side of the lake of the same name, about 1·5 kilometres from the modern village of Stymphalos. The limestone ridge which formed the acropolis is well described by Frazer.[12] It is evident that the acropolis actually occupied the lower, eastern half of this ridge (K.7 Tripolis in square 240E/390N), an area about 250 metres east to west by 50 metres north to south, divided from the western section by a dip.[13] On the south flank of the acropolis a section of rough walling is preserved, which resembles Cyclopean masonry in style, and may be of Mycenaean date. Conclusive evidence for Mycenaean occupation of the site was found by Hope Simpson and his wife in 1958, in the shape of chips of obsidian and at least two Mycenaean sherds, one from an LH IIIA *Kylix*, the other from an LH IIIB *Angular Bowl*. There is so far no evidence that the site was occupied in the Early Iron Age.

Παρρασίη (2. 608) MAP 4

This name is probably to be associated with the later district of Parrhasia (Pausanias 8. 38. 3, cf. 8. 27. 2 and 4, and 6. 8. 2). Pausanias (8. 27. 4) enumerates as among the Parrhasians *Λυκοσουρεῖς*, *Θωκνεῖς*, *Τραπεζούντιοι*, *Προσεῖς*, *Ἀκακήσιον*, *Ἀκόντιον*, *Μακαρία*, and *Δασέα*. Of these, Trapezous, Thoknia, Daseai, and Lykosoura are all located to west or north-west of Megalopolis, and it seems probable that the catalogue refers to this area.

That the Mycenaeans had thoroughly penetrated western Arcadia is proved by the discovery of Mycenaean remains on the Palaiokastro in Gortinia, an hour's walk to west of ancient Gortys (*Gazetteer*, No. 92 : K.6 Dhimitsana 789E/068N), with an extensive cemetery near the village of Palaiopyrgos,[14] and also by the apparently Mycenaean tombs found at Kalliani.[15]

Unless Rhipe, Stratie, and Enispe lay in western Arcadia, and apart from the reference to Parrhasia, the places mentioned in the Arcadian section of the Catalogue all lay in eastern Arcadia. But this is not surprising, since the main centres were always Tegea, Mantinea, and Orchomenos,[16] and it is dangerous to assume that the western boundary of Homeric Arcadia was less far to the west than in classical times,[17] for in one of Nestor's tales, a battle takes place between Pylians and Arcadians . . . *ἐπ' ὠκυρόῳ Κελάδοντι . . . Φειᾶς πὰρ τείχεσσιν, Ἰαρδάνου ἀμφὶ ῥέεθρα* (*Il.* 7. 133–5), and Pheia is presumably the same as classical Pheia, securely located at Ayios Andreas near Katakolon,[18] while the river Iardanos is presumably the stream immediately to north of the village of Skaphidia, and it has been suggested[19] that 'Keladon' might be an earlier form for 'Ladon'. Admittedly it would be hard to reconcile a conflict between Pylians and Arcadians at Pheia with a *contemporary* attack by Epeians on a Pylian fortress on the Alpheios (cf. *Il.* 11. 711–13), but the Homeric evidence suggests an unstable and fluctuating situation, with the Arcadians occasionally raiding as far as the coast, and this is believable enough. It is, perhaps, worth noting that although Agamemnon provides the Arcadians with their ships (*Il.* 2. 612–14), it is not specifically stated that this is because they have no seaport, but only . . . *ἐπεὶ οὔ σφι θαλάσσια ἔργα μεμήλει*—and this could be said of many Greek islanders to-day!

Of the places mentioned in the Catalogue[20] all, except the unknown Rhipe, Stratie, and Enispe, were occupied in Mycenaean times (assuming Parrhasia to refer to the later district of that name), and there is no major Mycenaean site which is not mentioned. But Pheneos, Tegea, and Mantinea, at least, were also occupied in the Early Iron Age, and Orchomenos and Stymphalos probably were, though there is as yet no evidence for it, so the Homeric picture of Arcadia cannot be said definitely to reflect the Mycenaean era. Yet the fact that the whereabouts of Rhipe, Stratie, and Enispe were unknown in historical times suggests that it does.

NOTES ON THE ARCADIAN SECTION

1. Frazer, *Pausanias* iii. 235–6.
2. Cf. *PAE* 1951, p. 104 fig. 15*a*.
3. Furumark, *MP*, form 267.
4. *JHS Arch.* for 1965/6, p. 8.
5. *KMK*, p. 10.
6. *RE*, Suppl. vi. 608.
7. Cf. Page, *HHI*, p. 122.
8. *BCH* 45 (1921), fig. 57 and p. 312.
9. Mr. and Mrs. M. S. F. Hood, Mr. D. H. French, and Hope Simpson.
10. Frazer, *Pausanias* iii. 201 and 221.
11. Frazer, loc. cit.
12. *Pausanias* iv. 269.
13. Cf. Burr, *NK*, p. 69.

14. Cf. *AJA* 65 (1961), No. 11; *JHS Arch.* for 1957, p. 11; Ålin, *EMF*, pp. 72 f.; Desborough, *LMTS*, p. 92.

15. *Gazetteer*, No. 93.

16. Cf. the numbers of hoplites from Arcadia at Thermopylae (Herodotus 7. 202): 500 from Mantinea, 500 from Tegea, 120 from Orchomenos, and 1,000 *ἐκ τῆς λοιπῆς Ἀρκαδίης*.

17. *CH*, p. 293. In Scylax (44) Arcadia comes down to the sea at Lepreon, and this is the only town mentioned near the coast.

18. *Gazetteer*, No. 258: K. 5 Pirgos 235E/245N. Cf. *AJA* 65 (1961), No. 1.

19. Wace and Stubbings, *CH*, p. 293.

20. For the *Αἰπύτιον τύμβον* (*Il.* 2. 604) cf. Pausanias 8. 16. 2–3. Aipytos' father was called Elatos: cf. Pausanias 8. 4. 7 and Pindar, *Ol.* vi. 33. 36 (*Αἴπυτος Εἰλατίδας*).

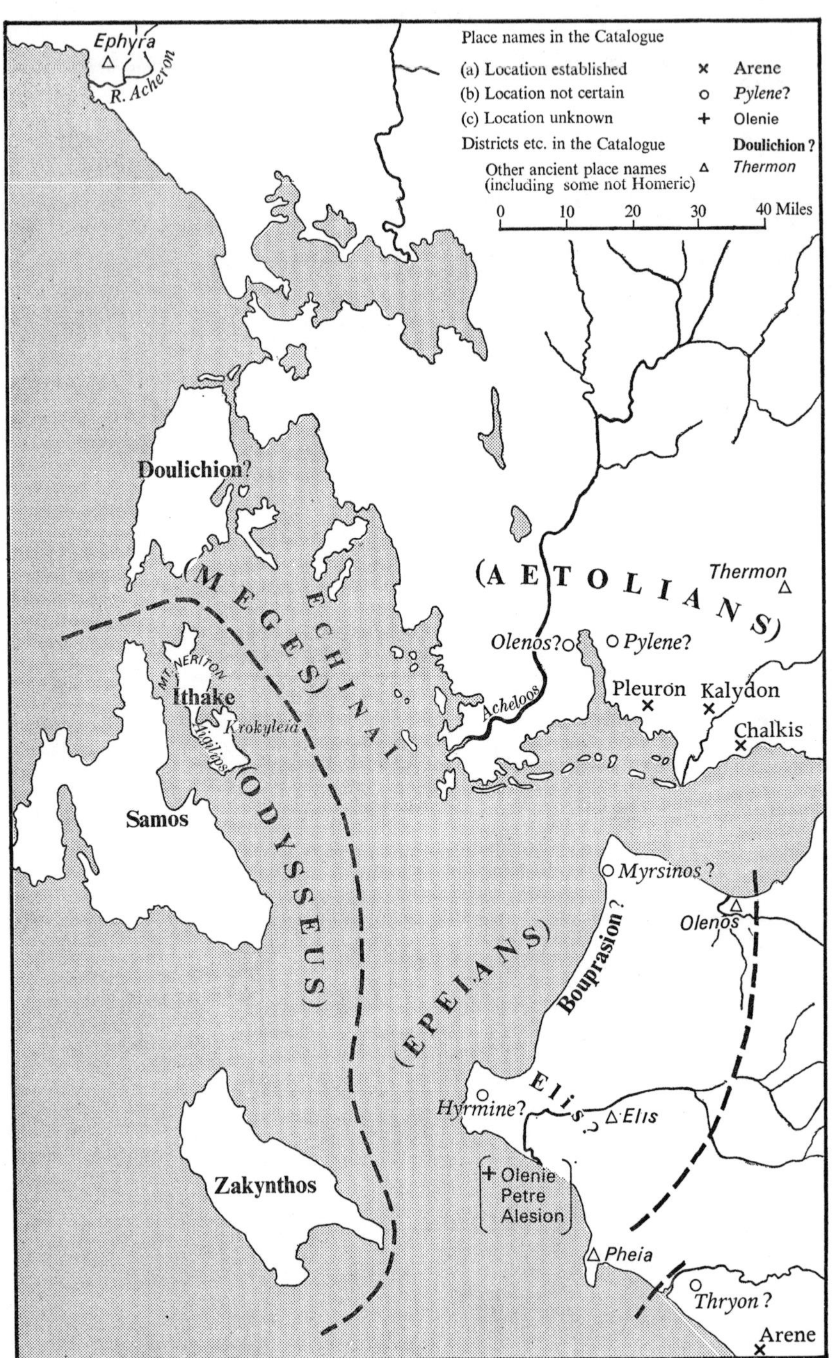

Place names in the Catalogue
(a) Location established
Arene
(b) Location not certain
Pylene?
(c) Location unknown
Olenie
Districts etc. in the Catalogue
Doulichion ?
Other ancient place names
(including some not Homeric)
Thermon
0
10
20
30
40 Miles
Ephyra
R. Acheron
Doulichion?
(MEGES)
ECHINAI
(AETOLIANS)
Thermon
Olenos?
Pylene?
MT. NERITON
Ithake
Krokyleia
Aigilips
Acheloos
Pleuron
Kalydon
Chalkis
Samos
(ODYSSEUS)
Myrsinos?
Olenos
Bouprasion?
(EPEIANS)
Elis?
Hyrmine?
Elis
Olenie
Petre
Alesion
Zakynthos
Pheia
Thryon?
Arene

MAP 5

THE EPEIANS

Βουπράσιον (2. 615) MAP 5

This is usually taken to mean the coastal district between Cape Araxos in the north and Cape Chelonatas in the south, lying, as Strabo says (8. 340; cf. 8. 345 and 387), between the city of Elis and the Dymaia. A passage (8. 340) in which Strabo appears to say that Bouprasion is a district of Elis having in it a settlement of the same name (*τὸ δὲ Βουπράσιον . . . τοῦτο*) is regarded by most editors as a gloss.

Ἦλις (2. 615) MAP 5

This also seems to be a district-name, to judge from other passages in the *Iliad* and the *Odyssey*, especially *Il.* 2. 626 and *Od.* 4. 635 and 21. 347. There is little warrant for regarding *Ἦλις* as referring to the city of that name, despite the opinion of Hecateus of Miletus (ap. Strabo 8. 341),[1] and the most natural explanation is that it refers to the district later known as *κοίλη Ἦλις*, comprising the main broad plain, between the eastern foothills and the promontory of Chelonatas.

Nevertheless, there is evidence that the site of the later *city* of Elis was occupied from EH times onwards,[2] so that the name may just possibly refer to a town on this site in Homer.

Ὑρμίνη (2. 616) MAP 5

REFS. *Gazetteer*, No. 280; J. Servais, *BCH* 85 (1961), pp. 1–9 (Palaeolithic), pp. 123–61 (esp. 157–61) (MH and LH III); *BCH* 87 (1963), p. 837; *BCH* 88 (1964), pp. 9–50; *JHS Arch.* for 1956, p. 16 (Geometric).

The recent investigations by Servais have considerably clarified the position with regard to the identification of Hyrmine. In particular, he pointed out that the 'Kyklopischen Burgmauer', noted by Curtius at Kounopeli, are a 'lusus naturae',[3] and this was certainly our impression when we visited the place in 1961: we saw nothing which could not be attributed to medieval or later periods.

All we know about Hyrmine is that there was an *ἀκρωτήριον πλησίον Κυλλήνης ὀρεινὸν . . . καλούμενον Ὅρμινα ἢ Ὕρμινα* (Strabo 8. 341). Servais has convincingly demonstrated that ancient Kyllene lay at the site of the medieval Glarentsa (the modern Kyllini), where he has found numerous classical and later remains,[4] and especially a fragment from an Attic amphora dated to the early 5th century B.C.[5] Hyrmine–Hyrmina–Hormina must therefore lie on the promontory of Chelonatas, and it seems probable that the actual site is that of the castle of Chlemoutsi (K.4 Zakynthos △ 24 FORT RUINS at 099E/515N), which dominates not only the coastal hills, but also the plain of Elis for miles around (PLATE 9*a*).

The trial excavations of Servais at Chlemoutsi have revealed considerable MH deposits, and some Mycenaean remains, including LH IIIB–C pottery.[6] A Mycenaean tomb has also been found between the castle and the village of Neochori, and a Geometric cemetery is reported near by.

Μύρσινος (2. 616) MAP 5

REFS. *Gazetteer*, No. 282; *JHS Arch.* for 1961/2, p. 12, for 1962/3, p. 21, for 1963/4, pp. 12f.; E. Mastrokostas, *Archaeology* 15 (1962), pp. 133–4; *Ergon* for 1962, pp. 171 f., for 1963, pp. 186f.; *BCH* 87 (1963), pp. 767f.; *BCH* 88 (1964), pp. 760–2.

Strabo (8. 341) says that Myrsinos was the Myrtountion of his day—a town which lay seventy stades from Elis on the road to Dyme. Myrtountion is now rather scantily represented by some ruins between the modern villages of Kalotikos and Kapaleto, seen by Gell,[7] but when we visited this area in 1961, we concluded that it would be extremely unlikely that any major Mycenaean settlement would be located in such a flat and marshy area, and Strabo may simply have been wrong to equate the Homeric Myrsinos with his Myrtountion: as Servais says,[8] the Catalogue strongly implies that the four places mentioned in Elis are on its frontiers, and Myrtountion 'n'est pas assez au Nord pour atteindre les confins de Bouprasion et marquer ainsi l'extrémité du pays épéien'.

Mastrokostas has recently discovered an impressive Mycenaean fortress, with Cyclopean walls preserved to a length of 200 metres on its north-west side and in one place standing ten metres high, at 'Kastro tis Kalogrias', south of Cape Araxos (I.5 Mesolongion 'Kalogria' at 323E/799N). He is almost certainly right in equating the fortress with the 'Teichos' mentioned by Polybius (4. 59. 4),[9] and we are strongly tempted to suggest that it is also the Homeric Myrsinos: the epithet *ἐσχατόωσα* for Myrsinos in the Catalogue suggests the Araxos promontory, and the situation of the 'Kastro tis Kalogrias', on a commanding promontory, resembles that of Hyrmine—assuming this is Chlemoutsi—with which Myrsinos is coupled in the Catalogue.

πέτρη Ὠλενίη (2. 617) MAP 5

As Sakellariou remarks,[10] the location proposed by Strabo (8. 341) for the 'Olenian Rock', at Skollis (the present Santameri), finds no followers. The fragment attributed to Hesiod (ap. Strabo 8. 342) which places the Olenian Rock on a river Peiros in fact supports a location near the later Olenos.[11]

Ἀλήσιον (2. 617) MAP 5

Alesion is called *Ἀλησίου κολώνη* in Nestor's tale (*Il.* 11. 757), as Strabo reminds us (8. 342), and it is presumably a polis, like the *Θρυόεσσα πόλις, αἰπεῖα κολώνη* of *Il.* 11. 711. Beyond this we have no reliable information to help us to its location, and the supposed connection between Ἀλήσιον and Ἀλισός[12] is no more than a philological guess: Servais suggests that it should be sought near the Alpheios,[13] and this would certainly fit in with the implication in the Catalogue that Hyrmine, Myrsinos, the Olenian Rock, and Alesion mark the confines of Elis, assuming that Hyrmine is Chlemoutsi, Myrsinos is 'Kastro tis Kalogrias', and that the Olenian Rock should be located near the later Olenos.

If Bouprasion and Elis are to be taken as districts, it may not merely be a coincidence that there are four other places mentioned in this section of the Catalogue, in view of the four commanders given to the Epeians (*Il.* 2. 618–24): Hyrmine and Myrsinos are presumably towns, and there is no reason to doubt that Alesion is one also, while *πέτρη Ὠλενίη* probably refers to one.

Bouprasion, the Olenian Rock, and Alesion recur in Nestor's tale (*Il.* 11. 756–7), and it has been suggested that the context requires them to be placed 'not very far from the Pylian frontier'.[14] Yet, as we saw, Strabo consistently locates Bouprasion between Hollow Elis and the Dymaia, and there is some reason to put the Olenian Rock in what was later western Achaea, near Olenos. In fact one wonders how far one should press the 'geographical requirements' of Nestor's tale: the further away Bouprasion, the Olenian Rock, and Alesion from Thryon, the greater the glory of Nestor's exploit! Nevertheless, if we are right to set the northern frontier of Nestor's kingdom at the Alpheios,[15] it follows that this was also the southern frontier of the land of the Epeians and, as we have seen, Alesion at least may have been located somewhere here.

Mycenaean settlements in Elis are at present few and far between, except in the Olympia district,[16] but Mycenaean remains have now been found at Chlemoutsi and Elis itself, and more finds may be expected in the hills to east of the great plain of Elis.[17] It is, perhaps, significant that the only Homeric place-names which can be firmly associated with specific sites are the seaside towns of Hyrmine and Pheia: it would not be surprising if Myrsinos, the Olenion Rock, and Alesion were also near the coast, since the hilly interior of Elis is separated from the sea by a wide and relatively barren plain, and it may be that the inhabitants of the hilly country were not Epeians—the fact that Doulichion and the Echinai also appear to have belonged to an Epeian,[18] also suggests such a division between a maritime race and the people of the interior.

The trouble with this, however, is that Odysseus is also said to have commanded men *οἵ τ' ἤπειρον ἔχον ἠδ' ἀντιπέραι' ἐνέμοντο* (*Il.* 2. 635), which presumably means that they lived in Elis, and this is apparently confirmed by *Od.* 4. 634–7 where Noemon of Ithaka is said to own land for stud-farming in Elis.[19] If this is to be taken seriously, the Epeians, far from being confined to the coastal region of Elis, would appear to be deprived of at least a part of it. But the problems involved in these western kingdoms are difficult, if not impossible, to solve, and it may be that we should not look for too rigid frontiers; nor need all the Homeric passages refer to the same period.[20]

NOTES ON THE EPEIAN KINGDOM

1. Cf. Allen, *HCS*, p. 80.
2. *Ergon* for 1961, pp. 177–8, for 1963, pp. 115 f.; *JHS Arch.* for 1961/2, p. 12, and for 1963/4, p. 12. Recent excavations near the Theatre have revealed an EH tomb, and graves of the transitional period between Sub-Mycenaean and Protogeometric (Desborough, *LMTS*, pp. 92 f.). In 1961 we picked up some Geometric sherds on the acropolis (Kastro Belvedere), and some which looked like LH III.
3. *BCH* 85 (1961), pp. 146–50, esp. fig. 14 on p. 149.
4. *BCH* 85 (1961), pp. 130 f.; cf. *Gazetteer*, No. 281 : K. 4 Zakynthos 105E/569N.
5. *BCH* 85 (1961), p. 143, fig. 11.
6. *BCH* 88 (1964), pp. 9–36.
7. Cf. Meyer, *RE* xvi (1st edn.), p. 1183.
8. *BCH* 88 (1964), p. 49. On p. 37 of the same article Servais is inclined to accept the equation Myrsinos = Myrtountion.
9. Cf. Frazer, *Pausanias* iv. 112–13.
10. *Peloponnesiaca* 3 (1959), p. 25.
11. For this site see especially Meyer, *Peloponnesische Wanderungen* (1939), pp. 119–22 and Abb. 10.
12. Sakellariou, *Peloponnesiaca* 3 (1959), pp. 34–5.
13. *BCH* 88 (1964), p. 50; cf. Strabo 8. 341.
14. Wace and Stubbings, *CH*, p. 293; cf. Bölte, *RhM* N.F. 83 (1934), pp. 319 f.; Sakellariou, *Peloponnesiaca* 3 (1959), pp. 17 f.
15. Cf. n. 42 on p. 89 above.
16. Successive excavators at Olympia have pronounced on the absence of Mycenaean finds there. Yet Dörpfeld's excavation house stood on a Mycenaean site (*AJA* 65 (1961), No. 7; *Gazetteer*, No. 266), and some of the finest sherds were found near its doorstep! For recent finds in the area see *JHS Arch.* for 1961/2, pp. 11–12, *JHS Arch.* for 1964, p. 12, *ADelt.* 17 (1961/2), pp. 105 f.
17. Some ten prehistoric mounds were reported in the area between Boukhioti and Amalias in *JHS Arch.* for 1960/1, p. 14.
18. Cf. *Il.* 13. 691–2; Strabo 10. 459; Allen, *HCS*, pp. 81–3.
19. See pp. 104–5 below.
20. See p. 87 above, on the wars between the Pylians and the Epeians and Arcadians.

THE KINGDOM OF MEGES

Δουλίχιον (2. 625) MAP 5

The identification of Doulichion is bound up with the whole question of the realm of Odysseus, but the most plausible suggestion is that it is Leukas. It must be an island,[1] it must be rich in grain and grass,[2] and—for those who believe in the authenticity of the ship-numbers[3]—it must also be populous enough to send the majority of Meges' ships, since, if the *Ἐχῖναι ἱεραὶ νῆσοι* are the Echinades (see below), they could hardly have contributed more than a few. More important, perhaps, it must be large enough to send almost as many suitors for Penelope's hand as all the other islands put together.[4]

Strabo's identification of Doulichion with 'Dolicha', one of the Echinades (10. 458), is a guess based on dubious etymology, and certainly will not do, since, as Page says,[5] Dolicha is a 'small, miserable and deserted island, rough living for a goat'. But it is very difficult to believe, as Page does, in the brutal bisection of Kephallenia into Doulichion and Samos, perpetrated by the antiquarians Pherekydes, Hellanicus, and Andron[6]—Strabo rightly rejected this.

In fact only Leukas will really do, and there seem to be only two objections to this hypothesis. The first is that Leukas is apparently mentioned under that name in the *Odyssey* (24. 11): *πὰρ δ' ἴσαν Ὠκεανοῦ τε ῥοὰς καὶ Λευκάδα πέτρην.* But the last book of the *Odyssey* may well be a late addition,[7] and the name 'Leukas' was known to have been a late arrival.[8] Moreover, the reference to the 'White Rock' does not by itself prove that the whole island was known as 'Leukas' when the passage was composed.

The second objection (Strabo 10. 452) is that Leukas was not an island until the Corinthians dug a canal between it and the mainland, in the 7th century B.C.—even then the canal seems to have silted up by the time the Athenian general, Demosthenes, attacked Leukas in 426 B.C.[9] But it seems likely that there was always *some* water between it and the mainland, and that all the Corinthians had to do was to widen and deepen the channel.

As Allen saw,[10] 'Dörpfeld's excavations, on which he relies to prove the identity of Leukas and Ithaka, show in reality that Leukas will do for Doulichion.' Mycenaean pottery has been found at Nidri,[11] Ayios Sotiros,[12] and in the cave of Choirospilia,[13] and the discovery of a Late Bronze Age settlement at Spartochori, on the neighbouring island of Meganisi,[14] suggests that there are other and more important Mycenaean sites still to be found on Leukas.

Ἐχῖναι ἱεραὶ νῆσοι (2. 625–6) MAP 5

These islands are securely identified with the Echinades, and that they were inhabited in Mycenaean times[15] is proved by the Mycenaean sherds strewn over the fields to the south of the village of Spartochori on Meganisi,[16] and by the Bronze Age site discovered on Kalamos.[17]

In the rest of the *Iliad* Meges is, as Page says,[18] 'an insignificant person', appearing only once, and that in the highly suspicious 'Little Catalogue' (*Il.* 13. 685–98), as one of three commanders of the Epeians. But although in the Catalogue, if we are to believe the ship-numbers, he is a powerful king, this sort of 'discrepancy' between the Catalogue and the rest of the *Iliad* is not at all uncommon.[19] His kingdom, provided that we accept the equation of Doulichion with Leukas, is in itself geographically reasonable and coherent, and could easily reflect a real Mycenaean kingdom.

NOTES ON THE KINGDOM OF MEGES

1. Despite Burr, *NK*, p. 74: cf. *Od.* 9. 22–4, 16. 122–3 = 19. 130–1.
2. Cf. *Od.* 14. 335, 16. 396.
3. See below, p. 161.
4. Telemachos tells his father (*Od.* 16. 247–53) that there are 52 suitors from Doulichion, 24 from Same, 20 from Zakynthos, and 12 from Ithaka: this alone makes it very difficult to believe that what was later called Ithaka was the Homeric Doulichion, as P. B. S. Andrews suggests, *BICS* 9 (1962), pp. 17–20.
5. *HHI*, p. 163.
6. Ap. Strabo 10. 456.
7. Cf. Monro, *Homer's Odyssey, Books XIII–XXIV*, pp. 321–3; *contra:* Stanford, *Odyssey, XIII–XXIV*, pp. 404–6 and 409–10; but see now Kirk, *SH*, pp. 248–51.
8. Strabo 10. 452; Allen, *HCS*, p. 86.
9. Cf. Thucydides 3. 94–5.
10. *HCS*, p. 87.
11. *Gazetteer*, No. 320; T. 3 Leukas 798E/439N; Wace and Thompson, *PT*, p. 229; *BSA* 32 (1931/2), p. 230; Dörpfeld, *Alt-Ithaka* (1927).
12. *Gazetteer*, No. 321: T. 3 Leukas † at 781E/404N; *AM* 59 (1934), pp. 182 f.; Dörpfeld and Göbler, op. cit., pp. 319 f.
13. *Gazetteer*, No. 322: T. 3 Leukas 758E/347N; Dörpfeld and Göbler, op. cit., p. 266.
14. See following note 16.
15. Though not apparently in the 5th century B.C. (cf. Thucydides 2. 102).
16. *Gazetteer*, No. 323: T. 4 Preveza 843E/388N approx.; *BSA* 32 (1931/2), pp. 230–2 and Pl. 18.
17. *BSA*, loc. cit., pp. 233–4.
18. *HHI*, p. 163.
19. See pp. 158–9 below.

THE KINGDOM OF ODYSSEUS

Ἰθάκη (2. 632) MAP 5

Considering the unanimity of ancient testimony on the location of Ithaka, it is surprising that any alternative should ever have been seriously considered. Everything we are told in the *Odyssey* about Odysseus' home fits modern Ithaki or Thiaki,[1] except 9. 25–6 (αὐτὴ δὲ χθαμαλὴ πανυπερτάτη εἰν ἁλὶ κεῖται / πρὸς ζόφον, αἱ δέ τ' ἄνευθε πρὸς ἠῶ τ' ἠέλιόν τε), and, as was shown by Lord Rennell of Rodd,[2] even this description is in fact reconcilable with the modern Ithaki.[3] At all events, it is not enough to cast a doubt on the belief that ancient traditions about the locations of major islands are unlikely to be wrong, however inapt we may feel the description to be. In particular, Dörpfeld's identification of Ithaka with Leukas not only fails to solve the alleged topographical difficulties, but also adds to them unnecessarily.[4]

Late Bronze Age sites have been discovered on Ithaka at the village of Stavros,[5] Tris Langadhas,[6] the cave of Polis,[7] Pelikata,[8] Aetos,[9] and Ayios Athanasios.[10] Desborough[11] remarks that the earliest pottery from Aietos appears to overlap with the latest LH IIIC from the Polis cave, thus providing evidence for continuity of occupation from the end of the Bronze Age to the beginning of the Iron Age.[12]

Νήριτον (2. 632) MAP 5

The *Odyssey* tells us quite plainly (9. 21–2; 13. 351) that Neriton was a mountain on Ithaka: it has nothing whatever to do with the Νήρικος of *Od.* 24. 377, described as ἐϋκτίμενον πτολίεθρον, ἀκτὴν ἠπείροιο, which is fixed on Leukas or the Leukadian peraea by Thucydides 3. 7. 4–5. Although elsewhere he recognizes this (10. 453–4), in 10. 452 Strabo apparently himself lapses into the error—for which he subsequently castigates another—of confusing Neriton(s) with Nerikos. Yet in the same passage he describes how the Corinthians dug a canal through the isthmus of the Leukas peninsula, and 'made Leukas an island', transferring the name 'Nerikos' (the reading of the MSS.) to the strait, and calling the island 'Leukas'. The 'Leukadithakistai',[13] without good warrant and for their own ends, follow the mistake made by Pliny the Elder in *NH* 4. 5,[14] and equate Neritos with Nerikos,[15] although Pliny himself writes elsewhere (*NH* 4. 55): 'Zakynthos . . . ab ea Ithaca xv m. distat, in qua mons Neritus.'

Neriton(s) has been conjecturally equated with the modern Mt. Anogi, the chief peak in the northern part of Ithaka.[16]

Κροκύλεια and *Αἰγίλιψ* (2. 633) MAP 5

If Neriton was a mountain on Ithaka, there is no reason to look elsewhere for Krokyleia and Aigilips, and in particular we should avoid the confused reasoning which led Strabo—or one of his sources—into locating them on Leukas (10. 452, cf. 8. 376). Modern heresies include the location of Krokyleia on the island of Arkoudhi.[17] It has been more plausibly suggested[18] that Krokyleia and Aigilips were districts in the southern half of Ithaka—Krokyleia the region around Vathy (so called from the *κροκύς* or white limestone found in it), and 'rugged' (*τρηχεῖα*) Aigilips the mountainous area from Aietos to the southern end of the island.

Ζάκυνθος (2. 634) MAP 5

At least there can be no doubt that Homer's Zakynthos is the island which still bears the name. Nor can there be any doubt that Zakynthos was inhabited in Mycenaean times. A tholos-tomb and a Mycenaean house were excavated in 1934 on the south-east side of the akroterion near Halikais, containing LH IIIB and local Bronze Age pottery;[19] a well was found on the property of Eleos, on the road from Katastari to the sea, full of LH IIIA–B pottery;[20] and there is a settlement on the headland of Kalogeros near Vasiliko, with pottery from LH IIIA onwards.[21]

Σάμος (2. 634) MAP 5

Strabo (10. 453) identified Samos with Kephallenia, where there was in his day (as there still is) a town called 'Samos' or 'Same'. Certainly, if Doulichion is Leukas, and Ithaka and Zakynthos are the islands which bear those names now, Samos can hardly be anything else but Kephallenia, particularly in view of the line describing the island where the suitors lay in wait for Telemachos (*Od.* 4. 671, cf. 845), *ἐν πορθμῷ Ἰθάκης τε Σάμοιό τε παιπαλοέσσης*.[22] The epithet *παιπαλόεσσα* is especially appropriate to Kephallenia: its towering mountains dwarf even the hills of Ithaka, when approached from the south, and perhaps justify the description of the latter as *χθαμαλή* in *Od.* 9. 25.[23] Nor should we forget that Odysseus' followers are called *Κεφαλλῆνες* (*Il.* 2. 631, etc.).

A large number of prehistoric tombs and cemeteries have been found on Kephallenia, and at least three settlements: on an acropolis now called 'Palaiokastro' near Korneli, with MH pottery, but no certain LH;[24] a major settlement, probably with circuit-walls and a megaron, and pottery from EH to LH (including LH IIIB), at Kranea;[25] and a settlement and cemetery of chamber tombs at Diakata.[26]

"*οἵ τ' ἤπειρον ἔχον ἠδ' ἀντιπέραι' ἐνέμοντο*" (2. 635) MAP 5

Strabo, presumably because he thought of Doulichion as one of the Echinades and of Leukas as a promontory of Acarnania, was led to suppose that the peraea of the Kephallenes lay in Acarnania (10. 452–3). But other indications,[27] combined with common sense, suggest that it should be located in Elis, where Noemon of Ithaka kept his mares and mules (*Od.* 4. 634–7): the coast of Elis is readily accessible from Zakynthos at least, to which there is now a daily ferry service from Kyllini.

It has been argued that a Kephallenian peraea in Elis is hard to reconcile with the dominion of the Epeians, and that *Il.* 2. 635 is 'a relatively late addition designed to rescue Odysseus from the poverty to which the Catalogue condemns him'.[28] But if Doulichion is Leukas, Odysseus in fact rules the whole of Kephallenia, Ithaka, and Zakynthos, and this is hardly 'poverty', even though he only brings twelve ships to Troy as compared with Meges' 40.[29] With Meges ruling Leukas and the Echinades, we have a natural and plausible division of power between him and Odysseus, and the latter's realm does not merely consist of 'scraps collected right, left, and centre from Meges' dominion'.[30]

Nevertheless, it does remain difficult to fit Odysseus' mainland possessions into Elis, and that Meges himself is once said to be in command of Epeians (*Il.* 13. 691–2) is an added difficulty.[31] Yet such is the obscurity of the names in the section of the Catalogue relating to the Epeians, that we cannot be sure how much of Elis the Catalogue in fact envisages as belonging to them.

NOTES ON THE KINGDOM OF ODYSSEUS

1. For a good modern discussion see Wace and Stubbings, *CH*, pp. 398–407.
2. *BSA* 33 (1932/3), pp. 1–21; *Homer's Ithaca: a Vindication of Tradition* (1927).
3. If we suppose that the description is that of someone approaching Ithaka from the south: cf. V. Bérard, *Les Phéniciens et l'Odyssée* (1902), ii. 412. In *BICS* 9 (1962), pp. 17–20, P. B. S. Andrews argues that this description fits *Corcyra*, but in what sense can 'many islands right close to each other' be said to 'lie about Corcyra', especially the islands of Kephallenia and Zakynthos?
4. Cf. Allen, *HCS*, pp. 82 f., and especially pp. 97–8.
5. *Gazetteer*, No. 324: I.3 Argostolion 720E/165N; *BSA* 47 (1952), pp. 227–42; *BSA* 40/1 (1939–45), pp. 2–3.
6. *Gazetteer*, No. 324: *BSA* 40/1 (1939–45), p. 10.
7. *Gazetteer*, No. 325: I.3 Argostolion 713E/160N; *BSA* 35 (1934/5), pp. 45 f., 75 f.; *BSA* 39 (1938/9), pp. 8–17.
8. *Gazetteer*, No. 326: I.3 Argostolion ⍖ at 721E/174N; *BSA* 35 (1934/5), pp. 1 f.; *BSA* 40/1 (1939–45), pp. 1 f., especially p. 9.
9. *Gazetteer*, No. 328: I.3 Argostolion 180 at 743E/061N; *BSA* 33 (1932/3), pp. 22–65; *BSA* 43 (1948), pp. 1–124.
10. *Gazetteer*, No. 327: I.3 Argostolion 717E/185N; *BSA* 35 (1934/5), pp. 1 f.
11. *LMTS*, pp. 109 f.
12. For a recent discussion on the location of Odysseus' palace see Wace and Stubbings, *CH*, pp. 414–19.
13. Cf. Allen, *HCS*, pp. 82 f.

14. Pliny says here: 'Dein sinus, ac Leucadia ipsa peninsula, quondam Neritis appellata . . . oppidum in ea Leucas, quondam Neritum dictum.'
15. Burr (*NK*, p. 79) begs the whole question when he writes, '. . . Neritos (Nerikos) . . .'!
16. *BSA* 33 (1932/3), p. 14.
17. Burr, *NK*, p. 79.
18. Sir Rennell Rodd, *Homer's Ithaca*, pp. 104–7.
19. *Gazetteer*, No. 344: K.4 Zakynthos 789E/485N; *BSA* 32 (1931/2), pp. 218–19 and Pl. 38; *AA* 1934, pp. 161–2.
20. *Gazetteer*, No. 345: K.4 Zakynthos 768E/478N approx.; *BSA*, loc. cit., p. 218 and Pl. 39, Nos. 1–8.
21. *Gazetteer*, No. 347: K.4 Zakynthos 950E/326N; *BSA*, loc. cit., pp. 213–17 and Pls. 38–9; cf. *AA* 1934, pp. 161–2.
22. Probably Daskyleio: Wace and Stubbings, *CH*, p. 405.
23. Cf. V. Bérard, *Les Phéniciens et l'Odyssée* ii. 412.
24. *Gazetteer*, No. 331: I.4 Ekhinadhes 790E/785N; *BSA* 32 (1931/2), p. 220 and Pl. 38.
25. *Gazetteer*, No. 333: I.3 Argostolion 576E/871N; *ADelt.* 5 (1919), pp. 82–94; *BSA* 32 (1931/2), pp. 223–5; p. 221, fig. 8; p. 228, figs. 9–11; *AJA* 36 (1932), pp. 9 f. The LH IIIB tomb at Gephyra probably belongs to this settlement: *Gazetteer*, No. 334 (cf. *BSA* 32 (1931/2), pp. 22–3 and refs. on p. 228; Furumark, *MP*, p. 647).
26. *Gazetteer*, No. 335: I.3 Argostolion 580E/860N approx.; *BSA* 32 (1931/2), p. 221, fig. 8, and refs. on p. 228; *AE* 1932, pp. 14f.; *BSA* 33 (1932/3), p. 63.
27. Allen, *HCS*, pp. 91–2.
28. Page, *HHI*, pp. 162–3.
29. The relative ship-numbers should probably in fact not be pressed, as Page himself admits elsewhere (op. cit., pp. 152–3), particularly not Meges' 40 (cf. p. 161 below).
30. Page, op. cit., p. 163.
31. See above, p. 99.

THE AETOLIANS

Πλευρών (2. 639) MAP 5

REFS. *Gazetteer*, No. 312; *BSA* 32 (1931/2), p. 239; Philippson, *GL* ii. 670, No. 58.

Strabo's notes on Pleuron are obscure, but it seems likely that 'Old Pleuron' should be located at the hill of Gyphtokastro (I.5 Mesolongion 381E/056N), south-west of the site of 'New Pleuron' on the hill of Kastro Kyra Eirene.[1] The rocky hill of Gyphtokastro, about 300 metres in diameter, is covered in sherds, tiles, and wall-foundations, but Miss Benton was unable to find any Mycenaean sherds,[2] and this was also the experience of Hope Simpson and his wife and Miss D. H. F. Gray in 1958. Miss Benton, however, noted that a wall on the north side might be Mycenaean, and this was confirmed by the latter party: the remains of the wall are 'Cyclopean' in appearance, over two metres thick, with smaller stones packed into the interstices of the larger blocks—a common feature of Mycenaean wall-construction. In 1960 Hope Simpson found some flakes of obsidian on the top of the site, and some sherds which seemed from their fabric to be LH, although certainty was still not possible. The cist-graves and the five pithos-burials revealed by excavations for water-channels on the east and south-east sides of the hill might be attributed to a period within LH IIIC–Geometric.

Ὤλενος (2. 639) MAP 5

According to Strabo (10. 451), Olenos was near New Pleuron, at the foot of Arakynthos, and it has sometimes been located at the 'Kastro Trion Ekklesion' which lies on a spur about two kilometres north-west of New Pleuron, in a position just below the junction of two routes from central Aetolia—the Klisoura pass, and the more westerly route which runs by Angelokastro.[3] Woodhead, however, identifies this site as that of Homeric Pylene.[4] We visited the place in 1961: it is a small spur (about 150 by 55 metres), of no great height, with remains of a small classical or Hellenistic fort (the walling is 'trapezoidal: quarry face'), and a spring at its western foot. Sherds are not numerous, and we found no Mycenaean. We also felt that this site was too near that of New Pleuron to have been an independent town.[5]

Woodhouse[6] placed Olenos at the hill of *Ἅγιος Ἠλίας σταὶς Μυγδαλιαίς*, some three kilometres to the south of the village of Stamna.[7] He argues that this was the site of Polybius' Ithoria, on the basis of Polybius' description of the Macedonian invasion of Lower Aetolia in 219 B.C. (4. 64f.), and suggests that Ithoria was 'the lineal descendant of the Homeric city'.[8] On the west flank of the hill Mastrokostas has recently found a Mycenaean chamber-tomb containing LH IIIA pottery and other finds, including a scarab from the reign of Amenophis III (1405–1370 B.C.). There is also a group of small tholos-tombs near by, the largest at a place called 'Seremeti', 300 metres south of the acropolis, the three smaller ones at a place called 'Marathiá', some 300 to 500 metres west of the acropolis.[9] Pottery from the latter group included an LH IIIC prochoos.[10]

Πυλήνη (2. 639) MAP 5

Strabo (10. 451) says that the Aetolians moved Pylene to higher ground, and changed its name to Proschion: Woodhouse[11] placed it at the 'Kastro Trion Ekklesion', but others have preferred a site near the village of Magoula, some eight kilometres north-west of New Pleuron, and near the foot of the Zygos.[12] The name 'Pylene' does slightly suggest a site near the Klisoura pass, and if this position is correct, we should not expect a further 'city' of Olenos beween Pylene and Pleuron, while the recent discoveries near Stamna (see above on Olenos) provide some support for the location of Olenos proposed by Woodhouse.

Χαλκίς (2. 640) MAP 5

REFS. *Gazetteer*, No. 310; *BSA* 32 (1931/2), pp. 238–9 with figs. 19–20; Poulsen and Rhomaios, *Kalydon*, Pl. liii and p. 51; Philippson, *GL* ii. 670, No. 12; Ålin, *EMF*, p. 136.

There is every reason to accept the identification of this place with the remains near Kryoneri, at the western foot of Mt. Varassova (PLATE 9*b*), which, as Woodhouse demonstrates,[13] is clearly the mountain called *Χαλκίς* or *Χαλκία* in ancient times (Strabo 10. 460). The early settlement lies on a low, much eroded terrace under the western cliffs of Mt. Varassova, about 600 metres to the north-east of Kryoneri (I.5 Mesolongion 534E/988N). The top measures about 150 metres north to south by 100 metres, and rises about 20 metres above the plain. The position gives a view over the whole plain, and to the north can be seen Kalydon, for which Khalkis may have served as a harbour-town in Mycenaean times.

Miss Benton[14] noted LH II–IIIB sherds, together with Neolithic and Geometric, and house-walls probably of MH date. Caves to the north have the appearance of robbed Mycenaean chamber-tombs. To east of Kryoneri are other walls, some apparently Hellenistic,[15] and the centre of the later town appears to have lain somewhat further to the south-east, on the lower slopes of Mt. Varassova.[16]

Καλυδών (2. 640) MAP 5

REFS. *Gazetteer*, No. 311; *PAE* 1908, pp. 99–100 (Mycenaean sherds and walls); Nilsson, *The Mycenaean Origin of Greek Mythology*, p. 186 (Mycenaean fortification-wall, house remains, and sherds); E. Dyggve, F. Poulsen, and K. Rhomaios, *Das Heroon von Kalydon* (1934), and preliminary report in *Kgl. Danske Videnskabernes Selskab. Historisk-filologische Meddelelser* xiv 3 (Copenhagen 1927), p. 5 and plan fig. 1; *AA* 31 (1916), pp. 220f.; *AE* 1937, p. 315 (Geometric); *ADelt.* 23 (1937), p. 231; Ålin, *EMF*, p. 136.

There is, fortunately, no dispute about the location of Kalydon. It lies at the strategic point which commands both the coastal plain of the Euenos and the pass into inner Aetolia via the Euenos valley (I.5 Mesolongion 485E/025N), and there can hardly be any doubt that this was the chief Mycenaean centre for the whole of this southern part of Aetolia. Strabo's source (cf. 10. 450) suggests that it controlled only *Αἰτωλία ἐπίκτητος*, but the situation of the site is such that it would rather control Strabo's 'Old Aetolia', i.e. the fertile coastal plain.

The higher and northernmost hill appears to have been the Mycenaean acropolis. Here Mycenaean fortification-walls, house remains (including one apsidal building), and sherds were found, but the excavators were mainly concerned with the Heroon, and paid scant attention to the acropolis. This completely dominates the plain to the west and south and Strabo's view (10. 460), that the Homeric epithets for Kalydon—*αἰπεινή* (*Il.* 13. 217 and 14. 116) and *πετρήεσσα* (*Il.* 2. 640)—described the district and not this site, is palpably false. Hope Simpson found LH IIIB and Geometric sherds on the highest part of the hill in 1960.

In the Catalogue the Aetolians occupy approximately that part of Aetolia which was known as 'Old Aetolia', defined by Strabo (10. 450) as the coastal area between the river Acheloos and Kalydon. Of the five towns listed, the positions of Kalydon, Pleuron, and Khalkis are well established, but Olenos and Pylene remain elusive, though both were evidently near Pleuron. The Mycenaean remains at Kalydon are substantial, and the site is impressive and strategically placed. This accords well with the Homeric traditions of Tydeus and Meleager (*Il.* 9. 529–99; 14. 116) and the legend of the Kalydonian Boar.[17] Khalkis was also inhabited in the Mycenaean period, and although definite proof is so far lacking, Pleuron probably was. But the territory of the Mycenaean Aetolians may not have extended far inland: to judge by the nature and quality of the pottery from Thermon,[18] this settlement was less Mycenaeanized than Kalydon or Khalkis.

But more field-work remains to be done in Aetolia[19] before the relationship of the Catalogue to any particular period can be properly assessed: it is noticeable that Khalkis and Kalydon have both produced evidence of Geometric occupation. In other words, the pattern of settlement reflected in the Catalogue could be said to suit both the Mycenaean and Geometric periods equally well.

NOTES ON THE AETOLIAN SECTION

1. Cf. Woodhouse, *Aetolia*, especially p. 55 and pp. 130f.
2. *BSA* 32 (1931–2), p. 239. The statement in *CH*, p. 294, that excavations here have shown that Pleuron was 'very important in very early Mycenaean times' is an unfortunate error.
3. e.g. Philippson, *GL* ii, No. 58.
4. Op. cit., pp. 137f.
5. For another suggested site in the vicinity cf. Kirsten, *RE* xvii (1937), pp. 2443–5.
6. Op. cit., pp. 153f.

7. Philippson, *GL* ii, No. 59.
8. Op. cit., pp. 154f., p. 158.
9. *BCH* 88 (1964), pp. 762–6. Elsewhere (*PAE* 1963 (published 1966), pp. 203 f.) Mastrokostas, while agreeing that Ayios Elias is probably the centre of ancient Ithoria, suggests himself that Olenos should be placed further south, possibly at a place called Skopas, described as a little island-like hillock, near the mouth of the Achelous.
10. *BCH* 88 (1964), fig. 14 on p. 767.
11. Cf. Woodhouse, *Aetolia*, Index, s.v. 'Proschium', and map, and p. 133.
12. Philippson, *GL* ii, No. 54. Mastrokostas (*PAE* 1963, pp. 203f.) inclines towards placing Pylene (= Proschion) at Lysimacheia.
13. Op. cit., pp. 63 and 107.
14. *BSA* 32 (1931/2), pp. 238–9.
15. Philippson, *GL* ii. 347f., 354, 603, 628.
16. In the region of 106 at 557E/982N: Woodhouse, *Aetolia*, Index, s.v. 'Chalcis'.
17. Cf. Nilsson, *The Mycenaean Origin of Greek Mythology*, pp. 185–6; Wade-Gery, *PI*, p. 57.
18. *Gazetteer*, No. 313; Rhomaios, *ADelt.* 1 (1915), pp. 225–79, and parart., pp. 46–7; *ADelt.* 2 (1916), pp. 179 f.; *RE*, Suppl. vi. 610; Fimmen, *KMK*, p. 4; *OpArch.* 6 (1950), p. 203; Philippson, *GL* ii. 670, No. 27.
19. Mastrokostas's recent work (cf. *PAE* 1963, pp. 203f. especially) has gone some way towards remedying the situation.

THE CRETANS

Κνωσός (2. 646) MAP 6

REFS. Sir Arthur Evans, *The Palace of Minos*; Pendlebury, *The Archaeology of Crete*, Index, p. 393; R. W. Hutchinson, *Prehistoric Crete*, Index, s.v. 'Knosos'; *BSA* 47 (1952), pp. 243 f.; *BSA* 51 (1956), pp. 81 f.; *BSA* 53/4 (1958/9), pp. 194–261, 281–4; *BSA* 55 (1960), pp. 128 f., 159 f.; *BSA* 56 (1961), pp. 68 f.; *JHS Arch.* for 1950 onwards (except 1954 and 1956).

A passage in Odysseus' lying tale to Penelope (*Od.* 19. 178–81) shows that Knossos was regarded as Idomeneus' capital, and there is, of course, no doubt that it was an important place from at least the end of the third millennium B.C. until historical times. If Ventris's decipherment of the Linear B tablets as Greek and Evans's date for these tablets are accepted, it seems probable that Knossos had passed into the control of 'Achaeans' (i.e. Greek-speakers, probably from the mainland) in the LM II period, and many scholars have in fact come to regard LM II as a mainland culture,[1] as Wace[2] and others had suggested even before the decipherment. It has been thought in fact that the widespread destructions elsewhere—at Phaistos, Ayia Triadha, Tylissos, Amnisos, Nirou Khani, Mallia, Pseira, Gournia, and Mochlos[3]—indicate that 'Knossos was trying to establish control over the centre of the island',[4] and the 'Warrior Graves' at Knossos[5] are quoted as corroboration of this view. But it is not certain whether these destructions are not rather contemporary with the destruction of Knossos *c.* 1375 B.C.,[6] or even due to natural phenomena.[7]

It is also difficult to decide the scale on which the palace at Knossos was reoccupied after the LM IIIA destruction.[8] Hutchinson[9] has the impression that the shrines revived before the secular life, but although it is true that the most important relics of the reoccupation period are the shrines, as Pendlebury says,[10] 'large parts of the Palace were cleared of debris and inhabited with little or no alteration', and the most recent studies[11] have tended to suggest that Knossos was perhaps a more important place in LM IIIB than is sometimes thought.

Γόρτυς (2. 646) MAP 6

REFS. D. Levi, *Ann.* N.S. 17–18 (1955/6), pp. 216 f.; *Ergon* for 1957, pp. 92–4; *JHS Arch.* for 1958, p. 17; *ILN*, 26 Dec. 1959, pp. 946–8, and 2 Jan. 1960, pp. 16–18; Desborough, *LMTS*, p. 167, and Index, s.v. 'Gortyn'.

The recent evidence for Minoan occupation of the acropolis shows that the Catalogue may refer to prehistoric Gortyn, even though the real importance of the place probably only dates from Archaic times. Apparently too, the acropolis was not intensively occupied until late in the Minoan period,[12] and although such negative evidence should not be pressed, it is possible that this may provide an indication of a 'terminus ante quem non' for the Cretan section

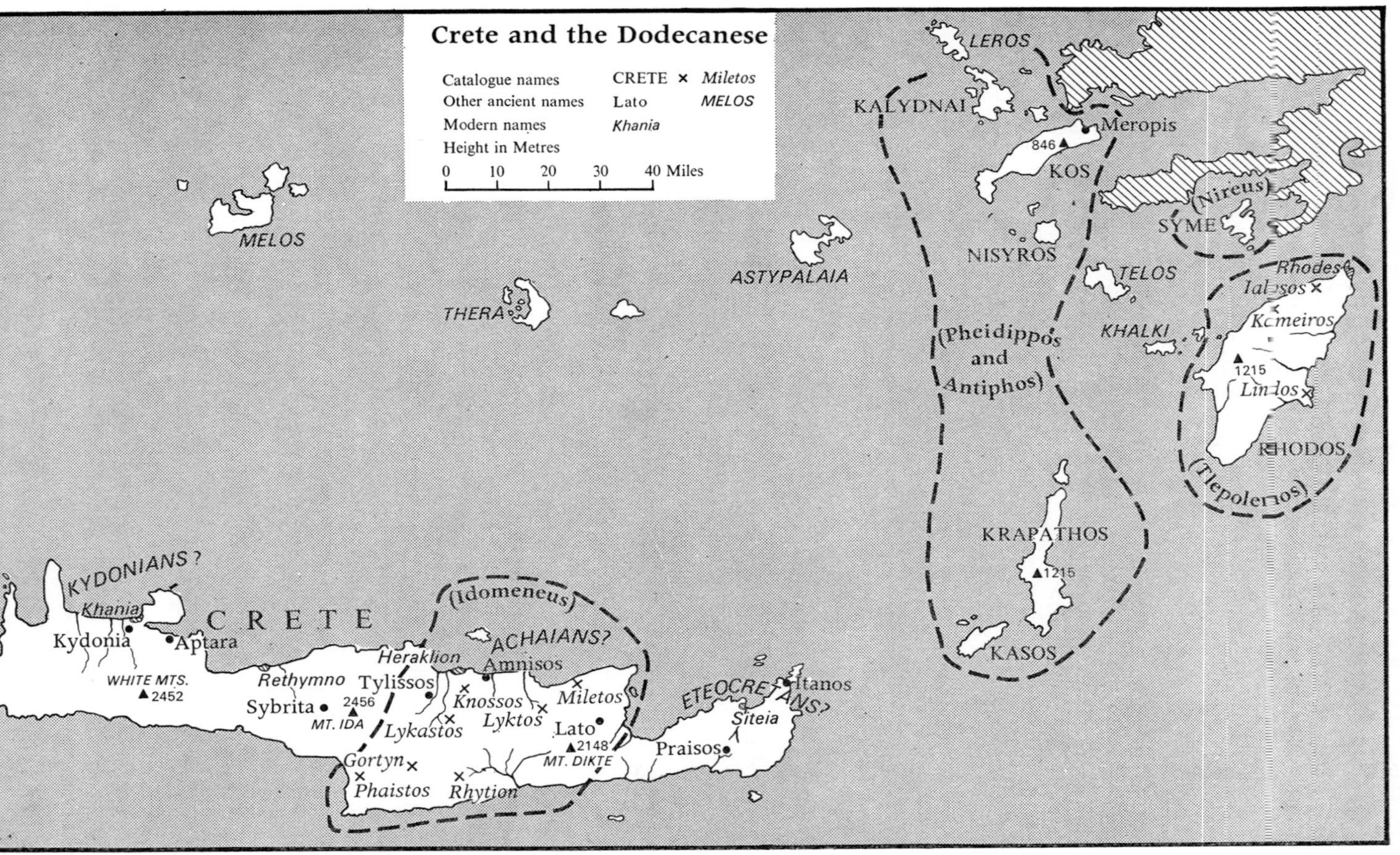
Crete and the Dodecanese
Catalogue names CRETE × Miletos
Other ancient names Lato MELOS
Modern names Khania
Height in Metres
0 10 20 30 40 Miles
MELOS
THERA
ASTYPALAIA
LEROS
KALYDNAI
Meropis
846
KOS
(Nireus)
SYME
NISYROS
TELOS
KHALKI
(Pheidippos and Antiphos)
Rhodes
Ialysos
Kameiros
1215
Lindos
RHODOS
(Tlepolemos)
KRAPATHOS
1215
KASOS
KYDONIANS?
Khania
CRETE
Kydonia
Aptara
WHITE MTS.
2452
Rethymno
Sybrita
2456
MT. IDA
Heraklion
Tylissos
(Idomeneus)
ACHAIANS?
Amnisos
Knossos
Lykastos
Lyktos
Miletos
Lato
2148
MT. DIKTE
Gortyn
Phaistos
Rhytion
ETEOCRETANS?
Itanos
Siteia
Praisos

Map 6

of the Catalogue. But there is also evidence for continuity of occupation into the Sub-Minoan and Protogeometric periods.

The reference in the *Odyssey* (3. 293–6) to a λισσὴ αἰπεῖά τε εἰς ἅλα πέτρη, ἐσχατιῇ Γόρτυνος, near Phaistos (cf. line 296), suggests that the territory of Gortyn had by this time expanded as far as the east coast, at the expense of Phaistos,[13] although the latter is still clearly in existence. Strabo (10. 479) records that, when the power of Gortyn increased, she destroyed Phaistos and incorporated Rhytion, and, if the reference in the *Odyssey* is to be taken seriously, the period reflected would appear to be *after* Phaistos had declined, but *before* her destruction by Gortyn.

Λύκτος (2. 647) MAP 6

REFS. Pendlebury, *The Archaeology of Crete*, pp. 294 and 344; *JHS Arch.* for 1955, p. 30; for 1957, p. 17; *BCH* 83 (1959), p. 733.

Strabo (10. 476) assumes an equation between Lyktos and the later Lyttos, and he is probably right. So far the only evidence for Minoan occupation appears to be a late Minoan seal-stone, said to have been found here,[14] though Polybius (4. 54. 6) describes Lyttos as *ἀρχαιοτάτη τῶν κατὰ Κρήτην πόλεων*. Recent excavations have revealed evidence of Archaic occupation.

Μίλητος (2. 647) MAP 6

REFS. Pendlebury, *The Archaeology of Crete*, pp. 251–2, 265 (and refs.), 324, 353; *BCH* 83 (1959), p. 732; Desborough, *LMTS*, Index, s.v. 'Milatos' and 'Mallia'.

It is commonly assumed[15] that this name refers to a settlement at Milatos where LM III chamber-tombs have been found, but Strabo (10. 479) says that *Μίλητος*, like Lykastos, 'no longer exists', whereas Milatos was almost certainly still inhabited in his day.

It has also been suggested[16] that *Μίλητος* in fact refers to the great Minoan palace and town at Mallia, and that it was from here that the Cretan Sarpedon (as opposed to the Lycian) was expelled by Minos to found Miletos in Asia Minor.[17] But the argument that Sarpedon ruled at Mallia depends on the analogy with Rhadamanthys' ruling at Phaistos, and the connection between Rhadamanthys and Phaistos in turn depends on the emendation *Φαιστός* for *Ἥφαιστος* in Pausanias 8. 53. 5, supported by the Cretan tradition (Pausanias 8. 53. 4) that Rhadamanthys was the father of Gortys.

In short, the argument that *Μίλητος* is Mallia is very tenuous, and, but for Strabo's statement that *Μίλητος* no longer existed in his day, one would have very little hesitation in supposing that it was Milatos. In view of Strabo's statement, however, certainty is impossible, and *Μίλητος* may in fact be neither Milatos nor Mallia.

Λύκαστος (2. 647) MAP 6

REFS. Pendlebury, *The Archaeology of Crete*, pp. 60, 177, 233, 316; Evans, *The Palace of Minos* ii. 71, etc.; Marinatos, *PAE* 1954 (published 1957), pp. 287–90.

Sir Arthur Evans equated Lykastos with the important Minoan site at 'Visala', to the east of the village of Kanli Kastelli and the rock upon which Nikephoros

Phokas built his great fortress of Temenos, after recovering Crete from the Arabs. There does not, however, appear to be any good evidence for the equation: Evans says: 'The wresting of its site by Gortyna from Knossos and its handing over to Rhaukos (Ayios Myros), distant only a few miles over the watershed to the west, squares well with this attribution.' But the source for this statement is unclear: all Strabo says (10. 479) is that the Knossians won control of the territory of Lykastos, after destroying the city.

Kanli Kastelli is a place of great strategic importance and would have been equally so in Minoan times, if in fact it lay on the principal route from Knossos to Komo, as Evans thought.[18] The quantity of LM IIIB pottery reported from Visala is also perhaps significant, but the equation must remain uncertain.

Φαιστός (2. 648) MAP 6

REFS. Pendlebury, *The Archaeology of Crete*, p. 234 and refs. (LM I), p. 264 and refs. (LM III reoccupation—cf. *Mon. Ant.* 12, p. 7, and 14, p. 313); D. Levi, *Ann.* N.S. 19–20 (1957/8), pp. 255 f.; *Ann.* N.S. 35–6, pp. 57 f.; *Studies in Mediterranean Archaeology* 11 (Lund 1964); *JHS Arch.* for 1958, pp. 16–17; for 1959/60, p. 19; for 1960/1, pp. 24–5; for 1962/3, p. 30; for 1963/4, pp. 26–7; for 1965/6, p. 23; Desborough, *LMTS*, Index, s.v. 'Phaestos'.

The Minoan palace at Phaistos was destroyed towards the end of the LM IB/II period, and the subsequent reoccupation seems to have been of little importance and to date to LM IIIB. But the frequent occurrence of the name 'Pa-i-to' (= ? Phaistos) in the Linear B tablets from Knossos[19] suggests that Phaistos was subordinate to the supposedly 'Achaean' dynasty at Knossos in the LM II period.[20]

The latest excavations indicate a new 'Mycenaean' settlement laid over the destruction debris,[21] when we also have a simple mainland type of megaron overlying the former Minoan palace at Ayia Triadha.[22] But Phaistos was clearly also an important place in the Early Iron Age.

The Catalogue certainly seems to reflect a period when Phaistos was subordinate to Knossos, and, as we have seen,[23] the *Odyssey* (3. 293–6) appears to refer to a time when Phaistos' power had so far declined that the territory of Gortyn cut her off from the east coast.

Ῥύτιον (2. 648) MAP 6

REFS. *BSA* 33 (1932/3), p. 86; Pendlebury, *The Archaeology of Crete*, pp. 327, 343, 353 (with refs.); *JHS Arch.* for 1958, p. 16; *BCH* 83 (1959), pp. 733–5; *Kretika Chronika* 1957, p. 339.

Spratt[24] identified this place with the extensive remains occupying the Kephala ridge above the village of Rotasi, at the eastern end of the Messara plain. The fine polygonal walling noted by Sir Arthur Evans[25] is attributed by Pendlebury[26] to the Archaic period, and classical and Orientalizing pottery has been found in many places. But Evans also found pithos-fragments which he thought to be LM I, and Huxley found some LM IIIA sherds on the site in 1958.[27]

Only seven towns in Crete are named in the Catalogue, and these are all confined to the centre of the island. Admittedly some of Idomeneus' men are described as ἄλλοι θ' οἳ Κρήτην ἑκατόμπολιν ἀμφενέμοντο (*Il.* 2. 649), but this does not necessarily mean that they were thought of as coming from all the other ninety-three cities, for the epithet, after all, describes the whole island, not necessarily the realm of Idomeneus.[28] The restriction of the realm of Idomeneus to the centre of the island in fact conforms to the picture of Crete in the *Odyssey* (19. 175–7), where it is divided between *Ἀχαιοί*, *'Ετεόκρητες*, *Κύδωνες*, *Δωριέες*, and *Πελασγοί*. For the location of the *'Ετεόκρητες* and the *Κύδωνες* in eastern and western Crete respectively is well established,[29] and this suggests that the *Ἀχαιοί* were thought of as occupying the centre of the island, whatever one makes of the *Δωριέες* and the *Πελασγοί*.[30] In other words, we seem to be dealing with a period in which the control of the whole of Crete by Knossos—if such control ever existed—has broken down[31].

The mention of *Δωριέες* in Crete (*Od.* 19. 177) is a problem. According to Strabo (10. 481), the Dorians were only led to Crete by Althaimenes, *grandson* of Temenos, which would put their immigration about 1050 B.C.[32] But Andron (*ap.* Strabo 10. 475) brings the Cretan Dorians direct from Histiaiotis, and this suggests that there was a tradition of an earlier immigration, although it does not necessarily follow that we should suppose a first wave of Dorian settlers arriving after the destruction of Knossos early in the LM IIIA period:[33] it seems equally possible that the Dorians only penetrated to Crete *after* the Mycenaean 'koine' period (LM IIIA:2–LH IIIB), and in this connection it is interesting to note the new settlement at Gortyn and Phaistos in LM IIIC.[34] If this was the case, the description in the *Odyssey* would strictly apply to a period later than the Trojan War.

It may be that the reference to *Δωριέες* in Crete in the Odyssey is a reflection of the Early Iron Age, and it is noticeable that there is evidence that all the towns mentioned in the Catalogue, with the exception of Rhytion, were inhabited at this time, assuming that *Μίλητος* is Milatos, and Lykastos is to be located at Kanli Kastelli. However, this need not be so if the tradition preserved by Andron is genuine, and Idomeneus himself seems, if anything, to belong to a period even earlier than the Trojan War, since he is only the grandson of Minos.[35] Thus there is no compelling reason to see in this section of the Catalogue a reflection of Early Iron Age Crete, rather than Late Minoan Crete, whatever one may feel about the passage in the *Odyssey*.

NOTES ON THE CRETAN SECTION

1. e.g. Miss Gray in *HHC*, p. 266; Wace in Foreword to *DMG*, pp. xxii f.; Hutchinson, *Prehistoric Crete*, pp. 302 f.
2. *Ap.* Pendlebury, *The Archaeology of Crete*, p. 229.
3. Hutchinson, op. cit., p. 300.
4. Gray, op. cit., p. 263 and n. 2.
5. *BSA* 47 (1952), pp. 243 f.; cf. *BSA* 51 (1956) pp. 81 f.
6. Hutchinson, loc. cit.
7. Cf. Marinatos, *Antiquity* 13 (1939), pp. 425–39.

8. Cf. Pendlebury, op. cit., pp. 237 f.
9. Op. cit., pp. 305–9.
10. Op. cit., p. 239.
11. Cf. M. R. Popham, *Studies in Mediterranean Archaeology* 5 (Lund 1964), esp. pp. 8–9; *Antiquity* 40 (1966), pp. 24–8; *Kadmos* 5 (1966), pp. 17–24; *contra*: M. S. F. Hood, *Kadmos* 4 (1965), pp. 16–44; *Kadmos* 5 (1966), pp. 121–41.
12. Desborough (*LMTS*, p. 183) regards the settlement at Gortyn as belonging to LM IIIC. As he makes clear on p. 167, he uses this term as equivalent to Levi's LM IIIB:2.
13. Evans (*Palace of Minos* ii. 86–8) identified this landmark with a headland of white rock, about a mile north of Matala, the naval arsenal of Gortyn, on the east coast south of Komo.
14. *AE* 1907, p. 184.
15. e.g. by Burr, *NK*, pp. 82–3.
16. G. L. Huxley, *Crete and the Luwians*, pp. 15–16.
17. Ephoros, *FGrH* 70 F 127; Strabo 12. 573; Herodotus 1. 173.
18. *PM* ii. 60–102. In 1963 we collaborated with Professor W. A. McDonald in an attempt to check Evans's statements about Minoan roads, and did find some possible traces of one near Visala.
19. Cf. *DMG*, pp. 32 and 141.
20. Cf. Huxley, *Crete and the Luwians*, pp. 15–16.
21. *JHS Arch.* for 1962/3, p. 30; for 1963/4, pp. 26–7; for 1965/6, p. 23; *Ann.* N.S. 35–6, pp. 57 f.; Desborough also regards this settlement as belonging to LM IIIC (*LMTS*, pp. 182–3, cf. n. 12 above).
22. Pendlebury, op. cit., pp. 240–1.
23. See above, on Gortyn.
24. *Travels and Researches in Crete* i. 333.
25. *Diary*, 2/4/1894.
26. Op. cit., p. 343.
27. We are indebted to Professor Huxley for this information.
28. Although there may be 'a reminiscence of days long past, like Ariadne's dancing-floor', as suggested by *CH*, p. 295. There is, of course, no need to follow Ephoros in his pedantic and unnecessary explanation (*ap.* Strabo 10. 479) of the 'discrepancy' between the hundred cities of the *Iliad* (2. 649) and the ninety of the *Odyssey* (19. 174). The reference to Phaistos and to *Μίλητος* (if this is Mallia) in the Catalogue might also be a reflection of the past glories of Minoan civilization, although, as we have seen, Phaistos certainly revived (at least in LM IIIC) and Mallia was still occupied in LM IIIB (*JHS Arch.* for 1964/5, p. 29).
29. Cf. Strabo 10. 475.
30. Huxley (*BICS* 3 (1956), p. 23) connects the *Πελασγοί* with the 'Sea Peoples'. For the *Δωριέες*, see above, p. 115.
31. The Linear B tablets from Knossos appear to name several places in western and eastern Crete (cf. *DMG*, p. 141), and this may indicate that Knossos' power extended further than the area of Idomeneus' realm suggested by the Catalogue, when the tablets were written. But if the tablets are in fact to be dated early in LM IIIA (cf. M. R. Popham, *Antiquity* 40 (1966), pp. 24–8), then they are considerably earlier than the Trojan War, which is ostensibly contemporary with the Catalogue.
32. Cf. Hammond, *The End of Mycenaean Civilization and the Dark Age* (*C.A.H.* Fasc. 13, pp. 46–7).
33. Huxley, *BICS* 3 (1956), p. 24 and n. 74.
34. Desborough, *LMTS*, pp. 182–3.
35. *Il.* 13. 446–54; *Od.* 19. 178–81.

THE RHODIANS

Ῥόδος (2. 655) MAP 6

Since the *city* of Rhodes was not founded until 408 B.C., the name in the Catalogue presumably refers to the whole island. Strabo (14. 653) notes that Lindos, Ialysos, and Kameiros existed before the foundation of the city of Rhodes, and remarks that they were once under separate governments of their own.

Λίνδος (2. 656) MAP 6

REFS. C. Blinkenburg and K. F. Kinch, *Lindos* (1931), i. 68–70; *Ann.* 6/7 (1923/4), pp. 252–3; Fimmen, *KMK*, p. 16; *CVA*, Denmark, Fasc. 1, Pl. 46:5; Desborough, *PG*, pp. 229–32.

The acropolis of Lindos is one of the most imposing in Greece, and the site is at once a fortress and a harbour. Mycenaean pottery (LH IIIB) was found during the Danish excavations,[1] and although there was not much of it, it must be remembered that the Mycenaean levels were probably extensively destroyed by building in later periods. The site was also inhabited in the Early Iron Age.

Ἰηλυσός (2. 656) MAP 6

REFS. *Clara Rhodos* i (1928), pp. 56–65; *Clara Rhodos* x (1941/2), pp. 41 f.; Furumark, *OpArch.* 6 (1950), pp. 150 f.; *Ann.* 2 (1916), pp. 271–4; *Ann.* 6/7 (1923/4), pp. 86–251; *Ann.* 13/14 (1930/1), pp. 254–345; Furumark, *MP*, p. 648 and refs.; Desborough, *PG*, pp. 225–7; Desborough, *LMTS*, Index, s.v. 'Ialysos'.

According to Wace,[2] the settlement at Trianda, near the village of Paraskeva, below the acropolis of Ialysos (now called Philerimos), was first established by the Minoans in the MM III period, although the earliest levels recorded in the reports are LM IA. Mycenaean colonists established them selves in Rhodes in the period LH II/IIIA, and there is a corresponding increase in the amount of Mycenaean pottery at Trianda during this period (Trianda level IIb). Then, at the beginning of the LH IIIA period, Trianda was suddenly deserted, and it is presumed that the Mycenaeans moved onto or nearer to the acropolis, for although later occupation has possibly removed traces of Mycenaean occupation on the acropolis itself, the Mycenaean chamber-tombs on the hillocks of Moschou and Makra Vounara below the acropolis are convincing proof of a major habitation-site, and there can be little doubt that it is to a settlement near here that the Catalogue refers. There is also evidence for occupation of the site in the Early Iron Age, but it was apparently deserted for a time at the end of LH IIIC.[3]

Κάμειρος (2. 656) MAP 6

REFS. *Boll. d'Arte* 9 (1915), pp. 226 f.; *Clara Rhodos* vi–vii (1923/4), pp. 1 f., 133–50, and 223 f.; Furumark, *MP*, p. 649 and refs.; Desborough, *PG*, pp. 227–9; Desborough, *LMTS*, pp. 6, 153, 157 f.

Although, as in the case of Ialysos, later building has apparently removed all trace of Mycenaean occupation from the acropolis of Kameiros, the Mycenaean cemeteries in the vicinity show that there was an important Mycenaean centre here, and it probably occupied the acropolis. The site was also occupied in the Early Iron Age, though, as in the case of Ialysos again, there is evidence that it was deserted for a time towards the end of LH IIIC.[4]

Some scholars have assumed that the description of Tlepolemos as Ἡρακλεΐδης marks him out as a Dorian hero, and they point to the phrases διὰ τρίχα κοσμηθέντες (*Il.* 2. 655) and τριχθὰ δὲ ᾤκηθεν καταφυλαδόν (*Il.* 2. 668) as indicating the Dorian division into three tribes.[5] It is possible, however, that *Il.* 2. 667–70 are an interpolation,[6] and, even if one does not wish to resort to this dangerous remedy, there is really nothing in the context to imply that the three-fold division of the Rhodians in the Catalogue refers to anything else than the three cities from which they come.[7] Nor need Tlepolemos' descent from Herakles mean that he was a Dorian hero, for there can be little doubt that Herakles was a Mycenaean hero long before he became particularly associated with the Dorians.[8] Indeed, the fact that Tlepolemos is later killed by Sarpedon the Lycian (*Il.* 5. 627–59) suggests that he was a local Rhodian hero. It is also clear from the story of Herakles' involuntary voyage to Kos (*Il.* 14. 250–6) that the Herakles myth was important in the Dodecanese, and there is no reason to think that it only became so after the Dorians had arrived. Admittedly, the evidence for the Protogeometric and Geometric occupation of Lindos, Ialysos, and Kameiros shows that this section of the Catalogue *could* refer to Early Iron Age Rhodes, but there is nothing in the entry which precludes a reference to Mycenaean Rhodes.

Page argues[9] that the description of Tlepolemos' flight to Rhodes (*Il.* 2. 661–7) cannot be a Mycenaean tradition because Rhodes had already been occupied by the Mycenaeans for several generations before the time of the Trojan War. But the passage does not necessarily imply that Tlepolemos was the founder of Achaean rule on the island.[10] Nor does the Rhodian entry in the Catalogue lend any support to Page's hypothesis that Rhodes is the 'Aḫḫijavā' of the Hittite tablets:[11] Tlepolemos' mere nine ships should not, perhaps, be pressed, but a Rhodes which is not even in control of the neighbouring islands would hardly have worried the Hittite king.

Page stresses the density of the Mycenaean population of Rhodes, the 'warlike' disposition of the colonists, and the arguments for regarding Rhodes as the principal source of Mycenaean exports to Syria, Palestine, and Egypt in the 14th century B.C.[12] But the mainstay of the argument is the famous 'Tavagalavaš Letter',[13] which probably belongs to the reign of either Mursilis II or Muvatallis (i.e. the late 14th or early 13th century B.C., early in the LH IIIB period). There are various clues in the letter to the location of Aḫḫijavā, but, as Huxley stresses,[14] 'the Tavagalavaš letter does not show where the centre of Aḫḫijavan power lay', and an examination of other Hittite texts shows that 'taken by themselves the references to Aḫḫijavā do not prove where the king of Aḫḫijavā resided'.[15] All we can conclude is that the king of Aḫḫijavā is independent,[16] of some importance,[17] and apparently safe from the clutches of the king of the Hittites.[18] Rhodes would adequately satisfy these criteria, but they certainly do not preclude a power on the mainland of Greece,[19] and Huxley rightly urges that archaeology and tradition alike should lead us to identify the king of Aḫḫijavā, whom even the king of the Hittites respected, with the lord of Mycenae.

Certainly, if Rhodes *was* Aḫḫijavā, it would be difficult to accept that the Catalogue here refers to the LH IIIB period, since one would have expected Aḫḫijavā to control at least the neighbouring islands, and their independence would make it hard to understand how Rhodes could interfere on the west coast of Asia Minor. Indeed, even if Rhodes is not Aḫḫijavā, as is probably the case, it seems likely that she controlled the neighbouring islands in LH IIIB, and the Catalogue may therefore refer to LH IIIC rather than LH IIIB here.[20] It could also, as we have seen, refer to the Early Iron Age in so far as Lindos, Ialysos, and Kameiros were all inhabited at that time, but there is nothing in the entry to compel this conclusion, and if the Catalogue as a whole reflects Mycenaean Greece, the Rhodian entry is an unlikely sort of 'interpolation'.[21]

NOTES ON THE RHODIAN SECTION

1. Omitted by Stubbings, *Mycenaean Pottery in the Levant.*
2. Foreword to *DMG*, p. xxv.
3. Desborough, *LMTS*, pp. 157 and 233.
4. Desborough, loc. cit.
5. Cf. the Δωριέες τριχάϊκες of Crete (*Od.* 19. 177); Lorimer, *HM*, p. 47, p. 466 n. 2; Wace in Foreword to *DMG*, p. xxx.
6. Page, *HHI*, n. 86 on p. 176.
7. A. Andrewes, *Hermes* 89 (1961), pp. 132–3.
8. Nilsson, *The Mycenaean Origin of Greek Mythology*, pp. 187–220; cf. p. 87 above, on Herakles' attack on Pylos.
9. *HHI*, pp. 147–8.
10. Cf. Wace and Stubbings, *CH*, p. 295.
11. *HHI*, pp. 1–40.
12. *HHI*, n. 55 on pp. 36–7; cf. Stubbings, *Mycenaean Pottery in the Levant*, pp. 6, 11, 68 f., 106; W. Taylour, *Mycenaean Pottery from Italy and Adjacent areas*, pp. 187 f.
13. *AU* i. 2–94; cf. Page, *HHI*, pp. 10–12 and n. 33 on p. 30; Huxley, *AH*, pp. 1–2, 11 f., 15 f.
14. Op. cit., p. 22.
15. Op. cit., p. 23.
16. Huxley, op. cit., p. 15.
17. In *AU* xvii, Kol. iv, 3, the name of Aḫḫijavā was crossed out in a list of kings of the same

rank as the King of the Hittites. As Huxley says (*AH*, p. 16), this 'does not prove that Aḫḫijavā was a lesser *power*, but only that it was thought politic not to admit her king's rank to be equal with the Hittite emperor's', and (as he goes on to say) 'the respectful tone adopted by the Hittite emperor in the Tavagalavaš text strongly suggests that about 1300 B.C. the King of Aḫḫijavā was a person of great importance'.

18. Page, *HHI*, pp. 13–14. As Gurney says (*The Hittites*, p. 49), 'one has the impression that the king of Aḫḫijavā is a somewhat remote figure'.

19. Huxley (*AH*, pp. 18 f.) argues convincingly that the Tavagalavaš letter, far from proving that the island to which Pijamaraduš fled and from which he threatened the coast of Asia Minor *was* Aḫḫijavā, proves that it was *not* Aḫḫijavā. Similarly, *AU* xvi, which mentions the King of Aḫḫijavā as being present *in person* on the coast of Asia Minor in the time of Tutḫalijaš IV, 'is far from proving that the Aḫḫijavan king lived close to the coast of Asia Minor' (Huxley, *AH*, p. 22).

As Huxley rightly argues (op. cit., p. 17), 'we cannot assume, without further argument, as some have done, that Aḫḫijavā in 1300 B.C. was identical in power and extent with Aḫḫijavā in the reign of Tutḫalijaš IV, fifty years later, and if we succeed in identifying a part of Aḫḫijavā we must not at once assume, as some have done, that the territory identified is the whole of Aḫḫijavā, or that the centre of Aḫḫijavan power lies within it' (cf. op. cit., p. 23).

Mellaart (*AJA* 52 (1958), n. 151 on p. 22, and *Minutes* of the London Mycenaean Seminar for 3 Feb. 1960) follows Goetze in locating Aḫḫijavā in north-west Anatolia (i.e. in the Troad): this may be an example of what Huxley warns against—identifying a part of Aḫḫijavā with the whole.

20. See pp. 161–4 below.

21. Allen, *HCS*, p. 102.

THE KINGDOM OF NIREUS

Σύμη (2. 671) MAP 6

REFS. *Gazetteer*, fig. 4, No. 5; Bean and Cook, *BSA* 52 (1957), p. 116 n. 205 and refs. there; Fraser and Bean, *The Rhodian Peraea and Islands*, pp. 139–41; Hope Simpson and Lazenby, *BSA* 57 (1962), pp. 156, 168–9.

The chief site on the island of Syme is the Kastro which dominates the harbour on the north-east, opposite the Turkish mainland. It lies on the spur separating the harbour-bay to the north from the more fertile land around the adjoining bay of Pedhi to the east.

In 1960 we found good 5th- and 4th-century B.C. black-glazed sherds on the north slopes, and two small, striped sherds which must, presumably, be either Mycenaean or Archaic, while in 1967 Hope Simpson found a piece of the rim of a Mycenaean monochrome *Kylix* associated with rough prehistoric sherds.

These sherds, though few in number, are enough to indicate that Syme was inhabited in the prehistoric period, and the Kastro hill would certainly be a suitable site for Mycenaean occupation.

THE KINGDOM OF PHEIDIPPOS AND ANTIPHOS

Νίσυρος (2. 676) MAP 6

REFS. *Gazetteer*, fig. 4, No. 6; Bean and Cook, *BSA* 52 (1957), pp. 118–19 and refs. in n. 213; Fraser and Bean, *The Rhodian Peraea and Islands*, pp. 138–54, esp. pp. 147 f.; Hope Simpson and Lazenby, *BSA* 57 (1962), p. 169.

The main town of Nisyros in ancient times probably occupied the Kastro above Mandhraki. Here again we found a number of striped sherds which could be Mycenaean, but were probably Archaic.[1] We did, however, find on the site several chips of the semi-translucent obsidian which comes from the tiny island of Yali, between Nisyros and Kos,[2] and prehistoric occupation is also indicated by the Cycladic idol reported to have come from Nisyros.[3]

Κράπαθος (2. 676) MAP 6

REFS. *Gazetteer*, fig. 4, Nos. 1–4; Fraser and Bean, *The Rhodian Peraea and Islands*, pp. 141–4; Hope Simpson and Lazenby, *BSA* 57 (1962), pp. 156, 159–68 and refs. there; S. Charitonides, *ADelt.* 17 (1961/2), pp. 32–76 (the Makelli tomb); *JHS Arch.* for 1960/1, p. 34, for 1962/3, p. 29.

This is clearly the island of Karpathos, and the main site of the island seems always to have been near the modern port of Pigadhia. This was once called 'Posin', which is probably a contraction of 'Potidaion' or 'Poseidion', the name of the classical town which lay there.

The discovery of some ninety vases of the period LH IIIA to early LH IIIB in the Makelli tomb near Pigadhia makes it certain that there was also a major Mycenaean settlement here, and we would locate this on the rocky acropolis which dominates the bay of Pigadhia on the east. We were unable to find any Mycenaean sherds there, largely owing to the overlay of later remains, but we did find part of an obsidian blade. The site we discovered on a low bluff, on the shore about 100 metres west-north-west of the Limenarcheion, although yielding a quantity of Mycenaean sherds, did not seem to us as suitable for the main Mycenaean settlement as the acropolis east of Pigadhia, and the Minoan influence (later giving way to Mycenaean) observable in the pottery from the Makelli tomb suggests a pattern of occupation similar to that at Trianda on Rhodes, with the Minoans occupying the low-lying site near the sea, and the Mycenaeans later moving to a higher, more readily defensible position on the acropolis east of Pigadhia.

The seven Mycenaean (LH IIIB) pots and the bronze sword, found near Yiafani at the north-east end of the island,[4] indicate that there was a Mycenaean settlement somewhere there too, and we would tentatively locate it on the broad promontory, with extensive cultivated terraces (now called Kambi), less than a mile south of the village of Yiafani, beyond the church of Ayios Nikolaos.

It is also obvious that the sites of the later towns of Brykous and Arkaseia[5] were places where Mycenaean settlement might be expected. At Brykous we did find what may be part of a Mycenaean *Kylix*, and some other possibly Mycenaean sherds, but certainty was not possible: the acropolis, on a promontory jutting some 500 metres into the sea, looks suitable for Mycenaean occupation.

Arkaseia occupied a spectacular high and steep-sided acropolis on a promontory on the south-west coast of the island. Again it would have been a place eminently suitable for Mycenaean occupation, but although we found five or six flakes of obsidian, and a few possibly Mycenaean sherds, we could find no conclusive evidence for Mycenaean occupation. The upper of the two sections of wall visible on the north-east corner of the site could be 'Cyclopean': it is built of large, roughly-dressed blocks, with small stones packed in between, and contrasts with the lower wall of well-jointed, polygonal blocks.

Κάσος (2. 676) MAP 6

REFS. Fraser and Bean, *The Rhodian Peraea and Islands*, pp. 152–3; *RE* x, Reihe ii (1919), pp. 2268–9; L. Ross, *Inselreisen* iii (1843), pp. 32 f.; Hope Simpson and Lazenby, *BSA* 57 (1962), p. 168.

The main centre of occupation on Kasos seems always to have been on the east side of the central valley, on and around the sharp-pointed hill called *Κάστρο στὸ μπόλιν*. We were unable to visit the island in 1960, but in 1967

Hope Simpson found some Late Bronze Age sherds of 'provincial' type on the Kastro, and one or two possibly Mycenaean pieces.

Κῶς (2. 677) MAP 6

REFS. Bean and Cook, *BSA* 52 (1957), pp. 120 f. and refs. there; Hope Simpson and Lazenby, *BSA* 57 (1962), pp. 154, 156, and 169–72; Desborough, *LMTS*, p. 153 and Index, s.v. 'Kos'; *Gazetteer*, fig. 4 Nos. 7–12.

By *Κῶς Εὐρυπύλοιο πόλις* is presumably meant a city on the site of the present town of Kos, called elsewhere *Μεροπίς*. Thus the *Hymn to Apollo* (line 42) refers to Kos as *πόλις Μερόπων ἀνθρώπων*. This is borne out by other references to Kos in the *Iliad* where it is given the epithet *εὖ ναιομένη*, which usually seems to be applied to cities.[6] That the site was occupied in Mycenaean times is proved by the excavations at the Seraglio,[7] but occupation was apparently continuous from LM IA to the Geometric period.[8]

νῆσοι Καλύδναι (2. 677) MAP 6

REFS. *Gazetteer*, fig. 4, Nos. 13–14; Bean and Cook, *BSA* 52 (1957), pp. 120 f. and refs. there; Hope Simpson and Lazenby, *BSA* 57 (1962), pp. 154–6 and 172–3; Desborough, *LMTS*, p. 154 and Index, s.v. 'Calymnos'.

The problem of what Homer meant by the *νῆσοι Καλύδναι* was already a subject for discussion in Strabo's day. He says (10. 489) that the general opinion was that it meant Kalymna (= Kalymnos) and the islands near by, Kalymna having once, perhaps, been called 'Kalydna'. But he also remarks that some held that Leros and Kalymna were meant, while Demetrius of Skepsis thought that *Καλύδναι* was a plural similar to *Ἀθῆναι* or *Θῆβαι* and thus referred only to Kalymna.

Certainty is not possible, but at least there does not seem to be any good evidence that Kalymnos alone was ever called *Καλύδνα* or *Καλύδναι*, although the Elder Pliny does mention a 'Calydna insula' as a source of excellent honey (*NH* 11. 32). On the other hand, the Athenian Tribute Lists do seem to refer to the *inhabitants* of Kalymnos as *Καλύδνιοι*, and this suggests that those who thought that the *νῆσοι Καλύδναι* meant Kalymnos *and Leros* were wrong, since the people of Leros were assessed separately or included in the assessment of Miletos.[9] Moreover Leros, unlike Kalymnos, seems always later to have been an Ionian island, whereas Kalymnos was Dorian,[10] and although this does not prove anything for a period much earlier than the Protogeometric era, it does emphasize the fact that although the two islands are only separated by a narrow strip of water, the inhabitants of Kalymnos have always lived mainly in the two southern valleys and looked naturally towards Kos rather than Leros, the northern part of the island being so barren. It seems, then, probable that the general opinion quoted by Strabo was right, and that *νῆσοι Καλύδναι* refers to Kalymnos, Pserimos, and Telendos, all of which are inhabited to this day, and form a natural group.

So far no evidence for prehistoric occupation of the two smaller islands has come to light, but Kalymnos must always have been the main centre, and there is no doubt that this was inhabited both in Mycenaean times and in the Early Iron Age. Long ago Paton found Mycenaean vases (including LH IIIC) in tombs 'on the hill to the west of the torrent . . . which finds its outlet in Pothia harbour',[11] and in 1960 we found a considerable number of Mycenaean sherds (LH IIIA–B) on the middle and lower slopes of the hill called 'Perakastro', particularly near the windmills on its eastern and southern sides. To anyone entering Pothia harbour, this hill stands out as the obvious site for a Mycenaean stronghold, and we have no doubt that this was the main centre in Mycenaean times.

Some of the vases in the archaeological collection at Pothia are said to have come from near Damos, up the valley to the north-west,[12] but we were unable to find any evidence for Mycenaean settlement in this area. Nor were we able to find a Mycenaean site in the Vathy valley, though Mycenaean pottery has been found in the cave of Daskalio,[13] and been reported from Phylakai.[14] The most likely site, perhaps, is a small, broad, and low spur, projecting slightly into the valley on its north-east edge, less than half a kilometre west of the Hellenistic tower which goes by the name of 'Phylakai'. Here we found sporadic black-glazed and Roman sherds, together with a coarse, micaceous ware which might be prehistoric.

Nothing much can be said about the realms of Nireus and of Pheidippos and Antiphos. Although Syme has produced some evidence for Mycenaean occupation, and nothing from the Early Iron Age, this does not prove anything, and it will probably never be possible to refer this entry to a particular period. Nireus' obscurity, however, and the weakness of his following, are perhaps some guarantee of antiquity, and the separation of his island from Rhodes and the rest of the Dodecanese seems more likely to reflect the historical reality of some period than to be mere fiction.

Pheidippos and Antiphos, like Tlepolemos of Rhodes, have been suspected because of their descent from Herakles, but, as was argued above, this provides no good warrant for regarding them as Dorian heroes.[15] According to Diodoros (5. 54), it was their father Thessalos, grandson of Eurypylos, king of Kos,[16] who brought the Kalydnai and Nisyros under the sway of Kos. However, one cannot avoid being suspicious of this sort of tradition, especially in this case, since Eurypylos was also the name of an important *Thessalian* hero. It is also odd that Diodoros does not mention Karpathos here—or Kasos for that matter: judging from the remains, Karpathos at least was an important centre of Mycenaean settlement, and Diodoros' earlier statement (5. 53. 1) that *τῶν μετὰ Μίνω τινὲς συστρατευομένων* colonized Karpathos during Minos' thalassocracy shows that there were traditions about the island, unlike Kasos.[17] Indeed, this particular tradition could almost be said to have been 'confirmed' by the discovery of a Minoan settlement on Karpathos.[18] A realm comprising Kalymnos, Kos, Nisyros, Karpathos, and Kasos has a certain geographical plausibility about it—though one might, perhaps, have expected Telos to be included—and, as in the case of Syme, the separation of these islands from Rhodes looks as though it does reflect historical reality.

The evidence for Early Iron Age occupation of the islands is, as usual, even scantier than for the Mycenaean, but there is no doubt that Kos (including Kos-town) and Kalymnos at least were inhabited in the Protogeometric and Geometric periods, and the other islands probably were.

NOTES ON THE KINGDOMS OF NIREUS AND OF PHEIDIPPOS AND ANTIPHOS

1. Cf. *BSA* 52 (1957), p. 119.
2. Cf. A. Furness, *PPS* 22 (1956), p. 193.
3. Bean and Cook, *BSA* 52 (1957), p. 119 n. 217.
4. Stubbings, *Mycenaean Pottery in the Levant*, p. 21.
5. Cf. Dawkins, *BSA* 9 (1902/3), pp. 201–4.
6. Bowra, *JHS* 80 (1960), p. 20.
7. Morricone, *Boll. d'Arte* 35 (1950), pp. 316–30, esp. 320 f.; *Ergon* for 1959, pp. 131–4.
8. Desborough, *PG*, pp. 222–4, *LMTS*, p. 153; *Ergon*, loc. cit. For other Mycenaean sites on the island of Kos see Hope Simpson and Lazenby, *BSA* 57 (1962), p. 171 and refs. there.
9. *ATL* i. 494, 510–11. In 1967 Hope Simpson found some LH IIIB sherds on the Kastro at Leros.
10. Cf. *BSA* 52 (1957), p. 134.
11. *JHS* 8 (1887), pp. 446–8; cf. *CR* 1 (1887), pp. 80 f.; Stubbings, *Mycenaean Pottery in the Levant*, p. 22.
12. *BSA* 52 (1957), p. 129 n. 287 *ad fin.*
13. *PPS* 22 (1956), p. 188.
14. *BSA* 52 (1957), p. 128 n. 282.
15. As, for example, Miss Lorimer does (*HM*, p. 47); cf. p. 171 and n. 7 on p. 173.
16. According to Pherekydes (*FGrH* 3 F 78), Thessalos was the son of Khalkiope, the daughter of Eurypylos, by Herakles (cf. Apollodoros 2. 7. 1, Schol. Pindar *Nem.* 4. 25. 40). But in other versions (Eustathius ad *Il.* 2. 677; Hyginus, *Fab.* 97) either Eurypylos himself was Herakles' son by Khalkiope, or Khalkiope was wife to Thessalos.
17. The only traditions about Kasos were that it was once called 'Akhne', 'Amphe', or 'Astrabe': Pliny, *NH* 5. 133; Stephanus of Byzantium s.v. Ἄμφη; Pliny, *NH* 4. 70; Stephanus of Byzantium, s.v. Ἀστράβη.
18. *BSA* 57 (1962), pp. 160–1.

THE KINGDOM OF PELEUS AND ACHILLES

τὸ Πελασγικὸν Ἄργος (2. 681) MAP 7

REFS. Allen, *HCS*, pp. 108 f.; Hope Simpson and Lazenby, *Antiquity* 33 (1959), p. 104.

This is usually taken to refer to a district, whether the plain of Malis,[1] or the Spercheios valley.[2] H. M. Chadwick, however, suggested[3] that it means what was later called Larisa Cremaste, an alternative name for which was 'Pelasgia' according to Strabo (9. 435).[4] Strabo himself thought that Larisa Cremaste belonged rather to Protesilaus' kingdom than to Achilles', but although the hills to the west and south cut it off from the plain of Malis to some extent, beyond it the country becomes wilder still, and there is certainly no pressing geographical reason to exclude it from the kingdom of Achilles. Certainty is not possible, but if τὸ Πελασγικὸν Ἄργος *is* Larisa Cremaste, our discovery of Mycenaean sherds there[5] becomes relevant.

The balance of this passage in the Catalogue would, perhaps, be enhanced if the first four names referred to towns, and the last two (see below) to districts, but elsewhere in the Catalogue[6] the district seems to be mentioned first, and Ἄργος Ἀχαιϊκόν normally seems to mean the Peloponnese (or southern Greece) generally, not the Peloponnesian *city* of Argos.[7]

Ἄλος (2. 682) MAP 7

REFS. Allen, *HCS*, p. 111; Hope Simpson and Lazenby, *Antiquity* 33 (1959), pp. 102–3, 105.

By Strabo's time (9. 432) the Greeks were already in doubt about the location of both Alos and Alope, and some even wondered whether the Locrian Alos and Alope were not meant. But in the case of Alos, there is certainly no reason to assume, as Burr does,[8] that Phthiotic Halos is meant, since that clearly lay within the boundaries of the kingdom of Protesilaus, and in any case was possibly only founded *after* the Trojan War.[9]

As Allen says,[10] the name is extremely common, and 'on a rapidly-growing alluvial coast, such as the delta of the Spercheus, places are stranded and forgotten'. A site such as the low mound of Platania,[11] on the fringes of the lower, marshy valley, would suit the name, and would at least lie within the boundaries of Peleus' probable kingdom.[12]

Ἀλόπη (2. 682) MAP 7

REFS. Béquignon, *La Vallée du Spercheios*, pp. 367–8 and Pl. xx. 2; Hope Simpson and Lazenby, *Antiquity* 33 (1959), p. 103; *JHS Arch.* for 1961/2, p. 31.

Alope is hardly less obscure than Alos, but at least Stephanus of Byzantium says that there was such a place (s.v.), between Larisa Cremaste and Echinous,

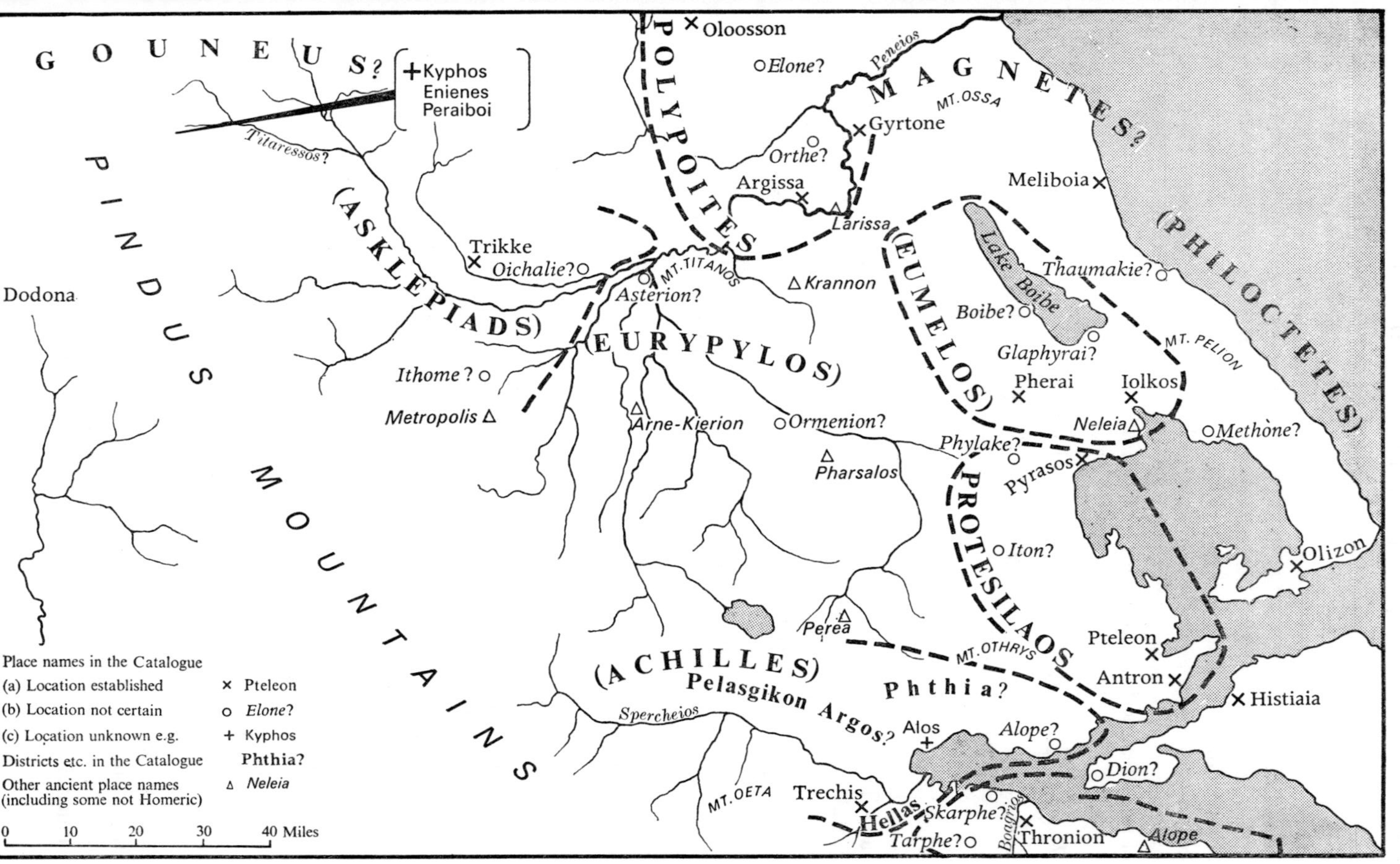
GOUNEUS?
+Kyphos
Enienes
Peraiboi
Titaressos?
PINDUS MOUNTAINS
Dodona
(ASKLEPIADS)
Trikke
Oichalie?
Ithome?
Metropolis
POLYPOITES
Oloosson
Elone?
Orthe?
Argissa
Gyrtone
Larissa
MT. TITANOS
Asterion?
Krannon
(EURYPYLOS)
Arne-Kierion
Ormenion?
Pharsalos
MAGNETES?
Peneios
MT. OSSA
Meliboia
(PHILOCTETES)
(EUMELOS)
Lake Boibe
Thaumakie?
Boibe?
Glaphyrai?
MT. PELION
Pherai
Iolkos
Neleia
Methone?
Phylake?
Pyrasos
PROTESILAOS
Iton?
Olizon
Pteleon
Antron
Histiaia
MT. OTHRYS
Perea
(ACHILLES)
Pelasgikon Argos?
Phthia?
Spercheios
Alos
Alope?
Dion?
MT. OETA
Trechis
Hellas
Skarphe?
Tarphe?
Boagrios
Thronion
Alope
Place names in the Catalogue
(a) Location established × Pteleon
(b) Location not certain ○ Elone?
(c) Location unknown e.g. + Kyphos
Districts etc. in the Catalogue Phthia?
Other ancient place names (including some not Homeric) △ Neleia
0 10 20 30 40 Miles

Map 7

and Livy's reference (42. 56) to the attack by a Roman fleet under Q. Marcius Rex on Larisa Cremaste and Alope in 171 B.C. suggests that the Alope in question was near Larisa Cremaste, though since the fleet eventually went on to Chalcis, it may be that the Locrian Alope is meant.

Béquignon identified some remains near the village of Rakhes with Alope, and, although these are insignificant, our discovery of a prehistoric site on the coast near by[13] supports the conjecture. We were even told that the area around the site was called *Ἀλοπεκά*, though one can never be sure that the statements of some wandering scholar are not behind such local traditions.[14]

Τρηχίς (2. 682) MAP 7

REFS. *Gazetteer*, No. 470; Allen, *HCS*, p. 110; Béquignon, *La Vallée du Spercheios*, pp. 243–60, fig. 4, Pls. ix–x; Hope Simpson and Lazenby, *Antiquity* 33 (1959), pp. 103–4; Pritchett, *Studies in Ancient Greek Topography* (Berkeley and Los Angeles 1965), pp. 81 f.

This is the only place in the kingdom of Peleus and Achilles which can be identified with any certainty: it is presumably to be located at the site of the later Trachis (T.7 Lamia 307E/426N), which was supplanted in its turn by Herakleia, founded by the Spartans in 426 B.C. The strategic importance of the place is obvious, commanding as it does the Asopos gorge, the approaches to the pass of Thermopylae, and the largest area of farming land between the mountains and the sea.[15]

In 1958 we found a few Mycenaean sherds on the lower slopes, and Mycenaean occupation of the site is suggested by the existence of a smaller Mycenaean settlement about a kilometre and a half away, west-north-westwards along the foot of the cliffs.[16] So far there is no evidence for occupation between the Mycenaean period and classical times.[17]

Φθίη and Ἑλλάς (2. 683) MAP 7

REFS. Allen, *HCS*, pp. 119–20; Hope Simpson and Lazenby, *Antiquity* 33 (1959), p. 104; Wace and Stubbings, *CH*, pp. 296–7.

It is probable that these names refer to districts rather than to towns, although this was already disputed in Strabo's day (9. 431). Achilles often refers to his home as Phthia,[18] occasionally as Phthia and Hellas,[19] but if they were towns it would be difficult to account for the Phthians under Protesilaus and Philoctetes,[20] and the Panhellenes under Aias, son of Oileus (*Il.* 2. 530), whereas, if they were districts, we may suppose that the Phthians once occupied a wider area, but were pushed out of the Spercheios valley by the Myrmidons and Achaeans, leaving the name behind them, for Achilles' *men* are never called Phthioi. Similarly, the Hellenes under his command could have come from the part of his father's kingdom which adjoined that of Aias (see below). It is also easier to explain the extension of the name 'Hellas'[21] if it was originally the name of a district than if it was the name of a town.

It may be possible to locate Hellas more precisely: the presence of *Ἕλληνες* under Achilles (*Il.* 2. 684) and of *Πανέλληνες* under Aias, son of Oileus (*Il.* 2.

530), suggests a district south of the Spercheios, in the region of the Asopos and on down the coast, and this is confirmed by Phoenix' story of his flight from his father's home at Eleon in Boeotia *through* Hellas to Phthia.[22] It is also notable that, as was noted by Leake,[23] and later by Wace and Thompson,[24] the name 'Helladha' was applied to the Spercheios until quite recently.

The ancient heresy[25] that Phthia was the later Pharsalos has recently been revived by Verdelis, following his excavations there.[26] But, as we have seen, it is fairl cleary that in the epics Phthia meant an area and not a town, and it is probable that the theory that it was a town sprang from the desire of the Kreondai of Pharsalos to secure a mention for their own home in the national poems.[27] Béquignon[28] neatly disposes of the identification of Phthia with Pharsalos, and administers the *coup de grâce* by demonstrating that 'Palaio-pharsalos' (cf. Strabo 9. 431) most probably lay at Palaiokastro Derengli, and not at the modern Pharsalos at all.[29]

As for the ruined city called 'Hellas' pointed out by the Pharsalians (Strabo, loc. cit.), it is clear that they meant the site at Ktouri,[30] but they can hardly have been right.[31]

Page argues[32] that the kingdom of Peleus and Achilles in the Catalogue is completely at variance with Achilles' importance elsewhere in the *Iliad*, and that elsewhere, too, Peleus' power is implied to extend as far as Mt. Pelion. But Achilles' importance is essentially personal and dramatic: his refusal to fight deprived the Achaeans of their finest warrior and was the essential theme of the story; but, although the Myrmidons were formidable fighters, there is never any suggestion that it was *they* who were missed.[33] As for the extent of Peleus' kingdom elsewhere in the *Iliad*, the only evidence that it may have extended as far as Mt. Pelion seems to be that the famous spear which Cheiron gave him came *Πηλίου ἐκ κορυφῆς* (*Il.* 16. 143–4 = 19. 390–1), and that Cheiron taught his son (*Il.* 11. 832). But this proves nothing: Cheiron might have taught Achilles how to apply healing ointments to wounds (for this is all his teaching amounts to in the *Iliad*) on some such visit as Idomeneus paid to Helen and Menelaus (*Il.* 3. 230–3) or Odysseus to his grandfather Autolykos (*Od.* 19. 392 f.). Nor is the gift of the spear any proof that Peleus lived on Cheiron's doorstep: Agamemnon's breastplate came from Cyprus (*Il.* 11. 19 f.), Odysseus' bow was the result of a chance encounter with Iphitos *ἐν Μεσσήνῃ* (*Od.* 21. 11 f.), and the boar's-tusk helmet started its adventurous career at Eleon in Boeotia, and thence travelled via Kythera to Crete (*Il.* 10. 266–71).

The only real indications of the whereabouts of Achilles' home, apart from the indications in the Catalogue itself, are his close connections with the Spercheios: his sister, Polydore, bore a son to the Spercheios (*Il.* 16. 173–6), and he himself dedicated his hair to the river in return for a safe home-coming (*Il.* 23. 141 f.). These passages suggest that the Spercheios valley was the heart of his father's realm, and its fertility is appropriately described by the epithets *ἐρίβωλαξ*, *βωτιανείρῃ*, *ἐρίβωλος* and *μήτηρ μήλων* applied to Phthia in the *Iliad* (1. 155, 9. 363 and 479).

Taking the evidence of the Catalogue and the rest of the *Iliad* together, we can possibly define the boundaries of the kingdom more precisely. Unless *τὸ Πελασγικὸν Ἄργος* refers to a town on the site of the later Larisa Cremaste, it seems likely that the frontier here lay to the west, and if Alope was near Rakhes, then the frontier probably lay between Rakhes and Larisa Cremaste. To the south the Thermopylae pass would form an obvious boundary, while Phoenix' position, ruling over the Dolopes *ἐσχατιὴν Φθίης* (*Il.* 9. 484), suggests that Peleus' power extended west of Tymphrestos, for this is where Dolopia lay in historical times.[34] The Othrys and Oita ranges provide natural barriers north and south of the valley, and there is no good evidence that Peleus' power extended beyond them.

NOTES ON THE KINGDOM OF PELEUS AND ACHILLES

1. Allen, *HSC*, pp. 108 f.
2. Wace and Stubbings, *CH*, pp. 296–7.
3. *The Heroic Age*, p. 280 n. 1.
4. That there was some very ancient connection between the names 'Argos' and 'Larisa' and the Pelasgians is suggested by *Il.* 2. 840–1, and by the name of the main acropolis of the Peloponnesian Argos.
5. *Gazetteer*, No. 478: T.8 Atalandi 668E/589N; *Antiquity* 33 (1959), p. 102.
6. Cf. *Il.* 2. 536, 581, 603, ?615.
7. Cf. *Il.* 9. 141 = 283; *Od.* 3. 251. At *Il.* 19. 115, however, it would more naturally mean the city.
8. *NK*, p. 89.
9. Cf. Strabo 9. 433.
10. *HCS*, p. 111.
11. *Gazetteer*, No. 474: T.7 Lamia 360E/535N; cf. *Antiquity* 33 (1959), pp. 102–3, 105.
12. It is possible, though there is no evidence for it, that the name *Ἄλος* refers to a town on the site later occupied by Lamia. This great citadel dominates the Spercheios valley and it seems incredible either that it should not have been occupied in Mycenaean times, or that it should not figure in any list of towns of the region. Surface-sherding has so far revealed no evidence for Mycenaean occupation, but the existence of the site at Platania near by makes it all the more likely that the castle-hill of Lamia was the site of a Mycenaean stronghold. An alternative possibility is that Lamia is *τὸ Πελασγικὸν Ἄργος*, though again there is absolutely no evidence for it.
13. Béquignon, *La Vallée du Spercheios*, pp. 367–8; *Gazetteer*, No. 477: T.8 Atalandi 630E/507N; *Antiquity* 33 (1959), p. 103; *JHS Arch.* for 1961/2, p. 31. Sherds included LH IIIA:2–LH IIIB.
14. An alternative suggestion is that Alope lay at the site of the later Echinous (*Gazetteer*, No. 476: T. 8 Atalandi 564E/520N), which was certainly inhabited in Mycenaean times (*Antiquity* 33 (1959), p. 102 and n. 7), and which was probably a more important place than the site near Rakhes. However, although one might argue that Alope was the old name for Echinous, and that Stephanus of Byzantium or his sources were induced to put Alope elsewhere because they knew of Echinous, it seems better to accept that there was another place called Alope, and to locate it near Rakhes.
15. Cf. Herodotus 7. 199.
16. *Gazetteer*, No. 471: T.7 Lamia 302E/432N; *Antiquity* 33 (1959), pp. 103–4.

17. For the topography of Trachis/Herakleia see now W. K. Pritchett, *Studies in Ancient Greek Topography*, Part I (Berkeley and Los Angeles 1965), pp. 81 f.

18. e.g. *Il.* 1. 155, 9. 363–4.

19. e.g. *Il.* 9. 395.

20. *Il.* 13. 693, cf. 2. 704 and 727.

21. Wade-Gery (*JHS* 44 (1924), p. 64 n. 34) produces evidence which suggests that the spread of the name *Ἕλληνες* is to be connected with the Amphictyony.

22. *Il.* 9. 447 f., esp. 478–9. That Eleon was the home of Phoenix' father is indicated by *Il.* 10. 266 (cf. 9. 448)—presumably the Eleon in Boeotia is meant (cf. *Il.* 2. 500). When Phoenix says that he left Hellas (*Il.* 9. 447), he implies that Eleon was in Hellas too (cf. *CH*, p. 297).

23. *Travels in Northern Greece* ii. 8.

24. *PT*, p. 255.

25. Pherekydes, *FGrH* 3 F 1, and Jacoby, *FGrH*, pp. 887 f.; cf. Euripides, *Andromache* 16 f., etc.; Allen, *HCS*, pp. 119–20.

26. *PAE* 1951, pp. 154–63; *PAE* 1952, pp. 185–204; *PAE* 1953, pp. 127–32; *Ergon* for 1955, pp. 44–7; cf. *JHS* 73 (1953), p. 120, and *JHS Arch.* for 1955, p. 21; *RA* 1958, pp. 93–5.

27. Allen, *HCS*, loc. cit.; Page, *HHI*, p. 161 n. 29.

28. *RA*, 1958, pp. 93–5.

29. *BCH* 55 (1931), pp. 492–3; *BCH* 56 (1932), pp. 89–119.

30. *BCH* 56 (1932), pp. 137–91; *Gazetteer*, No. 538: H.7 Farsala 213E/067N. The mention of the spring Hypereia in *Il.* 2. 734 led Wace to conjecture that Ktouri was Ormenion (cf. Allen, *HCS*, p. 125, and p. 142 below).

31. The Melitaeans also claimed a Hellas (Strabo 9. 432).

32. *HHI*, p. 126, referring to Leaf, *Homer and History*, pp. 110 f.

33. For those who believe in the ship-numbers, it is perhaps worth noting that there were only 2,500 Myrmidons (cf. *Il.* 16. 168–70) as against 6,000 Boeotians (*Il.* 2. 509–10), and the presumably far more numerous followers of Agamemnon, Nestor, Diomedes, and Idomeneus. In fact, although there is some doubt about the entries relating to them, it is noticeable that two of the other great heroes—Aias and Odysseus—have insignificant followings (cf. *Il.* 2. 537 and 637).

34. Cf. Thucydides 2. 102. 2 and Polybius 21. 25. Hammond (*BSA* 32 (1931/2), pp. 131 f.) notes the importance of the Karpenision pass.

THE KINGDOM OF PROTESILAUS

Φυλάκη (2. 695) MAP 7

The exact location of Phylake remains unknown. Strabo (9. 435) says that it was near Phthiotic Thebes, and in historical times Phylake appears as a *κώμη* of Phthiotic Thebes, while its hero is found on some later coins.[1] Two sites have been proposed for it: one is just south of Kitik,[2] but this is rather remote from Phthiotic Thebes; the second is the kastro to the south of the village of Persouphli,[3] on the route between Pherai (Velestino) and Phthiotic Thebes. Both sites are of the 'high mound' type.

The ancient testimony is insufficient for a firm identification, though the second site, being closer to Phthiotic Thebes, is the more likely. But evidence from inscriptions is required—or perhaps the discovery of a half-completed Mycenaean palace (cf. *Il.* 2. 701)!

Πύρασος (2. 695) MAP 7

REFS. *Gazetteer*, No. 489; Wace and Thompson, *PT*, No. 59; *AM* 71 (1956), p. 176; *BCH* 81 (1957), p. 596; *Thessalika* 2 (1959), pp. 29–67; cf. *Ergon* for 1954, 1955, etc.

According to Strabo (9. 435), Pyrasos was the old name for Demetrion, a town which had been razed to the ground by his day, but which had originally lain twenty stades from Phthiotic Thebes, and possessed a good harbour. The identification of the place with the ancient site at Nea Anchialos (H.8 Volos △28 at 676E/936N) is thus virtually certain, especially in view of the later cult of Demeter there (cf. the Homeric description *Δήμητρος τέμενος* in *Il.* 2. 696), for Strabo says there was a grove of Demeter and a sacred precinct two stades from Pyrasos–Demetrion.

The ancient acropolis was the high mound above the harbour, measuring about 110 metres north to south by 80 metres at the top. The south and west slopes have been partially excavated, and rich Neolithic deposits were found, but the later levels have suffered considerably from erosion. On the west slope a few MH, Mycenaean, and Geometric sherds were found, but the Mycenaean pottery was mostly found to the south of the hill, in the flat ground later occupied by the city of 'Christian Thebes'. Here, at a depth of about three metres, MH and Mycenaean (LH IIIA–B) pottery was found in trenches near Basilica Δ.

Ἴτων (2. 696) MAP 7

REFS. *Gazetteer*, No. 493; Wace and Thompson, *PT*, No. 61, and pp. 150–66, with refs. there; Åline, *EMF*, p. 145; Desborough, *LMTS*, p. 130.

Strabo (9. 433) says that Iton was 60 stades from Phthiotic Halos, and Wace,

Droop, and Thompson[4] provisionally identified it with the site at Zerelia (H.7 Farsala △159 at 573E/817N), a high mound lying between two small lakes in the foothills to the south-west of the Krokian plain. Excavation here yielded some MH *Minyan* ware and LH III sherds, and a bronze double axe-head was found on the surface. Classical Itonos is probably to be located on the west side of Karatzadagli, about an hour's walk to the south of Zerelia.[5]

Ἀντρών (2. 697) MAP 7

From Strabo (9. 435) we learn that Antron lay near a submarine reef in the Euboean strait, up the coast from the island of Myonnesos, but south of Pteleon. Antron is called πετρήεις in the *Hymn to Demeter* (line 491), and is also mentioned by Stephanus of Byzantium (s.v.). The site (*Gazetteer*, No. 479: T.8 Atalandi 809E/588N) was discovered by Leake,[6] and visited by us in 1961: there is really no other place on this coast which would fit the directions given by Strabo, and the caves below the cliffs on the shoreward side support the identification.

Parts of the polygonal walling look 'Cyclopean', but we could find no sherds earlier than Hellenistic or Roman, though we were convinced that our failure was entirely due to chance. This is a clear case where a small trial excavation might yield positive results.

Πτελεόν (2. 697) MAP 7

REFS. *Gazetteer*, No. 496; *PAE* 1952, pp. 164–80; *PAE* 1953, pp. 119–27; cf. also *JHS Arch.* and *BCH* reports for 1951–3; Ålin, *EMF*, pp. 145 f.; Desborough, *LMTS*, pp. 130 f.

Ancient Pteleon lay on the rocky hill now called 'Gritsa', on the inner edge of the bay of Pteleon, about three kilometres to the south of the modern village (H.8 Volos 769E/645N). The summit of the hill measures some 350 metres north to south by 200 metres, and here MH and LH sherds (mainly the former) can be picked up, together with local Bronze Age wares. On the lower part of the west slope, or, more precisely, on the lower spur running westward from the hill of Gritsa proper, two tholos-tombs have been found. The westernmost contained LH IIIC:2–Protogeometric vases; the other, about fifty metres away to the south-west, and west of the main road, held contents ranging from LH IIIA to LH IIIC:1.

Yet another tholos, presumably belonging to the Gritsa group, has been found at Ayios Theodoros, on the top of a hill a few hundred metres north of the main road, and overlooking the bay of Pteleon.[7]

The kingdom of Protesilaus in the Catalogue forms a natural geographical unit, extending from the hill country around the later Larisa Cremaste, which divides it from the Kingdom of Peleus, along the western side of the Gulf of Pagasai, to the frontiers of the Kingdom of Eumelos. Of the five places mentioned, two—Pyrasos and Pteleon—were certainly inhabited in the Mycenaean period, and Antron probably was, while the exact location of Phylake and

Iton remains uncertain. Admittedly, Pyrasos and Pteleon were also inhabited in the Early Iron Age, but the absence of Phthiotic Thebes—the most important centre in historical times[8]—and the obscurity of Phylake and Iton suggest that the Catalogue reflects an early period, and probably the Mycenaean.

NOTES ON THE KINGDOM OF PROTESILAUS

1. Head, *Historia Numorum* (2nd edn. 1911), p. 31.
2. Wace and Thompson, *PT*, No. 69.
3. Wace and Thompson, *PT*, No. 37; cf. *RE* xx (1941), pp. 983 f., and *RE*, Suppl. vii. 1022, plan 2. This location is shown on our map.
4. *BSA* 14 (1907/8), p. 199.
5. Philippson, *GL* i. 306, No. 100.
6. *Travels in Northern Greece* iv. 348–51.
7. *Gazetteer*, No. 497: H.8 Volos 754E/633N. The contents included vases of the period LH IIIA/B: *PAE* 1951, pp. 150–4; *PAE* 1952, pp. 181–5; cf. contemporary *JHS Arch.* and *BCH* reports.
8. The site in fact seems to have been inhabited continuously from the Neolithic period: *Gazetteer*, No. 490; *PT*, No. 68 and pp. 166 f.; *PAE* 1907, pp. 166 f.; *PAE* 1908, pp. 163 f.; *AM* 31 (1906), pp. 5 f.; Desborough, *PG*, p. 153.

THE KINGDOM OF EUMELOS

Φεραί (2. 711) MAP 7

REFS. *Gazetteer*, No. 498; Béquignon, *Recherches Archéologiques à Phères* (1937); Kirsten, *RE*, Suppl. vii. 984–1026 (especially plan I on p. 990); Åhlin, *EMF*, p. 142; Desborough, *LMTS*, p. 132.

The acropolis of ancient Pherai (H.8 Volos 611E/052N) is a magoula of the 'high mound' type, with steep sides, about 400 metres north-east to south-west by 100 metres. Mycenaean finds were recorded from the area of the temple,[1] and it was argued that there was continuity of cult here from the Mycenaean period onwards.[2] But the majority of the graves in the necropolis were of the Iron Age.[3] Surface sherds include Neolithic, MH *Grey Minyan*, LH IIIA–B, Geometric, and classical.

As Allen remarks,[4] this is the only Thessalian city of first-rate importance in later times which Homer mentions. The description *παραὶ Βοιβηΐδα λίμνην* might possibly suggest that Lake Boibe was originally more extensive than it is now, since Velestino (the modern town on the site of Pherai) is now a considerable distance from the modern Lake Karla. But the argument cannot be pressed, since the juxtaposition of *Φεράς* and *παραὶ Βοιβηΐδα λίμνην* may be partly due to the exigencies of the metre: Allen[5] takes the description as applying to all the towns in this section.

Βοίβη (2. 712) MAP 7

REFS. *Gazetteer*, No. 499; V. Milojčić, *AA* 1955, pp. 222–30, esp. Abb. 22 on p. 227; *AA* 1960, pp. 150–67, esp. Abb. 2–3 on p. 154 and Abb. 9–10 on p. 163; Cf. *BCH* 84 (1960), pp. 764–5; *BCH* 80 (1956), p. 311; *BCH* 81 (1957), p. 597; *AM* 62 (1937), p. 60 n. 1 and Taf. 37; Åhlin, *EMF*, p. 142.

This place is probably to be identified with the site on the promontory of Petra, opposite the islet of the same name in Lake Karla (the ancient Boibe) (H.8 Volos △119 at 630E/181N). If the circuit-walls are Mycenaean, as Milojčić maintains, this is by far the largest Mycenaean fortress known, since they run for nearly five kilometres. At all events, there is no doubt that the site was occupied in LH III, since there are abundant sherds, and Mycenaean houses and cist-graves have been excavated on one of the hills.

Wace[6] placed Boibe at Kanalia, the village on the east corner of the lake, where some rough 'Pelasgian' walls were found on a rocky hill called 'Palaiokastro' (one of three sites so named in this area). But a party from the British School at Athens[7] which visited the site in 1958 noted nothing of importance, and was inclined to doubt the existence of a Mycenaean settlement here.

Γλαφύραι (2. 712) MAP 7

There is no evidence for the whereabouts of this place. Wace[9] assumed a location near Lake Boibe, and proposed a site at Prophitis Elias, near the village of Kaprena, south of the lake. But the circuit-walls were only 1·25 metres thick, and this hardly suggests the Mycenaean period. The name *Γλαφύραι* itself suggests that it was a seaport,[9] and if it was somewhere near Volos, it might be located at Pevkakia, where there is an important Mycenaean settlement.[10] But this is mere conjecture: the excavator remarked on the traditions of Pelias and Neleus (cf. *Od.* 11. 254 f.), and suggested that the site might be that of ancient Neleia (cf. Strabo 9. 436), 'the city of Neleus before he had to flee from Thessaly'.

Ἰαωλκός (2. 712) MAP 7

REFS. *Gazetteer*, No. 480; Wace and Thompson, *PT*, p. 207; *BCH* 45 (1921), p. 530; *BCH* 46 (1922), pp. 518 f.; *AA* 1922, p. 247; *Ergon* for 1956, pp. 43–50; for 1957, pp. 31–2, cf. *Archaeology* 11 (1958), pp. 13–18; *Ergon* for 1960, pp. 55–61; for 1961, pp. 51–60; (cf. also *JHS Arch.*, *BCH*, and *AJA* reports for these years); Ålin, *EMF*, pp. 143 f.; Desborough, *LMTS*, Index, s.v. 'Iolkos'. (There is a good photograph of the site in Wace and Thompson, *PT*, p. 2, fig. 2.)

The existence of a Mycenaean palace on the Kastro at Volos (H.8 Volos 773E/029N) has long been known, and there can be no doubt that this was the site of the ancient Iolkos. The recent excavations have revealed much of the history of the site in the Mycenaean and Protogeometric periods: the evidence for a catastrophic fire during the LH IIIC:1 period accords with evidence from other Mycenaean capitals in mainland Greece,[11] but there are also indications of continuity from the Mycenaean to the Protogeometric periods on some parts of the site.[12]

The kingdom of Eumelos occupies a good strategic position, commanding the anchorages at the head of the Gulf of Pagasai and the main pass into the Larisa plain. The importance of the area in Mycenaean times is shown by the quantity and quality of the Mycenaean remains, and in historic times by the cities of Pherai and Demetrias–Pagasai.

The limits of the kingdom are, however, hard to define. Wace[13] thought that the lands of Pherai probably included some of the hills to the west 'which are today included in the commune of Velestinos'. Allen[14] has an interesting note on the position of Pereia, where Eumelos' horses were bred (*Il.* 2. 766), but the location of Pereia does not tell us anything more about the boundaries of the kingdom.

The evidence for the occupation of Pherai and Iolkos in the Early Iron Age shows that one cannot assume that the Catalogue here reflects the Mycenaean period, though it is equally clear that there is no evidence which precludes this, and Iolkos itself was certainly a centre of great importance in the Mycenaean period.

NOTES ON THE KINGDOM OF EUMELOS

1. *BCH* 45 (1921), p. 529; cf. *PAE* 1925/6, p. 38.
2. Wrede, *AA* 1926, pp. 429 f. We cannot understand why Desborough says (*LMTS*, p. 132): 'No Mycenaean settlement or tombs have as yet been found here.'
3. Cf. Desborough, *PG*, p. 133. Surface-sherds were collected by Miss D. H. F. Gray and the Hope Simpsons in 1958.
4. *HCS*, p. 139.
5. *HCS*, p. 114.
6. *JHS* 26 (1906), p. 163.
7. Miss D. H. F. Gray and the Hope Simpsons.
8. *JHS* 26 (1906), p. 262; cf. Burr, *NK*, p. 96 n. 9. We show Wace's proposed location on our map.
9. The adjective *γλαφυραί* is constantly used of ships in Homer (e.g. *Il.* 2. 454), and one is also reminded of the ancient conjectures (Strabo 9. 436) about the derivation of the name 'Pagasai' from *ναυπηγία* (of the Argo), and of 'Aphetai' from the *ἀφετήριον* of the Argonauts (cf. Herodotus 7. 193).
10. *Gazetteer*, No. 482: H.8 Volos 782E/007N. *Ergon* for 1957, pp. 32–6; *JHS Arch.* for 1957, p. 12; *BCH* 82 (1958), pp. 749–53; *Archaeology* 11 (1958), pp. 13–18; Ålin, *EMF*, p. 144; Desborough, *LMTS*, pp. 128 f.
11. Cf. Desborough, *LMTS*, pp. 9, 128 and 227: the destruction appears to be later than those further south, and not to have affected the buildings around the palace.
12. Desborough, *LMTS*, pp. 31 f., 136 f., 234 f.
13. Allen, *HCS*, p. 115.
14. *HCS*, pp. 115–16.

THE KINGDOM OF PHILOCTETES

Μηθώνη (2. 716) MAP 7

What little the ancient sources have to say about this place[1] does not enable us to locate it with any confidence, but the identification with the hill of Nevestiki near Lechonia (H. 8 Volos 878E/981N),[2] although only a guess, is at least not inconsistent with the ancient evidence.

The site is an acropolis lying on the north-eastern edge of the fertile plain of Lechonia. It rises about 100 metres above sea level in a fine situation overlooking the Bay of Volos. There are remains of 'Cyclopean' walling on the south side, and prehistoric occupation is indicated by obsidian and coarse micaceous and 'oatmeal' wares. But the recognizable sherds all appear to be classical or Hellenistic, and no Mycenaean has yet been found, although Mycenaean occupation seems probable.[3]

Θαυμακίη (2. 716) MAP 7

Strabo (9. 436) appears to put Thaumakie on the east coast of Magnesia,[4] but, although it has been identified with Theotokou[5] or with some ancient remains near Skiti,[6] there is really no good evidence for either identification. They are both, however, more plausible than Burr's apparent assumption[7] that Thaumakie lay on the east coast of the Gulf of Pagasai.

Μελίβοια (2. 717) MAP 7

This name is normally associated with the site of the Kastro at Kato Polydendri[8] where an inscription was found bearing a dedication to Hermes.[9] The Kastro was partly explored by H. Biesantz,[10] who recorded the walls and sherds of the Greek and Roman periods. We visited the site in 1961: the small acropolis is covered in dense scrub and undergrowth, and it was difficult to search, except on the lower slopes above the promontory. This projects into the sea to the south of the beach of Ayiokambos (a summer resort for the villagers of Ayia and other near-by communities), and the site is well placed to give a wide view of the shores to north and south. It is also worth noting that the beach at Ayiokambos is one of the few places on this whole coast where ancient ships could have been drawn ashore in safety.[11]

The location of Meliboia at the Kastro of Kato Polydendri is, however, uncertain. An inscription containing the name of one *Παρμενίσκα Μενάνδρου Μελιβόισσα* was found at Thanatou[12]—now called Meliboia—about four kilometres to the north-east of Ayia and seven kilometres to the north-west of Kato Polydendri, and Georgiades placed Meliboia at a site between Thanatou and the sea,[13] where he found the ruins of a Byzantine fort, partially constructed of large squared blocks, which he conjectured to have come from an ancient acropolis on the same site. It is this site which is apparently indicated by the 'Meliboia' on Allen's map, although in the text[14] he places Meliboia at the Kastro of Kato Polydendri.

Ὀλιζών (2. 717) MAP 7

REFS. *Gazetteer*, No. 487; *JHS* 26 (1906), pp. 148–9; Stählin, *Die Hellenische Thessalien*, pp. 54 f.; *PAE* 1910, pp. 217 f.

The epithet τρηχεῖα suggests a rugged coastline, and Strabo (9. 436) locates the place on the coast. A plausible guess is that it should be identified with the ancient site at Palaiokastro, a steep hill on the narrow part of the isthmus which connects the Trikeri peninsula with the rest of Magnesia (H.8 Volos 999E/756N).

The summit of the little acropolis measures about 100 by 70 metres, and is surrounded by fortifications made of large blocks. Surface-sherds appear to be classical or Hellenistic, but the site could also be Mycenaean.[15] The identification with Olizon must, however, remain uncertain.

The kingdom of Philoctetes is made up of shreds and patches, and its borders are hard to define, particularly since, if the locations for Methone and Meliboia suggested above are approximately correct, this would appear to deny the Magnetes their access to Pelion (cf. *Il.* 2. 756 f.).[16]

NOTES ON THE KINGDOM OF PHILOCTETES

1. Cf. Scylax, *Periplous* 65; Strabo 9. 436.
2. *Gazetteer*, No. 485; *JHS* 26 (1906), p. 153; Stahlin, *Die Hellenische Thessalien*, p. 53.
3. Miss D. H. F. Gray and the Hope Simpsons visited the place in 1958.
4. Reading ἥ τε Θαυμακία καὶ ὁ Ὀλιζὼν καὶ ἡ Μελίβοια ἃ τῆς ἑξῆς παραλίας ἐστίν for . . . ἣ τῆς ἑξῆς παραλίας ἐστίν.
5. Philippson, *GL* i, No. 144, pp. 161 and 286; *Gazetteer*, No. 488: H.9 Skiathos 118E/789N; Desborough, *LMTS*, pp. 22, 38, 138, and 259.
6. Allen, *HCS*, p. 116 and Map at end; Wace and Stubbings, *CH*, p. 286 fig. 3.
7. *NK*, p. 98 and Skizze 3.
8. Cf. Burr, *NK*, p. 98: Z.8 Ayia 761E/376N.
9. *LAAA* 3 (1910), pp. 157 f., No. 11.
10. *AA* 1959, cols. 78–82 and Abb. 4–8 on cols. 83–8.
11. Cf. Herodotus 7. 188, and Tarn, *JHS* 28 (1908), pp. 210–12.
12. *ADelt.* 5 (1889), p. 92; *JHS* 26 (1906), pp. 143–5; *JHS* 28 (1908), p. 210.
13. *Thessalia*, p. 144.
14. *HCS*, p. 116.
15. It was visited in 1958 by the same party as in n. 3 above.
16. Cf. p. 151 below.

THE ASKLEPIADAI

Τρίκκη (2. 729) MAP 7

REFS. *Gazetteer*, No. 546; *Ergon* for 1958, pp. 68–71; *BCH* 82 (1958), p. 754; *JHS Arch.* for 1958, p. 12; *Thessalika* 2 (1959), pp. 69–79; Åin, *EMF*, p. 142; Desborough, *LMTS*, p. 132.

The name 'Trikke' presumably refers to a city on the site of the modern Trikkala (Z.6 Trikkala 798E/290N), where recent excavations near the church of Ayios Nikolaos have proved occupation from Early Helladic times onwards, though LH I and II appear to be lacking: the range of the Mycenaean seems to be LH IIIA–LH IIIC:1. The centre of the Mycenaean settlement was presumably the kastro itself (PLATE 10*a*), though so far it has not been possible to excavate there, and if this is so, the discovery of Mycenaean pottery at some distance below the slopes of the kastro indicates a considerable extent of occupation.

There is so far no evidence for occupation in the Geometric period, but a Protogeometric or Sub-Mycenaean pithos-burial[1] provides some evidence of continuity into the Early Iron Age.

Ἰθώμη (2. 729) MAP 7

Strabo (9. 437) describes Ithome as lying 'between four fortresses, which lie as it were in a quadrilateral, namely Trikke, Metropolis, Pelinnaion, and Gomphoi', and as belonging to the territory of Metropolis. Leake[2] thought he had identified Strabo's quadrilateral, and placed Ithome at Phanari, about eight kilometres to the north-west of Metropolis. Stählin[3] noted remains of Hellenic walls on the north-west side of the medieval castle above Phanari, but no prehistoric remains have yet been found on the site. The epithet κλωμακόεσσα and the statement by Strabo's source (9. 437) that Ἰθώμη was later called Θώμη (implying an analogy with θωμός = σωρός meaning a 'heap' or 'heap of stones') would suggest a location on one or other of the hills on the western border of the plain, but the identification with Phanari must remain uncertain. However, the tholos-tomb at Metropolis[4] at least shows that this area had been penetrated in Mycenaean times.

Οἰχαλίη (2. 730) MAP 7

Two alternative locations have been proposed for Oichalia, both of which were visited by us in 1961. The first[5] is Kastri, about three kilometres to the north of Neochori and on the right bank of the river of the same name. The conical hill is ringed with circuit-walls of rough stones, and there was certainly an ancient town of moderate size on the lower southern slopes, but we had the impression that this was unlikely to have been a Mycenaean site. Local opinion (unsolicited) strongly supported the identification with Oichalia!

The second site is that of Palaio-Gardiki, near Petroporon. This has been identified as the historical city of Pelinna.[6] It has a strong position, with a fortified acropolis, lying between a marsh on the south, and a rugged mountain on the north, and it dominates the plain which extends to south and west, whereas the site near Neochori is almost completely shut off from the plain.

All we know for certain is that Oichalia lay in the neighbourhood of Trikke (Strabo 10. 448), but one slight piece of evidence in favour of its identification with Pelinna is that the eponymous hero of that city is described by Stephanus of Byzantium (s.v. *Πέλινος*) as an Oichalian. We could find no prehistoric sherds on the site, but were not at all convinced that it could not have been inhabited in prehistoric times.

The kingdom of the Asklepiadai corresponds roughly to the later Histiaiotis. The towns mentioned (if we accept the location of Ithome at Phanari and Oichalia at Palaio-Gardiki as approximately correct) dominate the northern and western flanks of the western Thessalian plain. Owing to the lack of ancient testimony as to the position of Ithome and Oichalia, it will probably never be possible to determine the period reflected by this section of the Catalogue, but the discovery of Mycenaean remains at Trikkala and of the tholos-tomb at Metropolis has shown that a kingdom of the Mycenaean period could be referred to here.

NOTES ON THE KINGDOM OF THE ASKLEPIADAI

1. *Ergon* for 1958, fig. 70.
2. *Travels in Northern Greece* iv. 510.
3. *Die Hellenische Thessalien*, p. 129.
4. *Gazetteer*, No. 545: H.6 Kardhitsa 847E/056N; *AJA* 61 (1958), p. 324; *BCH* 82 (1958), p. 754; *Thessalika* 2 (1959), p. 69; Åkerström-Åkerström? Ålin, *EMF*, p. 142, s.v. 'Georgikon' and 'Tsipousi'; Desborough, *LMTS*, p. 132.
5. Burr, *NK*, p. 100; Stählin, *Die Hellenische Thessalien*, p. 115.
6. *BSA* 5 (1898/9), pp. 20f.

THE KINGDOM OF EURYPYLOS

᾿Ορμένιον and the κρήνη ῾Υπέρεια (2. 734) MAP 7

Strabo (9. 438) identified Ormenion with the later Orminion, which he says lay near the Gulf of Pagasai, and located the Hypereian spring in the city of Pherai (9. 439), though, as he admits in the case of the latter, 'it is then strange that it should be given to Eurypylos'. Assuming these identifications to be wrong, since they would make nonsense of the Catalogue, we can only guess at the location of the places concerned. Georgiades' location of Ormenion at Ktouri,[1] near modern Pharsala,[2] is perhaps the best: there are springs on either side of the acropolis which could be identified with the springs Hypereia and Messeeis.[3] But the identification of Ormenion with Ktouri is still only a guess, and the *κρήνη ῾Υπέρεια* may be a different place altogether—this is the natural way to take the line in the Catalogue.

Ἀστέριον Τιτάνοιό τε λευκὰ κάρηνα (2. 735) MAP 7

With these names the problem is reversed: Asterion and Titanos are usually taken to be two separate towns, but although *κάρηνα* may be used of towns (as in *Il.* 2. 117 and 9. 24), possibly referring to battlements, it is also used of mountain peaks (as in *Il.* 1. 44 and 2. 869). Thus it is possible that the words *Τιτάνοιό τε λευκὰ κάρηνα* should be taken as a further description of the neighbourhood of Asterion.

As for Asterion, it has been deduced[4] from Apollonius Rhodius that the Argonaut Asterion, who was presumably its eponymous hero, was supposed to have lived at Peiresiai, at the confluence of the rivers Apidanos and Enipeus, near Mount Phylleion. This is copied in the Orphic Argonautica (163–5), except that there Peiresiai stands at the junction of the Apidanos with the Peneios. Thus Stephanus of Byzantium equated Asterion with the historical Peiresiai, and Leake[5] reflected that the description of Peiresiai in the *Argonautica* 'may be applied to the hill of Vlokho, which is situated between the junction of the Apidanos with the Enipeus, and that of the united stream with the Peneius' (Z.6 Trikkala △313 KASTRO VLOKHOU at 066E/239N). 'Peiresiae', Leake continues, 'was believed to be the same place as the Homeric Asterium and to have received this appellation from its situation on a high hill, as conspicuous as a star. Nothing can be more apposite to this etymology than the mountain of Vlokho, which by its abruptness, insulated situation, and white rocks attracts the spectator's notice from every part of the surrounding country. If the more ancient parts of the ruins of Vlokho are those of the Homeric Asterium, the words *Τιτάνοιό τε λευκὰ κάρηνα*, which the poet couples with *Ἀστέριον*, were intended doubtless for the conspicuous summit occupied by the acropolis of that city, and the white calcareous rocks of which are well suited to the name Titanus.'

Strabo, however (9. 439), while supporting Leake in his interpretation of the significance of the name 'Titanos',[6] says that the place was near Arne, and this place was equated with Kierion, located by an inscription[7] at Mataranga (H.6 Kardhitsa △183 Ouglari at 035E/081N). Wace[8] was attracted by the idea of equating this with Titanos, for this would complete a hypothetical system of three major fortresses, at Vlokho (Asterion), Mataranga (Titanos = Arne = Kierion), and Ktouri (Ormenion). As Wace says, 'all the three sites . . . are isolated limestone hills lying like islands in the plain, and also any two are easily visible from the third. Consequently they would be the natural sites to occupy for anyone who wished to dominate the western Thessalian plain.'

This view is certainly attractive, especially since both Ktouri and Mataranga were the sites of Mycenaean forts, but the strong traditions associated with Arne–Kierion, and the lack of any tradition precisely equating Arne with Titanos, weaken this link in the chain, and it may be better to take the *Τιτάνοιο λευκὰ κάρηνα* as referring to a range of hills rather than to a town and to identify them with the white limestone hills to the east of Vlokho (Asterion), which form the divide between the western and eastern Thessalian plains.[9]

In the absence of any positive identification of the names in this section of the Catalogue, it is obviously impossible to be at all precise about the boundaries of Eurypylos' kingdom, but it is clear that it is to be located in the south-eastern part of the western plain of Thessaly, between the kingdoms of the Asklepiadai to the west and north-west, of Polypoites to the north-east, of Eumelos to the south-east, and presumably of Peleus to the south. At all events, Eurypylos' kingdom does not appear to encroach upon the territory allotted to any other hero. Again, assuming that the proposed locations for the towns are approximately correct, the Mycenaean finds at Ktouri and Mataranga are at least sufficient to show that it is not impossible to see in this kingdom a reflection of a Mycenaean kingdom.

NOTES ON THE KINGDOM OF EURYPYLOS

1. *Thessalia*, pp. 37 and 213; cf. Wace, quoted by Allen, *HCS*, pp. 125–6.
2. *Gazetteer*, No. 537: H.7 Farsala △211 Khtouri at 222E/063N.
3. Cf. Strabo 9. 432; Allen, *HCS*, pp. 125 f. The people of Pharsalos said that these springs were to be found at what they thought was Homer's 'Hellas': see p. 129 above.
4. *Argonautica*, 1. 35 f.; Allen, *HCS*, p. 123.
5. *Travels in Northern Greece*, iv. 322; Edmonds, *BSA* 5 (1898/9), pp. 21 and 23; Wace, quoted by Allen, *HCS*, pp. 124–5.
6. 'Titanos' means 'white earth', 'gypsum', 'lime', or 'chalk'; cf. Strabo's remarks about *Ἰθώμη/Θώμη* (9. 437).

7. Stephanus of Byzantium (s.v.) identified Kierion with the Thessalian Arne (cf. Thucydides I. 12. 3). For the inscription see *IG* ix 2. 61, and Leake, op. cit., p. 498; for the Mycenaean site see *Gazetteer*, No. 541.

8. Quoted by Allen, *HCS*, pp. 124–5.

9. The 'heutige Dobrudschadag' of Burr, *NK*, p. 102. Allen also takes *Τιτάνοιο λευκὰ κάρηνα* as referring to a mountain (*HCS*, p. 125 and Map at end), but Leake may be right in his assumption that the summit of Vlokho itself is referred to, or Titanos may be the *ὄρος Φυλλήιον* of Apollonius Rhodius (*Argonautica* I. 37), which lay near Peiresiai.

THE KINGDOM OF POLYPOITES

Ἄργισσα (2. 738) MAP 7

REFS. *Gazetteer*, No. 515; Wace and Thompson, *PT*, No. 30; *AA* 30 (1955), pp. 192 f.; *AA* 31 (1956), pp. 141 f.; *AA* 32 (1957), pp. 37–52; *AA* 34 (1959), pp. 36 f.; *Historia* 4 (1955), p. 470; *Thessalika* 2 (1959), p. 69; *BCH* 82 (1958), pp. 754–6; *JHS Arch.* for 1958, p. 12; *Germanica* 36 (1958), pp. 319–24 (Palaeolithic); *JHS Arch.* for 1962/3, p. 23; Ålin, *EMF*, p. 138; Desborough, *LMTS*, pp. 133–4.

Argissa was equated by Strabo (9. 440) with the Argura of his day, and this has now been identified with the remains of an extensive Graeco-Roman city on the north bank of the Peneios, about eight kilometres west of Larissa.[1] The new identification may be regarded as firm, and replaces the outmoded identification with the ruins of Gounitsa.[2]

The prehistoric settlement was centred on the mound of Gremnos (*Κρημνός*), a little to the west of the Graeco-Roman remains (Z.7 Larisa 295E/388N). The mound (PLATE 10*b*) is of great size, much of it man-made deposit, measuring about 350 metres south-west to north-east by 120 metres at the top. Below it on the south is the marshy bed where the river used to run (before a natural diversion to the south). Although the attention of the excavators was focused mainly on the important Palaeolithic and Neolithic strata, there was no lack of MH and LH (ranging from LH IIIB to LH IIIC), and some Protogeometric was also found.

Γυρτώνη (2. 738) MAP 7

REFS. *Gazetteer*, No. 511; *PAE* 1911, pp. 334–7, esp. plan on p. 336; Philippson, *GL* i. 307, No. 183.

It appears from the Roman campaigns against Perseus[3] that the historical city of Gyrtone lay on the *left* bank of the Peneios, although Strabo (7, frag. 14) seems to place it on the *right* bank. It is usually located at the acropolis near the village of Bakraina, which has now been renamed 'Gyrtone' (Z.7 Larisa 186 at 391E/495N).

The site is marked 'Mycenaean to Hellenistic' by Kirsten[4] and, although when we visited it in 1961 we could find no evidence of Mycenaean occupation, we were of the opinion that it could very well have been occupied in Mycenaean times. It has some strategic significance because of its proximity to the Tempe pass.

Ὄρθη (2. 739) MAP 7

This place cannot, unfortunately, be certainly located. Strabo (9. 440) says that 'some have said that Orthe is the acropolis of the Phalannaians' and, if this equation with Phalanna is accepted, then the latter is usually located at Tatar Magoula (Z.7 Larisa △68 at 336E/456N)[5], inhabited in MH and LH IIIB–IIIC:1, and subsequently from classical to Roman times, though so far there is no evidence for continuity of occupation in the Early Iron Age.

But Phalanna has also been located at Kastraki near Turnavo[6] and, in any case, ancient sources other than Strabo[7] show that there was an *independent* city of Orthe in historical times, and this is confirmed by coins.[8] The principal reverse-type of these was a horse springing from a rock, and Wace[9] laid considerable emphasis on this, and on the parallel with the similar type on the coins of Pherai, which is taken as typifying the fountain of Hypereia there. Following this reasoning, he preferred to locate Orthe at Karatsoli,[10] near which 'a large spring named Mati gushes forth from the rock and forms at once a stream sufficient to work several mills'.

It is difficult, however, to decide what weight to place on this reasoning: Thessaly was, after all, famous for its horses, and the meadows near Tatar Magoula would have provided good pasture. But it must be admitted that our judgement is swayed by the desire to reserve the site at Karatsoli for Elone.

'Ηλώνη (2. 739) MAP 7

REFS. *Gazetteer*, No. 517; Wace and Thompson, *PT*, No. 81; Philippson, *GL* i. 305, No. 12; *JHS Arch.* for 1961/2, pp. 30–1.

Whether or not Strabo (9. 441) was right to equate the river Europos of his day with Homer's Titaresios,[11] he describes Elone as 'below Olympos and not far from the river Europos'. The site at Karatsoli (Z.7 Larisa ✝ Moni at 278E/582N) certainly fulfils the first condition, since it lies on the southernmost foothills of the Olympos range. It centres on the hill of Kastri (PLATE 11*a*), which bears the remains of a monastery and chapel of Ayia Paraskevi, north-west of and above the village (now called Argyropouli). There is a good spring near the east foot of the hill.

In 1961 we found considerable quantities of Mycenaean sherds here, especially behind the chapel on the neck which joins Kastri to the higher, rockier hill behind on the north. At this point erosion has created a large pit in which Mycenaean deposits nearly three metres thick can be seen, and in one side a Mycenaean house-wall standing to a height of two metres (PLATE 11*b*). It is plain that the main part of the settlement lay on the monastery-hill (an area about 250 by 100 metres in extent), but we also found some sherds on the higher hill behind—now covered with the remains of sheep-folds and other structures—and this too may have formed part of the citadel. To the north of it there is a steep drop to a ravine below. We recorded (?MH) *Yellow Minyan* and plentiful LH IIIA–C sherds of good quality—the range appeared to be LH IIIA:2 to LH IIIC:1. The classical sherds included good 5th-century B.C. *black-glaze*. The site is impressive, and the Mycenaean sherds cover a wide area. We could find no Protogeometric or Geometric.

The quantity and quality of the Mycenaean remains here, the nature of the site, and its strategic position at the southern end of the Meluna pass, all lend support to its identification with Elone, though not in themselves sufficient to prove it.

Wace[12] wished to place Elone at Magoula (Z.6 Trikkala 085E/575N), but this site seemed to us likely to have been important only in the pre-Mycenaean period, and Strabo's statement (loc. cit.) that the name 'Elone' was later changed to 'Leimone' seems to demand a site where remains of the historical period are also found.

Ὀλοοσσών (2. 739) MAP 7

REFS. *Gazetteer*, No. 519; Philippson, *GL* i. 305, No. 8; *AA* 34 (1959), pp. 85–90 and Abb. 14–16 on pp. 93–4.

There does not seem to be any good reason why Oloosson should not be equated with the historical city of Elasson (Z.6 Trikkala ‡ Moni at 180E/660N).[13] Kirsten[14] marks Elasson on his map as 'Pre-Mycenaean' and 'Mycenaean to Byzantine', but no remains earlier than classical have yet, to our knowledge, been recorded from there. There is, however, a straight-sided *Alabastron* in the Almyros Museum (marked No. 60), apparently of LH IIIB date, labelled Ἐλλασσῶνα, and the example of Trikkala encourages us to hope that definite proof of Mycenaean occupation will one day be forthcoming. We have not been to the site, but from a distance it looked eminently suitable for a Mycenaean fortress guarding the Meluna pass, and the Mycenaean site at Argyropouli, at the southern end of the pass, is an indication of its importance in Mycenaean times.

Polypoites and Leonteus are referred to as Lapithai elsewhere in the *Iliad* (12. 128), as are their subjects (*Il.* 12. 181; cf. *Od.* 21. 297), and the Catalogue tells us (*Il.* 2. 742 f.) that Polypoites' father, Perithoos, had driven the 'Shaggy Pherai' from Pelion into the territory of the Aithikes.[15] This is, of course, a reference to the wars of the Lapiths and Centaurs,[16] and the kingdom of Polypoites was in fact long-established in the traditions. In the Catalogue, assuming that the location of Gyrtone at the site of the historical Gyrton, Elone at Argyropouli, and Oloosson at Elasson, are correct, the kingdom is of great strategic importance, controlling as it does two of the principal exits from the Olympus range.

NOTES ON THE KINGDOM OF POLYPOITES

1. Cf. *BCH* and *JHS* reports for 1958, and *AA* 32 (1957), loc. cit. A tholos-tomb has recently been found near Larissa itself (*JHS Arch.* for 1963/4, p. 24).
2. Burr, *NK*, p. 102, following Stählin, *Die Hellenische Thessalien*, p. 100.
3. Livy 42. 54; Leake, *Travels in Northern Greece* iii. 381 f.
4. Ap. Philippson, *GL* i. 307, No. 183.
5. *Gazetteer*, No. 514; Wace and Thompson, *PT*, No. 36; Philippson, *GL* i. 307, No. 184; *BCH* 80 (1956), p. 311; *Historia* 4 (1955), p. 471; *Thessalika* 2 (1959), p. 69; *AA* 30 (1955), p. 221; Åလin, *EMF*, p. 139.

6. *AA* 35 (1960), col. 169 and 167 Abb. 13; cf. *AA* 30 (1955), col. 195 Abb. 5 for a map of the area.

7. Pliny, *NH* 4. 32; Stephanus of Byzantium, s.v. Ὄρθη; Hesychius, s.v. Ὄρθη.

8. Head, *Historia Numorum* (2nd edn. 1911), p. 303.

9. Cf. Allen, *HCS*, p. 129 n. 2.

10. See above, on Elone.

11. *Il.* 2. 751: see below, p. 149.

12. Quoted by Allen, *HCS*, p. 129 n. 2.

13. Oloosson has been placed at the hill of Mikros Elias near the village of Tsaritsani (*Gazetteer*, No. 518: Z.7 Larisa 218E/640N; cf. *PAE* 1914, p. 165). Arvanitopoullos thought he had found some small tholos-tombs to the north-east of the hill, and that there was a Mycenaean or Archaic settlement there. But it transpires that the only pottery that he actually *saw* on the hill was rough fragments of unpainted coarse ware, mainly from *pithoi*. Hope Simpson and his wife confirmed this on a visit in 1958, and concluded that the ancient remains had been much exaggerated. The Neolithic sherds (if they are really from this site) reported by Wace and Thompson (*PT*, p. 12) are, however, unimpeachable, and it is noticeable that Philippson only marks the site as 'Pre-Mycenaean'.

14. Philippson, *GL*, i. 305, No. 8.

15. Somewhere near the sources of the Peneios according to Strabo (7. 327).

16. Cf. Allen, *HCS*, p. 129.

THE KINGDOM OF GOUNEUS

Κύφος (2. 748) MAP 7

The location of Kyphos is, unfortunately, quite unknown, and the desperate straits to which the later Greeks were reduced in attempting to place it are illustrated by Stephanus of Byzantium's endeavour (s.v. *Γοννοί*) to connect Gouneus with Gonnos.

Δωδώνη and the Τιταρήσιος (2. 750–1) MAP 7

As Allen says,[1] the Enienes and the Peraiboi are 'wandering names', found in entirely different places in the historical period. Here they are said to live around 'wintry Dodona' and the 'lovely Titaresios', but the conjunction of these two names produces what is really an insoluble problem. For, if we are to reject Strabo's Thessalian Dodona near Scotoussa,[2] and to refuse to believe in any Dodona other than the Thesprotian—as we surely must—it follows that the Enienes and the Peraiboi must be located in the far north-west of Thessaly, and this is where Leake proposed to locate the river Titaresios also.[3]

Strabo, however (9. 441), identified the Titaresios with the Europos, and, although Allen[4] made a spirited attack on this identification on the basis of Leake's observations, his explanation of the natural phenomenon observed in *Il.* 2. 752–5 is perhaps based on a rather forced rendering of the epithet *ἀργυροδίνης* (applied to the Peneios): this means, literally, 'silver-eddying', and undertones of mud or pounded milkstone are not necessarily implied. Georgiades[5] recorded a similar if less spectacular phenomenon at the point of junction between the Europos and the Peneios: it was simply that, at first, the two streams did not appear to mix, and that for some distance they could be observed separately. Moreover, the gorge of the Europos (Sarandoporos) *is* of Stygian aspect, as Heuzey remarked.

Nevertheless, although there is no conclusive reason why the Enienes and the Peraiboi should not have spread over all the hill-country from the head-waters of the Peneios as far east as the Europos, this does give Gouneus rather an amorphous realm, and one, moreover, which appears to collide with that of Polypoites, since, if Elone and Oloosson are correctly located at Argyropouli and Elasson respectively,[6] we should expect Polypoites' kingdom to stretch at least as far as the Europos too. It is thus, perhaps, best to abandon Strabo's identification of the Titaresios with the Europos, and to cling to Dodona as the one fixed point in Gouneus' realm, locating the Titaresios somewhere near there also.

A certain amount of prehistoric pottery and a Late Bronze Age sword have been found at Dodona,[7] but the settlement is of a local Bronze Age character with pottery mainly of MH shapes. The earliest objects from the shrine[8] belong to the Late Geometric or Archaic periods. Other Bronze Age finds have been made in Epirus at Kastritsa,[9] Perama,[10] Grimpiani,[11] and Kalpaki,[12] but, apart from some very poor imitations of Mycenaean *Kylikes* at Kastritsa,[13] specifically Mycenaean finds consist of bronze weapons—if these are really Mycenaean[14]—and probably these indicate 'trade' imports and not settlement.

NOTES ON THE KINGDOM OF GOUNEUS

1. *HCS*, pp. 130–2.
2. Kineas (ap. Strabo 7, frag. 1 Meineke) implied that there was a city called Dodona in Thessaly, and that the oracle was transferred from there to Epirus; Strabo (7, frag. 1a Meineke) says that the oracle was once near the city of Scotoussa.
3. *Travels in Northern Greece* i. 415 and iv. 278.
4. *HCS*, pp. 133f.
5. *Thessalia* (1894), p. 23, quoted by Allen, *HCS*, p. 134.
6. See above, pp. 146–7.
7. *Gazetteer*, fig. 2, No. 1: Z.4 Ioannina 955E/371N; cf. esp. *Ergon* for 1959, fig. 80, and *AE* 1956, pp. 140–1; cf. also Philippson, *GL* ii. 667, No. 86; *BSA* 32 (1931/2), pp. 131f.; *Ergon* for 1955, pp. 54–8; for 1956, pp. 64–8; for 1957, pp. 42–6; for 1958, pp. 90–5; for 1959, pp. 75–7.
8. See, especially, *Ergon* for 1956, p. 58 fig. 55: a bronze figurine of a warrior in pre-Daedalic style.
9. *Gazetteer*, fig. 2, No. 2; *PAE* 1951, pp. 173–83; *PAE* 1952, pp. 362–86; *AE* 1956, esp. p. 151; *JHS* 72 (1952), p. 101; *JHS* 73 (1953), p. 121.
10. *Gazetteer*, fig. 2, No. 3; *AE* 1956, pp. 131f.
11. *Gazetteer*, fig. 2, No. 4; *AE* 1956, p. 131; Desborough, *LMTS*, Index, s.v. 'Gribiana'.
12. *Gazetteer*, fig. 2, No. 5; *AE* 1956, pp. 114–53; *AJA* 58 (1954), p. 236; Desborough, *LMTS*, Index, s.v. 'Kalbaki'.
13. Illustrated in *PAE* 1951, p. 182 fig. 7, and *PAE* 1952, p. 365 fig. 3.
14. Desborough, *LMTS*, pp. 37–8, 66, 102; Dakaris *AE* 1956, pp. 143f.

THE KINGDOM OF PROTHOOS

There does not seem to be very much room for Prothoos and his Magnetes between the realms of Philoctetes, Eumelos, and Polypoites, particularly since, as we saw,[1] if the locations proposed for Meliboia and Methone in Philoctetes' kingdom are approximately correct, the Magnetes are apparently shut off from *Πήλιον εἰνοσίφυλλον* (cf. *Il.* 2. 757–8), assuming this to refer, strictly, to the southern part of the Ossa–Pelion range.[2] Perhaps, however, we should suppose that the name *Πήλιον* is used loosely to refer to what are really the northern and western flanks of Mt. Ossa. If this is the case, we can locate Prothoos in the Vale of Tempe and the foothills and coastal strip to the north and south of the mouth of the Peneios. It is no wonder that no towns are named for so restricted an area, though at least the Magnetes (with their 40 ships!) have access to the sea—which is more than can be said for Polypoites, Gouneus, the Asklepiadai, or Eurypylos.[3]

NOTES ON THE KINGDOM OF PROTHOOS

1. Above, pp. 138–9.
2. As Miss Gray once remarked, Allen (*HCS*, pp. 137–8 and Map at end) seems to evade the difficulty by piling Pelion on Ossa—an error unfortunately repeated in Wace and Stubbings, *CH*, p. 286, fig. 3.
3. It is noticeable that there is no mention of people called *Θεσσαλοί* in the Catalogue. This is in accordance with the tradition that the Thessalians only entered the area *after* the Trojan War (cf., for example, Thucydides 1. 12. 3). Desborough (*LMTS*, pp. 234 f., 250 and n. 3) tentatively dates the arrival of the Thessalians, on *archaeological* grounds, to the 12th century B.C.

PART III · CONCLUSIONS

> The Achaean Catalogue depicts a world which stands already in the twilight between the long day of Bronze Age civilization and the darkness of the age of migrations.
>
> N. G. L. HAMMOND

THE Catalogue of the Ships poses a special problem for the historian—the question which period of Greek prehistory, if any, it reflects. But, in attempting to answer this question, we are immediately faced by the fact that we cannot even locate all the places mentioned in the Catalogue, and will probably never be able to do so. It is possible that more inscriptions may turn up, perhaps even Linear B tablets, which will enable us finally to locate all the places mentioned, but it is unlikely, and especially so in the case of that limbo of lost places which were unknown even to the Greeks of historical times.[1] We can probably assume that these places are not fictitious: they are intermingled with quite ordinary, real places in the text of the Catalogue, and later Greek writers always assumed that they were real enough. But in the absence of any clues, however tenuous, to their whereabouts, there is clearly no way in which we can set about locating them.

If, however, we do not even know where some of the places mentioned in the Catalogue were, we can hardly know anything of their history, and there will thus always be an unknown factor in any discussion of the period reflected. But even if we ignore these 'lost' places, and concentrate on those which can be more or less securely located, we still cannot really come to any clear-cut conclusions about the period reflected, for the Greece of the Catalogue will resemble the Greece of any period to some extent, since most of the places mentioned in it were inhabited throughout antiquity—many, for that matter, are inhabited to this day.

There are, however, a number of clues which clearly suggest that in the Catalogue we have a reflection, however partial and distorted, of Mycenaean Greece, and the most important of these is that the Catalogue refers to several places which can be fairly securely located, and which, on our present evidence at least, were inhabited in the Mycenaean period, but were not inhabited subsequently—or at least not until after the eighth century B.C., during which the Catalogue, together with the rest of the *Iliad*, probably reached substantially the form in which we have it.[2] Eutresis in Boeotia is the best example, but Krisa (Ayios

Georgios) in Phocis, Dorion (Malthi) and Pylos (Ano Englianos) in Messenia, and, perhaps, Hyrie (Dramesi) in Boeotia are others. There are not many such places, but for obvious reasons there cannot be: as we said above, most of the places mentioned in the Catalogue were inhabited throughout antiquity, and places deserted after the Mycenaean period are precisely those which are not likely to be locatable now. But that there are *any* such places is very difficult to explain unless the Catalogue here at least preserves Mycenaean tradition.

Moreover, these places, however few they may be, take on a much greater significance when it is realized that there is not a single place mentioned in the Catalogue which can be shown *not* to have been inhabited in the Mycenaean period. Precise statistics cannot really be given because of uncertainties about the location of many of the places concerned,[3] but it is probably fair to say that something like three-quarters of those which can be plausibly located have already been shown to have been occupied in Mycenaean times; and certainly, of those which have been *excavated*, none has so far failed to produce evidence of Mycenaean occupation.[4] Conversely, although we would be the first to admit that *negative* conclusions from surface sherding are unreliable, the fact remains that, of the locatable places where evidence for Mycenaean occupation has been found, about a third have so far failed to produce any evidence for Protogeometric or Geometric occupation.

Even the fact that the Catalogue mentions a number of places the whereabouts of which was unknown to the Greeks of historical times is itself an indication that the Catalogue reflects the Mycenaean period, for the most plausible explanation of their presence in the Catalogue is that they were real places which were destroyed or deserted when Mycenaean civilization came to an end. Excavation is constantly revealing evidence for the destruction and desertion of sites during the last century of the Mycenaean Age, and there are dozens of Mycenaean sites in Greece to which we can ascribe no ancient name. We should not fall into the error of equating such sites with Homeric names where there is no evidence for the equation, but they demonstrate clearly that places could be 'lost' in the collapse of Mycenaean civilization. It is very much harder to account for these 'lost' places if we suppose that the Catalogue reflects post-Mycenaean Greece, for, although there undoubtedly were local quarrels[5] which might account for the desertion of some sites, there does not appear to have been any widespread catastrophe such as is needed to account for the passing into oblivion of so many places: about a quarter of the places mentioned in the Catalogue fall into this category.

It may also be argued that the Catalogue betrays its Mycenaean origins in its failure to mention some of the important towns of historical Greece. Most of the great cities of historical times are, to be sure, mentioned, but this is only to be expected since many of the factors which made them important later must already have obtained in the Mycenaean period,[6] but Megara, Phlious, Chaeronea, Larisa Cremaste, Phthiotic Thebes, Pharsalos, and Larissa are examples of important historical centres which the Catalogue omits. Of course, some or all of these places may be referred to under another name—and their inhabitants certainly affected to think so[7]—but even then the change of name would require explanation, and the collapse of Mycenaean civilization would appear to be the most plausible.

However, too much should not be made of this argument, since the Catalogue equally appears to omit some places which were important in the Mycenaean period, such as Dendra and Gla.[8] It should be borne in mind that the Catalogue does not even purport to be a complete gazetteer of Greece: we might just as well argue that Herodotus' list of the states which sent ships to Salamis cannot reflect fifth-century Greece because it omits certain important fifth-century cities! When so much is unknown about the origins and transmission of the Catalogue, it is dangerous to argue from what it does *not* say; rather, we should look at what it *does* say about Greece. The only positive argument which could be advanced against the theory that the Catalogue reflects Mycenaean Greece, would be that a number of places mentioned in it did not exist in Mycenaean times and, as we have seen, our present evidence provides no basis for such an argument.

When we turn from the individual places mentioned in the Catalogue to the political divisions which it implies, we reach far more doubtful ground. The trouble here is that the nature of our evidence about Mycenaean Greece is such that in only two cases—the states which had Knossos and Pylos respectively as their administrative centres—do we really know anything about the extent of Mycenaean states. Indeed, if the generally accepted date for the Knossos Linear B tablets is the correct one,[9] they date from at least a century before the Trojan War, and obviously have little relevance to Idomeneus' kingdom in the Catalogue.

We are left, then, with Pylos, and here at least the date of the tablets is certain, and must fall within a generation or two of the time ostensibly depicted by the Catalogue. It must be admitted that, at first sight, there seems to be little resemblance between the realm of Nestor and the state administered from the palace at Ano Englianos: as we have seen,[10] most of the places mentioned in the Pylian section of the Catalogue do not seem to be referred to in the tablets, and Nestor's realm was apparently less extensive than the state which emerges from a study of the tablets. This is disturbing, and particularly so if we are to believe that the Catalogue actually reflects Greece as it was at the time of the historical

Trojan War (i.e. LH IIIB).[11] But, as we argued in the discussion of the Pylian section of the Catalogue, too much should not be made of the differences between the Pylos of the tablets and the Pylos of the Catalogue: the tablets themselves give us, at best, only a partial and uncertain picture of a Mycenaean state in the last year of its existence,[12] and the Catalogue may, after all, reflect a period either *before* or *after* that year.[13] The tablets certainly do not prove that Nestor's kingdom does not reflect Mycenaean Pylos.

If we forget about the tablets, we are left with no external evidence at all from the Mycenaean period to determine whether or not the political divisions implied by the Catalogue reflect those of Mycenaean Greece. Nevertheless, it is at least immediately obvious that they do not, in many cases, correspond to those of historical Greece: for example, although there were certain loose groupings of cities in the historical period, such as the Boeotian or Arcadian Leagues, and Herodotus, for instance, could talk of 'Phocians' or 'Locrians',[14] in general most of the cities grouped together under various princes in the Catalogue were later completely independent of each other, and there was certainly nothing later corresponding to the kingdoms of Agamemnon, Diomedes, Nestor, or Elephenor, to say nothing of the island-kingdoms of Odysseus or Meges in the west, or Pheidippos and Antiphos in the east. We must then ask, first, do these kingdoms reflect real political divisions which had once existed but had passed away before the historical period, and, secondly, if they do, at what period did these real political divisions exist?

To the first question, unfortunately, we can provide no conclusive answer, but the reality of most of the *places* mentioned in the Catalogue suggests that the way in which they are divided among the various heroes, also reflects reality: it is possible that they were divided in this way by imaginative poets, but it would be a little odd. Moreover, although at first sight many of the heroic kingdoms might appear to be what poets at any period might readily imagine, it is difficult to think of their inventing anything quite so strange as, for example, the kingdom of Agamemnon,[15] or the three *separate* kingdoms in the Dodecanese. It is difficult also, as Page has pointed out,[16] to imagine poets steeped in the traditions which lie behind the *Iliad* inventing, for important heroes like Achilles or Odysseus, the comparatively insignificant kingdoms accorded to them by the Catalogue. It is even more difficult, for that matter, to imagine their relegating Ajax, without good reason, to his lonely perch on Salamis.[17]

The probability is, then, that the political divisions implied by the Catalogue reflect a real situation which once obtained in Greece, and, if this is the case, it is most likely that this real situation obtained in the Mycenaean era, for we can hardly account for the differences between the political map drawn by the Catalogue and that of historical times except by supposing that the changes occurred when Mycenaean civilization collapsed. In short, the changes in the political map would have occurred at the same time as many of the places mentioned in the Catalogue were destroyed or deserted, and this seems likely enough.

Our final argument for supposing that the Catalogue reflects Mycenaean Greece is, as Thucydides said of the ultimate cause of the Peloponnesian War, ἀφανεστάτη λόγῳ. It is a feeling, derived from our knowledge of the characteristics of Mycenaean sites, that the majority of the places referred to in the Catalogue are typical *Mycenaean* sites. In our search for Catalogue cities we have been continually astonished at the way in which, with only the slightest clues to guide us, we have suddenly found ourselves on a Mycenaean site where a Catalogue-city ought to be. Between us we have now visited all but one or two of the places mentioned in the Catalogue and, with rare exceptions, we have invariably found an easily defensible, acropolis-type hill, usually with a good water-supply and either commanding good agricultural land or having some other strategic significance. Of course, this description could equally well be applied to the majority of historical Greek cities, and it is particularly necessary for more field-work to be carried out to determine the pattern of 'Dark Age' settlement. But the impression we have is that, although the later Greeks often continued to make use of the Mycenaean citadels, such sites were not as typical of later periods as they are of the Mycenaean. At Thisbe, for example, it appears that the Mycenaean town centred on the acropolis now called the Palaiokastro, whereas the later city lay on the plateau-like lower hill on the south side of the modern village.[18] Other examples of a similar shift in the focus of settlement can be seen at Hermione[19] and Aigeira.[20] In these particular places, clearly, we cannot just assume that the Homeric name refers to the Mycenaean town rather than to the later city, but they do suggest a slightly different pattern of settlement as between the Mycenaean and later periods, and the fact that the places mentioned in the Catalogue seem to conform to the Mycenaean type rather than the later constitutes a valid, though perhaps subjective, argument in support of the conclusion that in the Catalogue we can discern a reflection of Mycenaean Greece.

All in all, then, it is reasonable to suppose that the Catalogue reflects the Mycenaean period, and not some later period. This is the simplest hypothesis to account for the mention in the Catalogue of places which were inhabited in Mycenaean times but were then abandoned and lost, at least until after the Catalogue must have reached substantially its present form. It explains why the Catalogue refers to many places which were unknown in historical times, and why the political divisions it implies are, in some cases, unlike those of historical Greece. On the other side, there appears to be nothing which demonstrably refers to post-Mycenaean times, and when parts of it *must*, on our present evidence, refer to the Mycenaean period, and when none of it cannot, it seems perverse to deny that all or most of it does.

The most plausible way to account for the knowledge of Mycenaean Greece embodied in the Catalogue is to suppose that oral poets composing their songs after the decay of Mycenaean civilization inherited a list or lists of heroes and places which had come into existence, in some form, during the Mycenaean Age, and which preserved names which were unknown to them, and traces of a political situation which no longer existed in their day. The only real alternative is to suppose that the Catalogue took shape during the 'Dark Ages', but that there were traditions about certain places which were strong enough to secure a reference to them in the Catalogue, even though they no longer existed.[21] But although this is, perhaps, conceivable in the case of places like Pylos, Dorion, Krisa, and Eutresis, which obviously did have strong mythological associations, it does not seem very likely in the case of places like Eilesion, Arne, Mideia, and Nisa in Boeotia, or Rhipe, Stratie, and Enispe in Arcadia. In fact there is surely no other way to account for the preservation of the memory of so many obscure and defunct places than to suppose that their names were passed down from generation to generation in oral poetry.

Page is, indeed, probably right in suggesting[22] that the Catalogue embodies Mycenaean tradition in a purer form than the *Iliad* as a whole. As he says: 'The *Iliad* is the final product of a continuous development over a very long period of time, whereas the Catalogue, being essentially nothing but a list of names, has naturally changed comparatively little throughout the same period.' A list of heroes and places would, perhaps, have been less liable to change than details of weapons, armour, social and political organization, and the like, but to describe the Catalogue as 'essentially nothing but a list of names', is to undervalue its qualities as poetry: the names themselves have a glamour and mystery all their own and, as Page himself points out,[23] many of the epithets which occur in the Catalogue are unique and colourful. It is indeed not surprising that, for example, Lord Peter Wimsey should have 'delivered himself with fair accuracy, of a page or so of Homer's Catalogue of the Ships', when he had to think of something solemn and impressive to declaim,[24] or that elderly civil servants should recite it as a cure for insomnia![25] We can well imagine that as time went on poets felt that there was something almost mystical about this majestic parade of vanished people and places.

The Catalogue's apparent independence of the rest of the *Iliad* also suggests that it embodies Mycenaean tradition perhaps more purely than the Homeric poems as a whole. We could perhaps hardly have expected most of the places mentioned in it to be referred to elsewhere and, of all the heroes it records, only nine in fact fail to obtain at least a 'mention in dispatches' during the story of the quarrel between Agamemnon and Achilles.[26] But some of the peoples and heroes prominent in the Catalogue are of little or no importance elsewhere in the *Iliad*: more than a third of the places—and 200 of the ships for that matter—are assigned to the Boeotians and their neighbours,[27] but apart from Aias, son of Oileus, they play an insignificant part in the story. The Arcadians, for all their numbers and their knowledge of war (cf. *Il.* 2. 610–11), are never mentioned again; two of the four commanders of the Epeians, Thalpios and Polyxeinos, do not reappear, even to be killed; Nireus does not take advantage of Achilles' absence to flaunt his good looks (cf. *Il.* 2. 673–4), and his neighbours, Pheidippos and Antiphos, are also nowhere to be seen, while the sole function of many of the Thessalian barons seems to be to bring confusion to the Catalogue itself. Conversely the Catalogue appears to know nothing of the *Iliad*'s Patroklos, Teuker, or Antilochos, to say nothing of some of the commanders in the 'little catalogue' (*Il.* 13. 689 f.).

Page also follows Leaf in claiming[28] that 'the Catalogue and the *Iliad* are in most violent disagreement about the nature and extent of the kingdoms of three of the principal heroes—Achilles, Odysseus and Agamemnon'. We have argued[29] that the disagreements are in fact more apparent than real, but it remains true, and significant, that the Catalogue's account of the realms of these three heroes has clearly been unaffected by the parts they play in the story of the Wrath, and the same would appear to be true of Ajax.[30]

But the independence of the Catalogue in relation to the rest of the *Iliad* is not merely shown by the differences between them: 'It is indeed immediately obvious', as Page says,[31] 'that the Catalogue was not originally designed to occupy its present place in the *Iliad*.' In fact it clearly originally described, not the marshalling of the Greek army for battle in the tenth year of the war, but the assembling of the Greek forces at the beginning of the war: the size of the contingents is consistently expressed in terms of numbers of *ships*, although the description is ostensibly of the preliminaries to a battle on land,[32] and even the numbers of men, where given, are clearly intended to be the full strengths of contingents, not their strengths after nine years of war—though we could allow a certain poetic licence here. Some attempt has been made to harmonize the description with its present place in the *Iliad*, it is true: we are told, for example, that the Myrmidons were not actually present at this battle because of Achilles' withdrawal (*Il.* 2. 686–94), and that Protesilaus and

Philoctetes no longer commanded their respective forces, because the one had been killed as he leaped ashore—first of all the Achaeans to land (*Il.* 2. 699 f.)—the other because he had been left behind on Lemnos (*Il.* 2. 721 f.). Other lines are perhaps more suited to the impending land-battle than they would have been to forces assembling in Aulis Bay,[33] but Page probably goes too far in regarding as late additions most of the supplementary information about heroes given in the Catalogue:[34] apart from the passages referred to above, designed to fit the Catalogue into its present place in the *Iliad*, we have no real warrant for supposing that any of the rest are late. We should not just assume that there was an original Mycenaean Catalogue which simply gave a bare list of heroes, peoples, and places—indeed, such an assumption would bring us dangerously close to the 'muster-list' theory which Page rightly rejects.[35] Nevertheless, in general it is clear that a description originally of the gathering of the Greeks before they set out for Troy has been 'lifted' for its present dramatic purpose in the story of the Wrath.

Many scholars think that the Catalogue was only included in the story of the Wrath at a late stage in its development, and it must be admitted that the fact that it still betrays its original function is strong ground for supposing that it had not been included in its present position long before the *Iliad* reached the form in which it has come down to us. Whether or not this is, as Page claims,[36] 'a clear proof that the present form of our text owes something to editorial arrangement' need not concern us here, but he is certainly right to stress[37] that the question whether the Catalogue is in any sense an 'interpolation' has no bearing on the question of the age of the Catalogue itself and, as he clearly saw,[38] the Catalogue's independence of the rest of the *Iliad*, together with the evidence that it reflects Mycenaean rather than post-Mycenaean Greece, shows that it is 'substantially an inheritance from the Mycenaean era' which has 'survived independently of that version of the story which culminates in our *Iliad*'.

Some have even supposed that the Catalogue derives ultimately from an actual muster-list of the forces which sacked the historical Troy,[39] and this theory has derived support from a number of Linear B tablets from Pylos which possibly record certain military dispositions.[40] There is, to be sure, no doubt that people accustomed to the detail and intricacy of Linear B accounting *could* have drawn up a muster-list of contingents for an overseas expedition and, to judge from their attention to such things, they might very well have done so—though not perhaps on clay tablets![41] But, as Page saw,[42] the idea that the Catalogue actually stems from such a list is far-fetched: are we really to think that somehow or other a bard or bards—who would probably not have been able to read Linear B in any case[43]—acquired a muster-list and turned it into verse? It is much more likely that the Catalogue began as it ended, as poetry.

More difficult is the question whether, assuming that there really was a Mycenaean expedition against Troy VIIa, as was probably the case, the Catalogue, whether or not it goes back to an actual muster-list, in any sense preserves a record of those who took part. It is certainly difficult to believe in the numbers of ships for a start:[44] the numbers from Thessaly seem out of all proportion to the rest, especially since four of the Thessalian kingdoms have no seaboard—no suggestion here that Agamemnon, or anyone else,[45] lent the ships, as there is in the case of the Arcadians (cf. *Il.* 2. 612–14). There is, too, a suspicious ring about the constant refrain *τῷ δ' ἅμα τεσσεράκοντα μέλαιναι νῆες ἕποντο*,[46] while such contrasts as those between the 9 ships of Rhodes and the 33 from the neighbouring islands, or the 11 ships of Eumelos and the 30s and 40s of the other Thessalian princes, are hard to explain. Moreover, although the evident prosperity and systematic organization of the great Mycenaean centres suggest that they were probably capable of building and manning even as many as a hundred ships of some kind,[47] it is difficult to believe that the Greece of the thirteenth century B.C. either could or would have mounted an overseas expedition of anything like 1,186 ships of any kind. Only in one or two cases, unfortunately, does the Catalogue record the numbers of men in the various contingents, but if we suppose that the average complement of a ship was something like the mean between the 120 *κοῦροι Βοιωτῶν* in each of their ships (*Il.* 2. 509–10), and the 50 rowers in each of Philoctetes' (*Il.* 2. 719–20, cf. 16. 169–70), the total number of soldiers in the Greek army would have been over 100,000: even a total of nearly 60,000, if we suppose that 50 was the normal complement of a ship, seems far too high. Certainly, if the Catalogue does preserve a substantially accurate record of the forces involved, the Greeks took a sledge-hammer to crack a comparatively small nut.[48]

Nor is it really any easier to believe that the Catalogue even preserves, without much exaggeration, the *extent* of the confederacy which destroyed Troy VIIa. The evident cultural unity of LH IIIB *may* indicate a political unity,[49] and the references in Hittite documents of the fourteenth and thirteenth centuries B.C. to a state called 'Aḫḫijavā', if they do refer to mainland Greece,[50] show that it was a power to be reckoned with even by the Hittites. But it is still difficult to believe in co-operation, on the scale indicated by the Catalogue, in an overseas military expedition. Moreover, if the Catalogue does preserve a substantially accurate record of the confederacy, we should expect it faithfully to reflect Mycenaean Greece at the time of the destruction of Troy VIIa. Some scholars believe that it does: Huxley, for example, on the basis of an examination of the entries relating to Pylos, Boeotia, Athens, the

Dodecanese, and Crete, concludes that the Catalogue precisely reflects the time of the historical Trojan War.[51] But the arguments are largely inconclusive: in the case of the Pylian entry, it is questionable whether much reliance can be placed on Strabo's statement (8. 359) that it was only after the Trojan War that Lakedaimon grew weak and the Neleids occupied the territory around the Messenian Gulf: it is suggested that this is the period reflected by the tablets, while the Catalogue reflects the period before this, when Neleid power was confined to western Messenia and Agamemnon ruled the Pamisos valley, presumably through his brother Menelaus. But although the Catalogue does seem to confine Nestor's kingdom to western Messenia this could reflect a time of Neleid decline *after* the Trojan War (cf. Diodoros 15. 66. 2), and it certainly says nothing about either Agamemnon's or Menelaus' ruling any territory in Messenia. The reference to Ὑποθῆβαι in the Catalogue (*Il.* 2. 505) only provides a *terminus post quem* in the sack of the palace, as we have seen, and even this has been complicated by recent discoveries,[52] while the reference to the Boeotians themselves perhaps suggests a late date.[53] Similarly, the Athenian entry, even if it does imply that the synoecism of Attica has taken place—which is doubtful[54]—again only provides a *terminus post quem,* for it is dangerous to rely on the fact that the entry does not mention Pylian refugees or the refortification of the acropolis to prove that it must pre-date the sack of Pylos and the troubles of the late thirteenth century B.C. Finally, the entries relating to the Dodecanese and Crete could equally well be said to reflect the period after the Trojan War as the time of the destruction of Troy: the fact that the Dodecanese is divided into three separate kingdoms, of which that of Pheidippos and Antiphos is the most important if we are to put any faith in the ship-numbers, may reflect the loosening of ties which is detectable in the pottery of the twelfth century B.C.,[55] while the few places in Idomeneus' kingdom actually mentioned by name, and the reference to Phaistos and, particularly, Gortyn, may also reflect the twelfth century.[56]

Elsewhere the Catalogue seems to point more clearly to the period of Mycenaean decline. Desborough's recent book[57] has shed a flood of light on this hitherto neglected era. He shows that while the destructions at the end of LH IIIB brought to an end the cultural unity of the preceding period, and were followed by widespread depopulation and the flight of refugees to other areas, the invaders, whoever they were, did not settle in the parts of Greece they had devastated. Instead, the destroyed sites were either left deserted or were reoccupied by very much the same sort of people as had occupied them before. Even in some of the worst-hit areas, such as the Argolid, the Mycenaean way of life went on, and there was even a measure of recovery, though 'only a shadow of the former greatness remained',[58] while many areas—eastern Attica, Thessaly, the Islands—escaped altogether. But, for our purposes, the most significant thing is that, although the Mycenaean way of life went on, the unity of the Mycenaean world had been shattered.

If we look at some parts of the Catalogue, we seem to find the same picture of disintegration. In one or two other passages of the *Iliad*[59] there are hints of an overriding authority once exercised by the kings of Mycenae and, if ever there was a real situation corresponding to this, it was surely during LH IIIB. The cultural unity of the Mycenaean world at that time, as shown particularly by its pottery, taken together with Hittite references to a formidable 'Aḫḫijavā', led Desborough, for example, to the conclusion that 'there was one ruler over the whole Mycenaean territory',[60] and the splendour of the remains at Mycenae, the network of roads radiating out from the citadel, and the fact that the LH IIIB style was created in the Argolid and spread out from there[61] all indicate that Mycenae was the capital. But the Catalogue contains no hint that Agamemnon had any authority over the other kings—except possibly the lending of ships to the Arcadians—and even the lines (*Il.* 2. 577–80) which Page regards as an addition 'for the greater glory of Agamemnon'[62] only claim for him the finest and most numerous forces. Worse still, despite Page's ingenious arguments,[63] if the Catalogue's entry for Diomedes is taken at its face value, Agamemnon was even cut off from the Argive plain: it is surely impossible to believe that this was the case with Mycenae's ruler in LH IIIB, even if he did not exercise any authority over Greece as a whole. Rather, the Catalogue suggests a time when a much larger state, comprising at least the whole north-eastern corner of the Peloponnese, had split into two, leaving the great fortress of Mycenae as the back-door to a realm in Corinthia and Achaea, instead of the centre of a kingdom with the Argolid as its heart. It is not going too far to say that this is precisely the sort of thing which is suggested by the archaeological evidence for what happened at the end of the thirteenth century.

The same sort of thing is suggested by the entry relating to Orchomenos (*Il.* 2. 511–16). Recent excavation and surface exploration have shown that Gla and the forts on the northern shores of Lake Copais flourished in LH IIIB and, although direct archaeological evidence is still lacking, it is presumably to the same period that we should attribute the remains of the ancient drainage system still to be seen near Gla. All this presupposes a powerful central authority, and this must surely have been Orchomenos, the wealth of which became proverbial (cf. *Il.* 9. 381) and can still be glimpsed in the ruins of the magnificent tholos-tomb and the sheer extent of the Mycenaean settlement.[64] Yet in the Catalogue Orchomenos is huddled into one small corner of Lake Copais, with only

Aspledon to comfort her isolation and hostile Boeotians pressing in from either side at Koroneia and Kopai. This picture exactly fits the period after the great fortress of Gla had apparently been abandoned,[65] and when the dykes near Gla presumably fell into neglect. In fact, the very presence of the Boeotians in the Catalogue at all may indicate the same period of decay, for there was a tradition strong enough to survive to Thucydides' day, in the face of Homer's authority, that the Boeotians did not arrive in Boeotia until sixty years after the Trojan War,[66] and the lack of pedigree for any of the Boeotian leaders provides some confirmation of their late entry into the tradition.[67]

The Catalogue's picture of a Thessaly kaleidoscopically divided into eight or nine different kingdoms may also reflect the breaking-up of Mycenaean control in the area for, although the disasters elsewhere at the end of the thirteenth century apparently did not affect Thessaly directly,[68] there is some evidence that the prosperity of Mycenaean Thessaly, and particularly of the area corresponding to Eumelos' kingdom, was seriously affected.[69] We have already noted that the entries in the Catalogue relating to Pylos, the Dodecanese, and Crete may similarly reflect the period after the destructions of *c.* 1200 B.C.

The Catalogue then, and particularly the entries relating to Agamemnon and the Minyai, seems to betray traces of the period of Mycenaean decline, especially in the political divisions which it implies. Yet it is equally undeniable that if we considered the places mentioned in it alone, we should postulate a *terminus ante quem* of *c.* 1200 B.C., especially for the references to such places as Eutresis, Krisa, and Pylos, which are vital to the whole argument for believing that the Catalogue reflects Mycenaean Greece. But this apparent inconsistency between the political divisions implied by the Catalogue and the places to which it refers is, after all, only the sort of thing we should expect if, as we suggested above,[70] the Catalogue is the creation of oral poets, and not based upon some sort of muster-list of the forces which actually took part in the historical Trojan War, or even upon an accurate contemporary account of them.

In fact, the element of exaggeration which seems undeniable in the Catalogue is reminiscent of the vast forces arrayed against each other in the *Chanson de Roland* and other epic poems.[71] In the case of the *Chanson*, it seems certain that there is a kernel of historical truth in the story of Roland's last fight, and the same is almost certainly true of the story of the Trojan War. But the historical skirmish in the Pass of Roncesvalles has been blown up to huge proportions, and it seems likely that the same thing has happened with the siege of Troy. The fact that the Catalogue evidently preserves a memory of Mycenaean Greece leaves us to suppose that the bards who originally conceived the idea of recording in song the names of the heroes who took part in the Trojan War, and the places from which they came, were in a position to know something about the actual leaders and forces involved in the real expedition. But, just as what was probably in actual fact a swift raid on a relatively unimportant town[72] has through the medium of epic poetry assumed the proportions of a ten-year siege, so we should probably conclude that the forces arrayed on both sides grew in the telling:[73] just as we cannot leave the gods out of the story of the fighting before Troy and assume that the rest is history, so we should not think of the Catalogue as being something like Herodotus' list of the states which sent ships to Salamis.

It must be borne in mind that the story of Troy was probably not the first to be told in oral poetry. The search for the reality behind the *Iliad* has revealed evidence that the poem incorporates elements even older than the historical siege of Troy: a boar's-tusk helmet, for example, would probably have been an antique by the time Troy VIIa was sacked,[74] and so would the great body-shields which lie behind certain episodes in the *Iliad*.[75] Indeed, just as the siege of a city seems to have been a motif in Mycenaean art as early as the time of the Shaft Graves,[76] so it may have been the theme of oral poetry long before the siege of Troy.[77] But if this is so, then, when bards began to sing of the Trojan War, they would already have been using a traditional language, and thinking in terms of that language,[78] and this would inevitably have coloured the true facts from the first. Gradually thereafter heroes and tales from other sagas appear to have been attracted into the story: there are signs, for example, that in Ajax we have a hero of the days when the great body-shield was the principal feature of a warrior's equipment,[79] and even Achilles, with his sea-goddess mother, the aura of semi-divine power which surrounds him,[80] and his superhuman exploits, like the fight with the river, seems sometimes to belong to a more magical and perhaps more primitive world than the essentially human one of Homer.[81] This is not to suggest that the story of the Trojan War once did not include Achilles—though this is a possibility. But even if Achilles was a real Mycenaean chieftain who actually took part in the sack of Troy VIIa, he would appear to have acquired traits which did not originally belong to him, just as Odysseus clearly attracted sea-sagas which were probably once sung of other, perhaps nameless, heroes.[82] The *Iliad* is full of glimpses of a vast world of heroes and stories surrounding the saga of the Wrath of Achilles, and we can only speculate as to how much that now seems inextricably woven into that saga was once quite separate from it.

But if the story of the Trojan War absorbed other tales and other heroes, we can begin to see how an original catalogue might have been expanded in the same process until the kernel of historical truth in it became irretrievably overlaid by additions and alterations. For the *Iliad* still preserves traces of the sort of 'little catalogues' which were probably ready to hand for inclusion in the great catalogue: the notorious passage in Book 13 (lines 685 f.), describing a section of the Greek army in the desperate battle with Hector, is one such trace,[83] and the list of the 'Seven Towns' offered by Agamemnon to Achilles (*Il.* 9. 150 f., 292 f.) is another.[84] Other tales which are hinted at in the *Iliad* and which might have included 'catalogues' are 'The Seven against Thebes' (*Il.* 4. 376 f.), and 'The Kalydonian Boar' (cf. *Il.* 9. 527 f., esp. 544–5), while a saga of Nestor's fights with the Epeians (*Il.* 11. 670–761) and the Arcadians (*Il.* 7. 132–56) might very well have originally contained lists of the forces arrayed on either side. It is even possible that a list of Helen's suitors lies behind the splendid passage in *Iliad* 3 (lines 161 f.) in which she describes the principal Greek heroes to Priam and his counsellors. For Page is surely wrong to insist[85] that the Catalogue 'is a list of participants in a military campaign'. This is, of course, true of the Catalogue *as it now stands*, but this does not mean, first, that parts of it may not once have been connected with other campaigns, and, secondly, that some parts of it may not have been adapted from lists connected with other heroic events. For example, Page himself draws attention, in another context,[86] to the mention of Menestheus, son of Peteos, in the list of Helen's suitors attributed to Hesiod (fr. 94. 43 Rzach): *ἐκ δ' ἄρ' Ἀθηνέων μνᾶθ' υἱὸς Π[ετεῶο Μενεσθεύς]*. Here an oral poet had only to replace the words *ἐκ δ' ἄρ' Ἀθήνεων μνᾶθ'* with the formula *τῶν αὖθ' ἡγεμόνευ(ε)* (cf. *Il.* 2. 540, 563, 601, 740), to have a line referring to Menestheus as the commander in a military campaign. In this sort of way, by addition and adaptation from other stories, something like the Catalogue as we have it could have begun to emerge.

This sort of process *could* have gone on throughout the period of transmission, and many have suspected that it did: Miss Lorimer, for example, thought that the entries relating to Rhodes and the other islands of the Dodecanese betrayed 'the hand of the Dorian interpolator',[87] and Page, although he thinks that the Catalogue is substantially a Mycenaean account of the forces arrayed against Troy, argues that the entries relating to Ajax and Tlepolemos, at least, must be post-Mycenaean.[88] But there is nothing in these entries, or indeed in any of the others, which could not have been composed by Mycenaean bards,[89] once, first, we accept that the Catalogue developed out of a purely poetic attempt to describe the forces which took part in the Trojan War, in some such way as we have outlined above; and, secondly, we realize that Mycenaean bards singing of the Trojan War in the middle of the twelfth century, for example, would have been two or three generations removed from the war itself. The most we could allow, in view of the fact that the Catalogue as a whole seems to reflect the Mycenaean period, is that its various sections already existed as separate 'little catalogues' in Mycenaean times, but were only combined into the Catalogue as we have it after the close of the Bronze Age.

But even this is unnecessary if we bear in mind the second point mentioned above, namely that the tradition which culminated in our Catalogue could have undergone a fairly long development *within the Mycenaean period itself*. For if Blegen and his colleagues are right, Troy VIIa was sacked some time before the end of LH IIIB,[90] and Mycenaean civilization certainly survived in some form for at least a century longer.[91] We have suggested above that the Catalogue in fact does appear to show traces of the disintegration of the last generations of the Mycenaean era, but there is little or no reason to believe that it was substantially altered or expanded *after* the collapse of Mycenaean civilization, for, as we have seen, there are very few, if any, demonstrably post-Mycenaean elements in it, even as it now stands.

Nor is it difficult to see why the development of the Catalogue should have 'frozen' towards the end of the Mycenaean period: after the disasters of the late thirteenth century there was a measure of recovery—men could still hope that life would go on much as it had been. But by the end of the twelfth century, with their world finally crumbling to pieces around them, it would have been natural for poets and audiences alike to cling desperately to the traditions of more glorious days, and the Catalogue in particular would have been a constant reminder of what Greece had once been like.[92] If, as seems likely, many of the places mentioned in it had been sacked or abandoned at the end of the thirteenth century, even poets of the immediately succeeding generations would have begun to have the same sort of attitude to the names in the Catalogue they inherited as, we suggested, would account for their preservation later. Some of these names, such as Krisa and Pylos, would have become ineradicably embedded in the tradition, and there would have been plenty of survivors to remember the splendour that had gone. The more obscure places would already have taken on the glamour of mystery and age.

But if, as is probably the case, the unity of the Mycenaean world had been disrupted and, with the sack of the great administrative centres, the complicated organization revealed by the Linear B tablets had broken down, the actual boundaries of the great kingdoms might well have been forgotten. We can, for example, readily imagine Pylian refugees in Athens or elsewhere[93] keeping alive the memory of 'sandy Pylos' itself, but would they have remembered the 'Hither' and 'Farther' provinces? Similarly, bards in Argos—which apparently survived the disaster[94]—though they may have known that they once owed allegiance to

Mycenae's king, may well have wished to furbish up the new-found independence of their own princes by suggesting that their ancestors were already independent at the time of the Trojan War, while the incoming Boeotians, if the tradition preserved by Thucydides is true,[95] may have been anxious to secure a mention in the heroic story now that they ruled many of the places already referred to in the Catalogue: they may not have been able to dim completely the glory of 'Minyan Orchomenos', but they could lay claim to Koroneia and Kopai and other towns over which Orchomenos had perhaps once ruled.

It is, indeed, often supposed that the Catalogue was composed in Boeotia, partly because of the prominence of Boeotia in it, partly because of the other 'catalogues' alleged to have been composed in Boeotia.[96] But although we may perhaps allow that Boeotian poets may have had some influence on the *order* of the Catalogue, there is no good reason to believe that they materially altered its substance, except perhaps to secure the two explicit references to *Βοιωτοί* (*Il.* 2. 494 and 510).[97] Admittedly, the Boeotian entry mentions more than twice as many towns as any other,[98] but Mycenaean Boeotia was extremely rich and populous and, as we have seen,[99] with the exception of Koroneia, all the places in it mentioned by the Catalogue which can be located were certainly inhabited in the Mycenaean period. If the Catalogue had been composed in Boeotia, we should surely have expected the five Boeotian leaders to have had splendid pedigrees.[100] Instead, they, by contrast with the leaders of the next contingent—from insignificant Orchomenos—and most of the rest, have no pedigrees at all.[101]

Nor need the position of the Boeotian entry at the head of the Catalogue necessarily be due to Boeotian poets:[102] the Catalogue had to begin somewhere, after all, and although we may feel that it would have been more fitting to begin with Agamemnon, we simply cannot tell what factors determined the order. The Boeotians may clearly have been put first because the place of assembly was traditionally in their country.[103] Thereafter the order may have arisen as a sort of *periplous* round the outer coast, as Arkwright suggested,[104] or as a result of a process of what Jachmann called 'nachbarlicher Anschluß' (i.e. a transition from one contiguous district to another),[105] though neither of these hypotheses really explain the leaps from Aetolia to Crete and the Dodecanese, and then back again to Thessaly.[106] But at least some such suggestion as this is likely to be far nearer the truth than Burr's idea that the order may represent the actual order in which contingents arrived at Aulis![107]

Thus, although the theory that the Catalogue was composed in Boeotia may be correct, it is certainly not proved by the internal evidence of the Catalogue itself, and even the assumption that this sort of poetry was particularly at home in Boeotia is really based on nothing more than the existence of the so-called 'Catalogue of Women' and other 'catalogues' attributed to Hesiod: it may once have been more widespread.[108] This assumption apart, one could possibly make out a case for the Catalogue's having been composed in Athens, Argos, or even Thessaly, on internal evidence alone.[109] But such speculations are really quite idle:[110] various versions of the Catalogue may have come into being independently in various Mycenaean centres, and we have no means of telling how or where the version which has come down to us became canonical. But wherever it was composed, the Catalogue was probably *preserved*, as Page suggests,[111] independently of the tradition which culminated in the *Iliad*, though we must bear in mind that the particular part of the tradition upon which the *Iliad* draws was bound to appear to be independent of the Catalogue to some extent, simply because it concerns an incident in the tenth year of the war, and not the war as a whole: if we possessed the whole range of material from which the *Iliad* selects only a part, the Catalogue *might* appear to be fully consistent with it.

To sum up, then, we suggest that the Catalogue probably originated in an attempt by oral poets contemporary with the historical Trojan War to record in their songs the names of the princes who took part, and the places from which their forces came. This record would have been coloured from the first by the traditional language through which the poets had to express what they wished to say and, as time went on, for reasons which are no longer ascertainable but which find their parallel in other epic traditions, the siege of Troy became a focal point in the Greek epic tradition, absorbing other tales and other heroes. At the same time, as the Trojan War took on these vast proportions, so the list of those who had taken part grew longer, partly at least through absorbing other 'little catalogues' which had originally belonged to different stories. If the arguments we set out above are accepted, it would appear that, as far as the Catalogue itself is concerned, many of the place-names had already appeared in it by the end of the thirteenth century and that, although there was some further development during the succeeding generations of Mycenaean decline, by the end of the Bronze Age the Catalogue had reached substantially the form in which it has come down to us. Thus, during the 'Dark Ages' the Catalogue was preserved more or less as it stood. Finally, although it was actually a description of the Greek forces as they mustered before they set out for Troy, it was incorporated into the story of the 'Wrath of Achilles' in the tenth year of the war in order to set that particular episode against the stupendous background of the war as a whole. Nor is there, really, anything to prevent us believing that, if a single great poet was responsible for moulding the stuff of which the *Iliad* is made into its present complex and splendid whole, he could not also have been responsible for bringing in the

Catalogue to play its present part. For, when all is said and done, the alleged 'inconsistencies' between it and the rest of the *Iliad* are very slight, and are far outweighed by its own inherent qualities and by the colourful and evocative way in which it does, in fact, fulfil the purpose for which it has been used.[112]

But perhaps the most important conclusion to be drawn from a study of the Catalogue is that, whatever its origins and its relationship to the rest of the *Iliad*, it does appear to reflect Mycenaean Greece and, if this is so, it should have an important bearing on the whole question of the extent to which the Homeric poems preserve Mycenaean tradition. It is becoming fashionable nowadays, while recognizing that the *Iliad* and *Odyssey* do owe something to Mycenaean civilization, to think that the Mycenaean element in them is slight, and that the really formative period in the growth of the tradition was the Early Iron Age.[113] But although the Catalogue may have differed from the rest of the tradition in the extent to which it survived unaltered from the Bronze Age, there remains the possibility that it was not unique in this respect. We argued in the first part of this book that the core of Mycenaean tradition in the poems as a whole may well be larger than many scholars think and, in particular, that many of the alleged certainly post-Mycenaean elements in them may in reality not be post-Mycenaean at all. We can now see that the Catalogue is not only the best proof that the poems ultimately look back to the Mycenaean period, but that it is also an indication that quite lengthy and detailed fragments of Mycenaean *poetry* could be preserved through all the centuries that followed the collapse of Mycenaean civilization in something like their Mycenaean form.

We are aware that few if any of the arguments we have advanced in this book are conclusive. Discussion will continue to rage about the Catalogue as about the Homeric poems as a whole, and with increasing knowledge of the 'Dark Ages' the certainly Mycenaean elements in the tradition may be partly whittled away. In the ultimate resort, judgement on the questions we have been discussing will probably become more and more subjective, just as the answer to the great question of the authorship of the poems must now depend, largely, on subjective feelings about them, with the revelation that they are oral poetry. In this book we have tried to confine ourselves to sober reporting of archaeological evidence and to scholarly argument, but we are fully aware that others may draw different conclusions from the same evidence. But on one thing we insist, and that is that any discussion of the Catalogue should at least begin with the concrete archaeological and topographical considerations we have endeavoured to set out.

Yet we would be the first to admit that we cannot just stop there. It is undeniably hard for anyone with any imagination to turn, for example, from the Lion Gate and the thought that perhaps over that very slab of corrugated stone Agamemnon rode out to war, to the cold consideration of a few miserable sherds which may or may not date the gateway—and, for all our doubts that the Catalogue is a true record of the actual Greek forces involved in the sack of Troy, we are convinced that men from at least some of the places we have seen were there.

Homer, after all, has a habit of being proved right, and it is a salutary reminder to be humble in his presence, to recall the words of Kinglake[114] as he gazed out to sea from what he took to be the site of Troy, a generation before ever Schliemann put spade to ground, and saw 'aloft over Imbros—aloft in a far-away heaven—Samothrace, the watchtower of Neptune':

> So Homer had appointed it, and so it was: the map was correct enough, but could not, like Homer, convey *the whole truth*. Thus vain and false are the mere human surmises and doubts which clash with Homeric writ.

NOTES TO PART III

1. For example Eilesion, Arne, Mideia, and Nisa in Boeotia; Kalliaros, Bessa, and Augeiai in Locris; Eiones in the Argolid; Aipy, Pteleon, and Helos in Messenia; Rhipe, Stratie, and Enispe in Arcadia; Alision in Elis; and in Thessaly, Alos, Glaphyrai, Ormenion, and Kyphos.
2. For a recent discussion of the date of the composition of the *Iliad* see G. S. Kirk, *The Songs of Homer*, pp. 282–7.
3. For previous attempts see, for example, Burr, *NK*, p. 111, and Page, *HHI*, pp. 120f.
4. Mykalessos might be thought an exception to this, but the excavation was concerned only with the cemetery and, in any case, Mycenaean sherds have now been found on the site (see pp. 22–3 above).
5. Such as, for example, the early wars between Sparta and Argos (cf. G. L. Huxley, *Early Sparta*, pp. 26–31), or the First Messenian War.
6. Cf., for example, p. 65 above, on Corinth.
7. e.g. Megara was identified with Nisa (*Il.* 2. 508: cf. p. 32 above), Phlious was held to be the descendant of Araithyrea (*Il.* 2. 571: cf. p. 67 above), and the people of Chaeronea laid claim to Arne (*Il.* 2. 507: cf. p. 31 above).
8. Unless Gla is Arne (cf. p. 31 above). The omission of Dendra is the more puzzling, if it is in fact Midea (cf. Frazer, *Pausanias* iii. 231–2; *RE* 15, Cols. 1541–3). But it is noticeable that the Homeric poems make no mention of other places in the Argolid equally prominent in mythology—e.g. Lerna and Nemea.
9. Cf. now, M. R. Popham, *JHS* 85 (1965), pp. 193–6, *Antiquity* 40 (1966), pp. 24–8.
10. See pp. 86–7 above.
11. See pp. 161–4 above for a further discussion of this point.
12. The tablets presumably only refer to the administrative year during which the palace was sacked (Ventris and Chadwick, *DMG*, p. 138; Palmer, *Mycenaeans and Minoans*, pp. 52–3).
13. Huxley (*BICS* 3 (1956), pp. 21–2) suggests that 'the state of affairs in the Catalogue is

earlier than that reflected by the Pylos tablets'. We think that it is possible that it rather reflects the state of affairs after the date of the tablets (see above, p. 162).

14. See, for example, 7. 203.
15. Thus J. K. Anderson (*BSA* 49 (1954), p. 72) says: 'The boundaries of the Kingdom of Mycenae in the Catalogue are too strange to be accepted.' We would agree with Page (*HHI*, p. 165 n. 36) that this dictum is unjustified: see pp. 70–2 above, and n. 26 on p. 73. But these boundaries are, perhaps, too strange to be *invented*.
16. *HHI*, p. 132.
17. See p. 59 above.
18. See pp. 27–8 above.
19. See p. 62 above.
20. See p. 67 above.
21. Cf. Kirk, *SH*, especially pp. 117–18.
22. *HHI*, p. 136.
23. *HHI*, pp. 123–4, but cf. Kirk, *SH*, pp. 117–18.
24. 'Great stuff this Homer', as Lord Peter himself says (D. L. Sayers, *Hangman's Holiday*, p. 41).
25. See the obituary of Sir Louis Rieu (late of the I.C.S.) in *The Times* for 12 November 1964.
26. Page, *HHI*, pp. 135–6. Allen (*HCS*, p. 169) says eight, but there are nine including Polyxeinos (*Il.* 2. 263). Page (*HHI*, p. 168 n. 53) notes that the *Iliad* knows of some 70 Achaeans not mentioned in the Catalogue, and knows more about some of those who are.
27. Page, *HHI*, p. 125.
28. Ibid.; cf. Kirk, *SH*, p. 154.
29. See pp. 129–30 above, on Achilles; p. 105 on Odysseus; and pp. 70–2 on Agamemnon.
30. See above, p. 156 and p. 59.
31. *HHI*, p. 124.
32. Beye (*AJP* 82 (1961), pp. 370–8) suggests that *ΝΑΥΣ* might mean 'ship-load', but this is far-fetched, and still would not explain why, for example, the Catalogue begins by describing the contingents of Achilles, Protesilaus, and Philoctetes as though they were there, and then has to explain why they were absent.
33. e.g. 2. 525–6, 542–4, 577–80, 587–90.
34. *HHI*, pp. 149–50. Page notes (op. cit., p. 150) that 'it appears that the text of the Catalogue recognized by the Alexandrian editors of the *Iliad* as being canonical included nearly all of the persons and places, but excluded much of the explanatory comment'. One would, however, like to know more of their grounds for such exclusions: if the passages in question did not appear in some of their texts, this is one thing; if they were excluded on other, more subjective, grounds, it is quite another.
35. See above, p. 160.
36. *HHI*, p. 134.
37. *HHI*, p. 128.
38. *HHI*, p. 134.
39. e.g. Burr, *NK*, pp. 119 f.; Webster, *MH*, p. 122.
40. *DMG*, pp. 183 f.; cf. (*inter al.*) L. R. Palmer, *Minos* 4 (1956), pp. 120–45; H. Mühlestein, *Die Oka-Tafeln von Pylos* (Basel 1956); V. Burr, *Die Tontafeln von Pylos und der homerische Schiffskatalog* (Festschrift . . . des Peutinger-Gymnasiums Ellwangen, Jagst, 1958) pp. 71–81; Webster, *MH*, pp. 21, 99, 121–2, 180, 185, 218. Attention has also been drawn to an inscription from Ugarit which records information of a similar nature: Burr, *NK*, pp. 121 f., with Abb. 41; Wade-Gery, *PI*, pp. 54–5 and n. 111; Webster, *MH*, p. 21, etc.

41. Cf. C. M. Bowra, *Homer and his Forerunners*, pp. 5–6.

42. *HHI*, n. 21 on pp. 158–9.

43. Cf. *DMG*, p. 110.

44. Cf. Page, *HHI*, pp. 152–3. Huxley (*Greek, Roman and Byzantine Studies* 7 (1966), pp. 313–18) makes out a case for the numbers' being Mycenaean in origin, like the Catalogue as a whole, but even then they need not be authentic: Mycenaean bards would have been just as likely to exaggerate as their successors.

45. Allen (*HCS*, p. 144) suggested that Eumelos 'must have provided transports for the potentates of the interior, as Agamemnon did for the Arcadians'. If so, Eumelos was generosity itself, providing 132 transports for the others, and keeping only 11 for himself!

46. Particularly in the case of the Phocians (*Il.* 2. 524), Locrians (*Il.* 2. 534), and Euboeans (*Il.* 2. 545), who come one after another, and again in the case of Eurypylos (*Il.* 2. 737), Polypoites (*Il.* 2. 747), and Prothoos (*Il.* 2. 759), who only have Gouneus and his 22 ships in between. Cf. also Meges (*Il.* 2. 630), the Aetolians (*Il.* 2. 644), and Protesilaus (*Il.* 2. 710).

47. The numbers of men involved in the operations recorded in the Pylos oka-tablets are, however, very small (Page, *HHI*, pp. 193–4).

48. It has been suggested (e.g. by Huxley, op. cit. in n. 44 above) that the greater part of the Greek forces were employed in raiding towns in the vicinity of Troy, but this does not meet the other objections to the ship-numbers outlined above.

49. Cf. p. 163 above.

50. For the whole question see (*inter al.*) Page, *HHI*, pp. 1–40; Huxley, *Achaeans and Hittites* (Oxford 1960).

51. *BICS* 3 (1956), pp. 19–31. Huxley also believes that the Trojan Catalogue reflects LH IIIB (op. cit., pp. 24–5, cf. *AH*, pp. 31–6), but cf. Appendix, esp. pp. 178–80 below.

52. See p. 30 above, and n. 47 on p. 36.

53. See p. 53 above, and n. 76 on p. 37.

54. See p. 56 above.

55. Cf. Desborough, *LMTS*, p. 155.

56. See pp. 111–14 and 115 above.

57. *The Last Mycenaeans and their Successors* (*LMTS*), Oxford 1964. For what follows see especially pp. 225–30.

58. *LMTS*, p. 226.

59. See pp. 70–2 above. The most important passage, clearly, is *Il.* 2. 100–8.

60. *LMTS*, p. 218.

61. Desborough, *LMTS*, pp. 4 and 219.

62. *HHI*, p. 150.

63. *HHI*, pp. 127–32.

64. See pp. 38–9 above.

65. See Blegen, *The Mycenaean Age*, p. 23, for the date of the destruction of the south and south-east gates at Gla.

66. Thucydides 1. 12. 3. Huxley (*BICS* 3 (1956), p. 22) accepts the other tradition recorded here by Thucydides, that some Boeotians had already arrived before the Trojan War, but it is difficult not to suspect that this tradition owed its origin to an attempt to explain how, if the Boeotians only arrived after the Trojan War, Homer could say they were already there.

67. See p. 34 above.

68. Desborough, *LMTS*, pp. 127–38, especially p. 135.

69. Desborough, *LMTS*, p. 128.

70. See p. 161.

71. Cf. C. M. Bowra, *Heroic Poetry*, pp. 518–20, and Appendix, pp. 180–1 and n. 29 on p. 183.

72. Though the wealth and prosperity of Troy VI is sufficiently shown by its magnificent walls, it was a comparatively small place, the circumference of its walls measuring only some 600 yards (as against the 1,400 yards of Mycenae's walls, for example). Moreover, after the earthquake which wrecked Troy VI *c.* 1300 B.C., the place was never the same again: as Page says (*HHI*, pp. 71–2), Troy VIIa was 'a pinched and meagre offspring, unworthy of its robust and monumental parent'.

73. For the allies of Troy see the Appendix (pp. 176–81, especially pp. 180–11).

74. Cf. H. L. Lorimer, *HM*, pp. 217–19; Page, *HHI*, pp. 218–19, and n. 1 on p. 265.

75. Cf. *HM*, pp. 146–53, especially p. 153.

76. See above, p. 9, and n. 70 on p. 13.

77. Cf. Webster, *MH*, pp. 58 f.

78. Cf. p. 9 above, and n. 71 on p. 13.

79. Cf. Page, *HHI*, pp. 232–8, especially p. 233.

80. Cf. *Il.* 18. 203–31.

81. Achilles' spear is also shown to be very ancient by the unique term *μελίη* used of it (cf. Page, *HHI*, pp. 238–42).

82. Cf., for example, W. J. Woodhouse, *The Composition of Homer's Odyssey*, pp. 41–5.

83. Cf. Page, *HHI*, p. 133.

84. See n. 37 on p. 89.

85. *HHI*, pp. 134 f. Page also argues that the Trojan Catalogue must have been inspired by an expedition to the north-east, connected with the sack of Troy VIIa (*HHI*, p. 144), but see Appendix, esp. p. 181.

86. *HHI*, n. 79 on p. 173.

87. *HM*, p. 47 (cf. p. 466 n. 2, and p. 473 n. 6), but see p. 118 above.

88. *HHI*, pp. 147–9.

89. See pp. 59 and 118 above.

90. For recent discussions of the date of the Trojan War see G. E. Mylonas, *Hesperia* 33 (1964), pp. 363 f.; G. S. Kirk, *CAH* Fasc. 22, especially pp. 19–20.

91. Cf. Desborough, *LMTS*, *passim* and esp. p. 241. Much of what Kirk says about the 'Poetical Possibilities of the Dark Age' (cf., especially, *SH* Ch. 6, pp. 126–38) would apply equally well to the 12th century and, as Desborough has shown (see esp. *LMTS*, pp. 251 f.), the present archaeological evidence tends to suggest that the Dorian *settlement* did not actually take place until *c.* 1075 B.C. in the Argolid, and perhaps even *c.* 1000 B.C. in the south and west Peloponnese.

92. As we noted above (p. 158), the Catalogue is less likely to have been altered than other parts of the poem.

93. Pausanias 2. 18. 8–9; Mimnermus (fr. 12 Diehl) refers to Pylian refugees at Colophon.

94. Desborough, *LMTS*, pp. 80–1.

95. See pp. 34, 162, and 163–4 above.

96. Cf. Page, *HHI*, p. 152.

97. Elsewhere the *Iliad* calls the inhabitants of Boeotia *Καδμεῖοι* (4. 388, 391; 5. 807) or *Καδμεΐωνες* (4. 385 and 5. 804).

98. Yet Oldfather (*AJA* 20 (1916), p. 43 n. 2) could argue for a disproportionately high number in Locris!

99. See p. 33 above.

100. The names of the five Boeotian princes presumably go with the name *Βοιωτῶν*, and might have replaced the names of one or more pre-Boeotian heroes.

101. Cf. G. L. Huxley, *BICS* 3 (1956), p. 22.

102. In particular, as Allen points out (*HCS*, p. 33 n. 1), though the title *Βοιωτία* for the second book of the *Iliad* is ancient, it is merely an instance, on a large scale, of 'the ancient habit of referring to a passage from its beginning. It cannot be appealed to as a sign of the importance of the Boeotians.'

103. It may be no more than a coincidence, but it is none the less interesting that the first two places mentioned in the Catalogue should be precisely Hyrie, where the strange ship-carvings were found (see p. 19 above), and Aulis.

104. Allen *HCS*, p. 39 n. 1.

105. *Der homerische Schiffskatalog und die Ilias*, pp. 179 f.

106. The isolated position of the Thessalian contingents at the end is, in any case, a problem: Jachmann (op. cit., pp. 184 f.) regards *Νῦν αὖ* in *Il.* 2. 681 as indicating the beginning of an originally separate Thessalian (or Aeolic) Catalogue. But this theory is weakened by the *Αὐτὰρ* of lines 517 and 631, and the *αὖ* of line 671: surely all these can be explained as simply bringing variety into the way in which each contingent is introduced.

107. As for Burr's further suggestion (*NK*, pp. 86, 106 f., 115, 129) of a separate assembly-point for the Thessalian contingents at Halos (why not Iolkos?), although it is accepted by Wade-Gery without criticism (*PI*, pp. 54 f.), and tentatively by Kirk (*SH*, p. 224), surely if there ever had been a tradition of a separate assembly-point at Halos or anywhere else, we should have received a hint of it somewhere.

108. Webster, for example, argues for 'a common ancestor in pre-migration poetry' for Hesiod's 'Catalogue of Women' and the 'Catalogue of Heroines' in *Od.* 11 (*MH*, pp. 178 f.).

109. If we are right in thinking that the Catalogue reached substantially its present form in LH IIIC rather than LH IIIB, it may be significant that the invasions at the end of LH IIIB apparently passed Attica and Thessaly by, and did not even result in the destruction of Argos itself.

110. 'It is all mere guesswork', as Page remarks (*HHI*, p. 162).

111. *HHI*, pp. 124, 134, and 176 n. 93.

112. Page (*HHI*, p. 133 and n. 44 on pp. 166–7) accepts Jacoby's arguments for believing that the Catalogue is an 'insertion', but Jacoby's theory virtually denies that any action taken *before* the parade could possibly be described: only at *Il.* 2. 464 are we expressly informed that any men have actually left either huts or ships, and only at line 473 that they are actually on parade. As for the 'two marches' (lines 455–8 and 780–5), the first is really just the coming on parade, and is a fine preparation for the final and more resplendent marching out to battle (cf. Wade-Gery, *PI*, pp. 51 f.).

113. Cf., for example, G. S. Kirk, *SH*, pp. 126–56.

114. *Eothen* (Everyman edn.), p. 36.

APPENDIX

THE TROJAN CATALOGUE (*Iliad* 2. 816–77)

THE Trojan Catalogue occupies only 62 lines in the *Iliad*, as compared with the 266 lines of the Achaean Catalogue, and the information it conveys is correspondingly meagre. The allies of Troy are listed in sixteen contingents beginning, naturally enough, with the Trojans under Hector,[1] and ending with the Lycians under Sarpedon and Glaukos. The contingents seem to be grouped together in five geographical areas—the Troad, the European allies from beyond the Hellespont, the Far Eastern allies (Paphlagonians and Alizonians), the Near Eastern allies (Mysians and Phrygians), and the allies from south of the Troad—and in the last four cases, the list appears to begin with the contingent from nearest Troy, and to end with the one from farthest away.[2]

Of the thirty geographical locations mentioned,[3] including five rivers and five mountains, the majority can be more or less precisely located,[4] but since only one or two have been systematically explored or excavated, it is impossible to be certain whether they were inhabited in the Mycenaean period or not, or whether there have been any significant gaps in their occupation subsequently. For the time being, therefore, we lack the evidence to examine the Trojan Catalogue in the way we can now examine the Achaean Catalogue, and it is not the purpose of this appendix to discuss the precise location of the places mentioned.[5] Instead, we intend merely to discuss the general conclusions which may be drawn from a study of the Trojan Catalogue, in the light of our present knowledge.

A number of arguments have been advanced to show that the period reflected by the Trojan Catalogue is the Mycenaean period, or at least a period before the migrations from Greece to Asia Minor during the 'Dark Ages', and these have perhaps been set out most forcibly by Page.[6] First, in contrast to the knowledge of Greece shown in the Achaean Catalogue, the knowledge of Asia Minor shown in the Trojan Catalogue is extremely scanty, and it is thus very difficult to believe that the latter can have been composed after the migrations. Of the twenty-four names that occur in it, excluding the names of peoples, and the six in the dubious lines 853–5, all but four or five (Zeleia, ? Alybe, ? Askania, the Gygaian Lake, and Mt. Tmolos) refer to places or geographical features which are either on the coast, visible from the coast (Mt. Ida, Tereia, ? Mt. Phthires), or come down to the coast (the rivers Aisepos, Axios, Maiander, and Xanthos). The interior of Asia Minor is thus almost a complete blank as far as the Trojan Catalogue is concerned, and there are significant gaps too, in its knowledge of the coast—in particular, nothing about the Bosphorus, nothing about the south coast of the Black Sea (unless lines 853–5 are genuine), and nothing about even the west coast of Asia Minor from Larisa to Miletus,[7] or thence southwards to the Xanthos valley. In other words, with the exception of Abydos and Miletus, there is no reference to any of the later important towns on the coast of Asia Minor and, although the Asiatic Greeks might have been too faithful to the epic tradition, or too patriotic, to include their cities in a list of Troy's allies, it would have been an almost irresistible temptation to insert at least some reference to them, unless a list of Troy's allies already existed which made no mention of them. In short, the Trojan Catalogue is much easier to explain as a pre-migration list, representing something like Mycenaean knowledge of Asia Minor, than as a post-migration composition.

Secondly, the Trojan Catalogue is even more independent of the *Iliad* as a whole than the Achaean Catalogue: it is largely ignored in the rest of the poem—for example, eight of the heroes mentioned in it (out of twenty-seven) never re-appear, and only five are at all important elsewhere. More significantly, it is often contradicted in the rest of the poem: for example, different commanders of the Cicones, Paionians, and Mysians are mentioned in the body of the poem,[8] and the Mysians are elsewhere (*Il.* 13. 4–5) said to live in Thrace, not in Asia Minor as is implied in the Catalogue.[9] In other words, it is very difficult to believe that the Trojan Catalogue can have been constructed out of what the *Iliad* tells us about the Trojans,[10] and its independence of the main tradition of the *Iliad* suggests that it is very ancient.

Thirdly, a number of the places which are mentioned in the Trojan Catalogue were evidently unknown to the Greeks of historical times. The most interesting of these, perhaps, is Alybe, 'the birth-place of silver' (*Il.* 2. 857): as Page points out,[11] it is clear from the discussions of its location by ancient authors, beginning with Hecataeus, that no one really knew where it was, nor even whether Ἀλύβη was the correct form of the name. Yet if the Trojan Catalogue first came into being in the ninth or eighth centuries, it seems unlikely that all knowledge of such a place would have been lost by the fifth century, at a time when Greek knowledge of Asia Minor should have been on the increase. In fact, the name Ἀλύβη is possibly the Greek form of a Hittite name, which would strongly suggest that it was passed down in the epic tradition from the thirteenth century B.C.[12] Another interesting name in the Trojan Catalogue is that of Mt. Phthires (*Il.* 2. 868). Strabo (14. 635) records that Hecataeus thought this was Latmos, but that others thought that Grion was meant. But it is surprising that there should have been this doubt, particularly since the Maiander and Mykale are both already in the Catalogue (*Il.* 2. 869). Again, the most likely explanation is that Phthires was the ancient name for a mountain near Miletus, preserved in the epic tradition from a time before the main immigration of the Greeks into Asia Minor.

Some scholars have even gone beyond this and argued that the Trojan Catalogue reflects precisely the time of the sack of Troy VIIa. Huxley,[13] for example, argues that the reference to Miletus as inhabited by 'barbarian-speaking Carians' reflects 'a period between Mycenaean penetration of Asia Minor at the beginning of the thirteenth century and the migrations at the end of the same century, namely the Mycenaean IIIB period', and that the location of Phorkys and the Phrygians in north-west Anatolia[14] reflects a time before the Phrygian migration. More recently,[15] Huxley has argued that there are certain similarities between the Trojan alliance and the alliance of 22 states forming the land of Aššuva with which the Hittite king Tutḫalijaš IV (*c.* 1250–1230 B.C.) fought a war. The 22 states include Ka-ra-ki-ša which is probably to be identified with Caria; Lu]-uk-ka which may be Lycia; Ú-i-lu-ši-i̯a and Ta-ru-i-ša or Ta-ru-ú-i-ša which may be *Ϝίλιος* and *Τροία*; and Ḫal-lu-u̯a which, as we have seen,[16] Huxley suggests may be Alybe. If these identifications are correct, Huxley argues, it is possible that Tutḫalijaš' campaign against the land of Aššuva explains the absence from the Trojan alliance of any people between the Pelasgians of Larisa and the Carians, except the Maionians: the Trojan Catalogue would reflect a time after Tutḫalijaš' victory when the extremities of the old alliance—the Troad and Caria and Lycia—were strong, but the centre had been shattered.

This is an attractive hypothesis, but one wonders how much weight should be placed on these alleged resemblances between the allies of Troy and of Aššuva, especially since the resemblances themselves have all been questioned:[17] Tutḫalijaš' list certainly includes many places unknown to the *Iliad*, and the Trojan Catalogue equally includes many places not in Tutḫalijaš' list. The mention of Miletus, which Huxley earlier saw as the best criterion of the date of the Trojan Catalogue, is also of dubious value: the archaeological evidence[18] shows that the site of Miletus was settled from Crete in the MM III–LM Ia period, and that Mycenaean influence became preponderant in LH II. A massive circuit-wall was built *c.* 1300 B.C. (LH IIIA: 2/IIIB), and destroyed in LH IIIC: 1, though there is some evidence for continuity into the sub-Mycenaean and Protogeometric periods. The site of Miletus thus seems to have been inhabited by Greeks from the mainland from the thirteenth century onwards, and this is confirmed by Hittite documents, for example the famous Tavagalavaš Letter, in which Miletus (Millavanda) is recognized as being in the sphere of influence of the King of Aḫḫijavā.[19] It is, then, very odd that in the Trojan Catalogue not only should Miletus be listed among the allies of Troy but that it should be said to be inhabited by *Κᾶρες βαρβαρόφωνοι* (*Il.* 2. 867–8). Huxley explains it by reference to Hittite sources which suggest that at some point after the Tavagalavaš affair Miletus came under the control of the Hittites:[20] he thinks that the Trojan Catalogue reflects a time when the Hittite vassal-ruler of Miletus, presumably a Carian, had broken away from Hittite control as well. The archaeological evidence, on the other hand, shows that if there were any *Κᾶρες βαρβαρόφωνοι* in Miletus during the thirteenth century B.C., they used Mycenaean pottery and were defended by a Mycenaean circuit-wall. In fact, the archaeological evidence suggests, if anything, that the reference to Miletus in the Trojan Catalogue reflects rather the brief period, *after* the Trojan War, when the Mycenaean circuit-wall was destroyed, and this would fit in with certain indications in the Achaean Catalogue which, as we saw,[21] tend to suggest that it may reflect the period after *c.* 1200 B.C.

Much more disturbing, however, for the theory that the Trojan Catalogue reflects the Mycenaean period, is the reference to the 'eddying Xanthos' (*Il.* 2. 877). There can hardly be any doubt that this refers to the river which swirls around the foot of the acropolis of the historical Xanthos, but there is so far no evidence that the valley was inhabited before the late eighth century B.C.: the earliest pottery so far found in the French excavations on the acropolis of Xanthos, which were in some places carried down to bed-rock, is Late Geometric.[22] If this negative evidence proves anything, it means that even if the Lukka of the Hittite texts are Homer's Lycians, they did not live where the Trojan Catalogue says they lived, at the time of the Trojan War. Thus, of the two places mentioned in the Catalogue for which we have evidence from excavation—Miletus and Xanthos—in the one case the evidence suggests that it was not inhabited by 'barbarian-speaking Carians', as the Catalogue says it was, at the time of the Trojan War, but by Greeks, and in the other, the evidence suggests that it was not inhabited at all at that time.

In a recent article,[23] moreover, J. M. Cook has pointed out that although the lack of detail in the Trojan Catalogue, apart from the sections concerning the Troad, may reflect the ignorance of Mycenaean Greeks about Asia Minor except for the area around Troy, it might also reflect the well-established tradition that the Greek settlement in western Asia Minor took place *after* the Trojan War. He suggests that the greater detail in the sections dealing with the Maionians and the Carians (*Il.* 2. 864–6 and 867–9) might reflect the greater knowledge of Lydia and the region of Miletus which Ionian poets might be expected to have had, Miletus in particular being permitted a reference because it was the one place which had 'a unique prehistory of which the Ionic poets were not altogether unaware'.

Cook also argues that the names of some of the leaders of the allies of Troy, for example Hodios and Epistrophos of the Alizonians (*Il.* 2. 856) and Nastes and Amphimachos of the Milesians (*Il.* 2. 870), are *invented* names, 'no more historical than MM. Aller et Retour'. This argument, however, seems very forced, and Allen[24] in fact argued the reverse—that although Homer provided many of the minor Trojans with pure Greek names, others appear to have Asiatic-sounding names, including Hodios or Odios.[25] Cook's other argument has more weight, but there are too many imponderables here: the Trojan Catalogue could clearly either reflect Mycenaean ignorance of Asia Minor or the knowledge of early Ionians, deliberately omitting reference to their own post-migration settlements; but Cook's arguments are obviously not conclusive that the latter is the case.

In fact the question of the period reflected by the Trojan Catalogue cannot really be settled until there has been more exploration of the places mentioned in it, and above all until more of those which can be more or less securely located have been excavated. Only then will we be able to say with any certainty whether any particular references must refer to the Late Bronze Age. As it is, on the one hand the lack of knowledge displayed in the Catalogue and the references to one or two places or geographical features, like Alybe and Mt. Phthires, unknown to the Greeks of historical times, are suggestive; on the other, the references to Miletus as inhabited by 'barbarian-speaking Carians' and to Xanthos are disturbing, and the comparative lack of completely unknown names —Strabo, for example, seems quite happy that most of the places could be located[26]—is in contrast to the many unknown names of the Achaean Catalogue. In short, it is by no means as certain that the Trojan Catalogue reflects the Mycenaean period as it is that the Achaean Catalogue reflects Mycenaean Greece, though in the ultimate resort we should be inclined to think that it does.

In view of this, however, we clearly cannot use the existence of the Trojan Catalogue, as Page does,[27] to bolster up the hypothesis that the Achaean Catalogue is a Mycenaean 'Order of Battle' connected with the historical sack of Troy VIIa. We have already seen reason to doubt whether this is true of the Achaean Catalogue,[28] and the Trojan Catalogue is obviously too weak a buttress for Page's purposes. Apart from the doubts about the extent to which it reflects the Mycenaean period, it is difficult to believe that it really does embody an accurate record of the actual allies of Troy VIIa, particularly that help really came to the beleaguered city from as far afield as Paionia, Paphlagonia, Caria, or

Lycia.[29] Rather the Trojan Catalogue looks like an attempt to match the Greek alliance with one for Troy, perhaps with Agamemnon's opinion in mind that the actual Trojans were outnumbered by the Greeks by more than ten to one (*Il.* 2. 123–8). As such, it may embody a kernel of historical truth[30] in so far as it may represent an attempt by Mycenaean poets to describe the forces arrayed against their heroes, but it seems just as likely to have been subject to the same sort of process of expansion and exaggeration as, we suggest, was the Achaean Catalogue.[31]

Page argues[32] that, assuming the Trojan Catalogue is of Mycenaean origin, the motive for its composition must have been an expedition to the north-east, and that therefore the Achaean Catalogue was connected with the same event. We have argued[33] that the Achaean Catalogue could have been made up out of 'little catalogues' originally quite unconnected with the Trojan War, and it is possible that the Trojan Catalogue was constructed in a similar way. Allen,[34] for example, suggests that parts of it may have been connected with an early saga about the voyage of the Argo: originally, the story may not have taken the Argo beyond the Propontis—as Demetrius of Scepsis remarked (ap. Strabo 1. 45), Homer seems to have had no idea that Jason went as far as Phasis—and if so, a list of names originally belonging to a saga of the Argo's voyage from Iolkos to the Propontis might very well lie behind the Trojan Catalogue's brief references to the Paionians and Thrace, and the much more detailed references to the shores of the Hellespont and the south-west corner of the Propontis. Mycenaean knowledge of Miletus and its environs and of the region around Sardis[35] might also account for the more detailed references to these areas, without the necessity of supposing that this knowledge could only have been embodied in poems about the Trojan War.

To sum up, even if it does embody Mycenaean tradition, as it probably does, the Trojan Catalogue seems more likely to represent the efforts of oral poets to list the allies of Troy, drawing upon existing references to Asia Minor in Mycenaean sagas and upon more general Mycenaean knowledge of Asia Minor, than a sort of Mycenaean intelligence report on the enemy forces.

NOTES TO THE APPENDIX

1. Hector's men are said to be πολὺ πλεῖστοι καὶ ἄριστοι, as are the followers of Agamemnon (*Il.* 2. 577–8). They are presumably thought of as inhabiting the city of Troy itself, since no other place-names are given.

2. In each case the description of the last contingent includes the word τηλόθεν (*Il.* 2. 849, 857, and 877) or τῆλ(ε) (*Il.* 2. 863). If this order is rigidly adhered to, as it seems to be, the Mysians should lie between Troy and the Phrygians (cf. Wace and Stubbings, *CH*, p. 305).

3. Including Kytoros, Sesamos, the river Parthenios, Kromna, Aigialos, and Erythinoi (*Il.* 2. 853–5). In fact these lines are very dubious (cf. Allen, *HCS*, pp. 156–9; Page, *HHI*, p. 147).

4. Cf., for the Troad, Leaf, *Troy: a Study in Homeric Geography* (London 1912), and, for the rest, Allen, *HCS*, pp. 147–67, Wace and Stubbings, *CH*, pp. 300–6.

5. For this we refer the reader to the works listed in n. 4 above. Systematic exploration of the places mentioned would of course be possible, but it would be extremely difficult, and we do not feel that we have the necessary expertise in Anatolian archaeology to undertake it.

6. *HHI*, pp. 137–45.

7. Cf. Leaf, op. cit., pp. 198f.; Wace and Stubbings, *CH*, p. 302, for the location of Larisa. Reference is made elsewhere in the *Iliad* to Thebe Hypoplakie (1. 366, 6. 394–7: Allen, *HCS*, p. 149; Wace and Stubbings, *CH*, pp. 302–3) and Tarne (*Il.* 5. 44), which probably refers to Atarneus (Allen, *HCS*, pp. 164–5).

8. Cicones: 2. 846, cf. 17. 73; Paionians: 2. 848, cf. 17. 348; Mysians: 2. 858, cf. 14. 511–12.

9. See n. 2 above.

10. Page (*HHI*, p. 169 n. 59) rightly castigates Burr for suggesting this (*NK*, p. 150). Another contradiction between the Trojan Catalogue and the *Iliad* elsewhere involves Pandaros: in the Catalogue he is placed north-east of Troy (Allen, *HCS*, pp. 151–2), but in Book 5 it is twice implied that he comes from Lycia (lines 105 and 173)—cf. Wace and Stubbings, *CH*, pp. 301–2.

11. *HHI*, pp. 141–2; cf. Allen, *HCS*, pp. 159–61.

12. Allen, following Sayce, suggests that it corresponds to Khaly-wa, 'the land of the Halys' (*HCS*, pp. 160–1; cf. Wace and Stubbings, *CH*, pp. 304). Huxley, however (*AH*, pp. 34–5), points out that the Hittite name for the Halys was Maraššantija, and suggests that Ἀλύβη is rather the Hittite Ḫal-lu-u̯a, which occurs in the list of the allies of Aššuva defeated by Tutḫalijaš IV. If Huxley is right, this would mean that the Trojan Catalogue misplaced the Alizonians, for Aššuva and her allies lay in western Asia Minor, not beyond the Paphlagonians as, it implies, did Alybe.

13. *BICS* 3 (1956), pp. 24–5; cf. *AH*, pp. 31–6, especially p. 36.

14. *Il.* 2. 862–3: Askanie is probably to be located on or near the Lake Askania upon which the later city of Nicaea was situated (Allen, *HCS*, pp. 162–3, Wace and Stubbings, *CH*, p. 305).

15. *Achaeans and Hittites* (Oxford 1960) [*AH*], pp. 31–6; cf. Page, *HHI*, pp. 102–10.

16. See n. 12 above.

17. Cf. Page, *HHI*, pp. 106–7 and notes 30–3 on pp. 115–16.

18. Wieckert, *Istanbuler Mitteilungen* 7 (1957), pp. 102 f., and yearly reports thereafter; *JHS Arch.* for 1959/60, pp. 48–9; Furumark, *OpArch.* 6 (1950), pp. 201–3; Huxley, *AH*, pp. 13–14.

19. Cf. Huxley, *AH*, pp. 1–2, 10–15, 16–18.

20. Op. cit., pp. 2–3 and 36.

21. See above, pp. 161–4. Stubbings (*Mycenaean Pottery from the Levant*, p. 23) considers that some of the LH IIIB and LH IIIC pottery found at Miletus, *particularly of the latest phase*, is of local manufacture.

22. *JHS Arch.* for 1959/60, pp. 54–5; cf. the article cited in n. 23 below, p. 106.

23. *Studi Micenei ed Egeo-Anatolici* 2 (1967), pp. 105–9. We are very grateful to Professor Cook for sending us an offprint of this article.

24. *HCS*, p. 153.

25. Allen (loc. cit.) compares Astyanax with Astyages, Deiphobos and Deileon with Deioces, and Kassandra with Kassandane, and also lists Odios (2. 856), Oukalegon (3. 148),

Dares(5. 9), Echemmon (5. 160), Atymniades (5. 581), Selagos (5. 612), Abarbareë (6. 22), Gorgythion (8. 302), Harpalion (13. 644), Maris (16. 319), Amisodaros (16. 328), and Perimos (16. 695). Unfortunately, of these only Odios belongs to the Trojan Catalogue. On p. 160, however, Allen suggests that both Odios and Epistrophos are translations of the Assyrian word 'damgaru' meaning 'commercial traveller'!

26. Cf., for example, 13. 587–90 for the location of Zeleia, Adresteia, Apaisos, Pityeia, Mt. Tereia, Perkote, and Praktion.

27. *HHI*, pp. 137 and 144–5.

28. See above, pp. 160–4.

29. One is reminded here of the Moslem forces said to have come to the aid of Baligant in the *Chanson de Roland* (*laisses* 232–4).

30. Achilles' estimate of the extent of Priam's dominions (*Il.* 24. 544–6) would roughly coincide with the first of the five geographical areas into which the Trojan Catalogue appears to divide the Trojan alliance.

31. See above, pp. 164–8.

32. *HHI*, p. 144.

33. See above, pp. 165–7.

34. *HCS*, pp. 158–9 and 166–7.

35. Cf. *Nestor* 1 (1961), p. 121, and *ILN*, April 1961, for Mycenaean sherds from Sardis.

INDEX

Names and Figures in heavy type refer to places mentioned in the Catalogue and the pages on which the relevant passages are discussed.

a. Boeotian Orchomenos: the tholos tomb from within

b. Boeotian Orchomenos: ceiling of side-chamber of tholos tomb

a. Copais: Mycenaean (?) dyke, looking towards Topolia (Kopai)

b. Copais: retaining-wall of dyke with Gla in background

a. Panopeus from north

b. Panopeus: Cyclopean walls on south-east flank

a. Pyrgos (? Kynos) from north-west

b. Mendhenitsa (? Tarphe) from east

a. Kasarma bridge: culvert from south

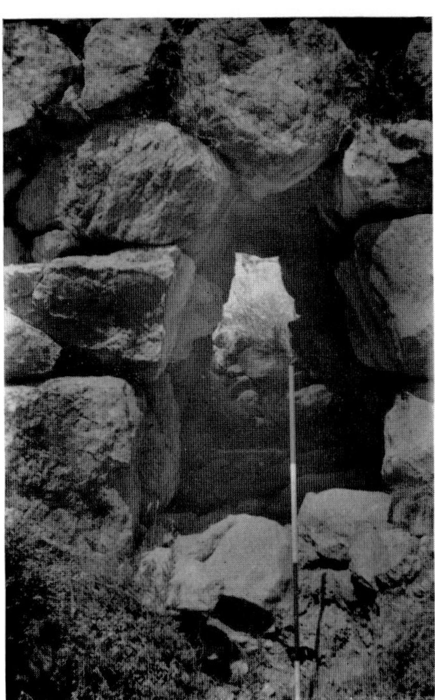

b. Kasarma bridge: interior of culvert

c. Mycenae: sally-port from north-east

PLATE 6

a. Kastro (? Orneai) from south

b. Tigani (? Messe) from south-east

a. Kyparissia from west

b. Pheneos from south

a. Gourtsouli (Mantinea) from south

b. Gourtsouli: Cyclopean walls on south-east flank

a. Chlemoutsi (? Hyrmine) from east

b. Kryoneri (Aetolian Chalcis) from Kalydon

a. Trikkala (Trikke) from north

b. Gremnos (? Argissa) looking west along the Peneios

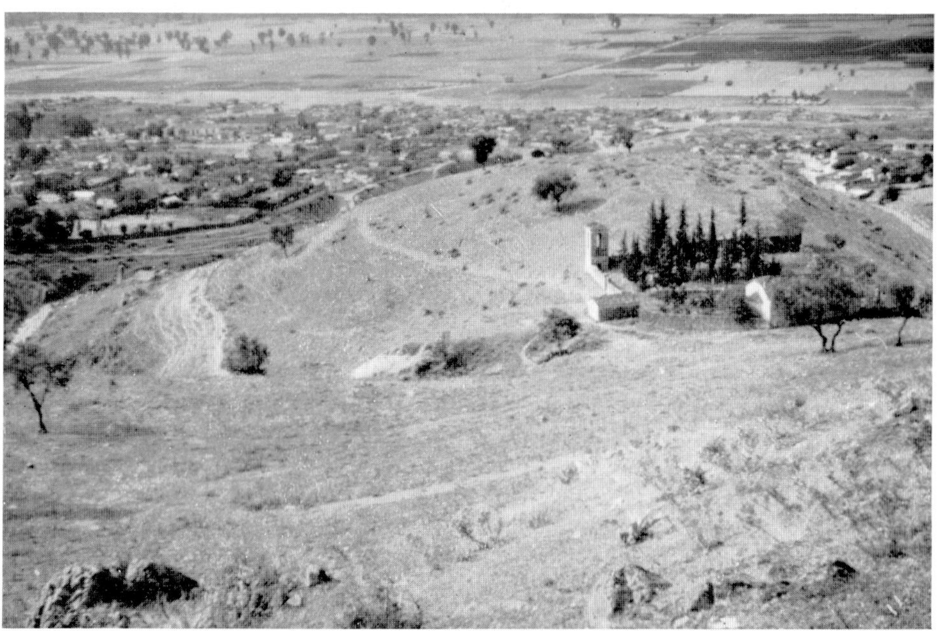

a. Argyropouli (? Elone) from north

b. Mycenaean house-wall on the east side of Argyropouli

PLATE 12

a. Mycenaean sherds from central and northern Greece

b. Mycenaean sherds from the Peloponnese